Paul B. Sturtevant is an audience research specialist at the Smithsonian Institution in Washington, DC. He completed his PhD at the Institute for Medieval Studies at the University of Leeds. He is also the founder and Editor-in-Chief of the very popular collaborative history web-magazine 'The Public Medievalist' (http://www.publicmedievalist.com/).

'Traditional medievalists have only scratched the surface of the broad and influential cultural phenomenon of medievalism. Paul Sturtevant's case study, instead of asking questions mainly important to professional historians, harnesses social-sciences theories and methodologies to help us comprehend how and why groups and individuals engage with representations of medieval culture around them. His book is an essential step towards providing scientifically valid information about the public's understanding of the medieval past.'

Richard Utz, Chair & Professor, School of Literature, Media and Communication, Georgia Institute of Technology

'Carefully researched and written in a lively and engaging style, this book is a must-read for anyone interested in the use – and abuse – of the medieval past in contemporary popular culture. Sturtevant skilfully integrates cutting-edge qualitative methods for studying audience reception with insights from culturally informed medievalism studies. This book demonstrates not only the broad significance of "the Middle Ages" for a wide public but also confronts its urgency in shaping present-day understandings of race, gender, religion, histories of violence, and geopolitics. Chapters examine how audience perceptions of the medieval past are influenced by *Game of Thrones* and fantasy fiction, Arthurian myths, Crusade themes in video games and films, and the varied afterlives of *Beowulf* and Robin Hood. This book is an invaluable resource for enthusiasts, educators, journalists, students, historians, and anyone who cares about what the medieval past means for us today.'

Jonathan Hsy, Associate Professor of English at George Washington University and blogger at *In The Middle*

'*The Middle Ages in Popular Imagination* reveals the preconceptions today's students have about the Middle Ages thanks to their representation in popular film. Sturtevant takes a fresh approach to studying medievalism in a book that crosses disciplinary boundaries and interrogates the divide between academic and public medievalism.'

Amy Kaufman, Director of Conferences, International Society for the Study of Medievalism

New Directions in Medieval Studies

Series editors:
Andrew Elliott, University of Lincoln
Helen Young, University of Sydney

This wide-ranging series responds to emerging themes and interdisciplinary research methods in medieval scholarship, including the reception and reworking of the medieval in the post-medieval period. Particular concerns involve cataloguing the rich variety of experience of medieval people and exploring cultural transfer across different periods, places and groups. These are expressed in the many scholarly themes highlighted below and, taken together, seek to contribute to the future directions and debates of medieval studies.

KEY THEMES:

- Medieval lives including marginal voices, variation and dissimilitude
- Cultural exchange and interconnectedness across medieval Europe
- The reception and re-use of the Middle Ages in later periods
- Re-evaluating medieval history from a global perspective

We particularly welcome proposals from scholars working in the following areas:

- religious and ethnic minorities
- gender and queer history
- emotional communities
- postcolonial perspectives
- travel, trade and migration
- work that extends reception of the Middle Ages beyond the predominantly British perspectives of published work to date
- digital and new media receptions
- work responding to the idea of an 'ethical turn'

For further information, or to submit a proposal, please contact:
ahenderson@ibtauris.com

THE MIDDLE AGES IN POPULAR IMAGINATION

Memory, Film and Medievalism

PAUL B. STURTEVANT

BLOOMSBURY ACADEMIC
LONDON · NEW YORK · OXFORD · NEW DELHI · SYDNEY

BLOOMSBURY ACADEMIC
Bloomsbury Publishing Plc
50 Bedford Square, London, WC1B 3DP, UK
1385 Broadway, New York, NY 10018, USA

BLOOMSBURY, BLOOMSBURY ACADEMIC and the Diana logo
are trademarks of Bloomsbury Publishing Plc

First published 2018 by I.B. Tauris & Co.
Paperback edition first published 2019 by Bloomsbury Academic

A catalogue record for this book is available from the British Library.

A catalog record for this book is available from the Library of Congress.

ISBN: HB: 978-1-7883-1139-7
PB: 978-1-3501-2490-5
ePDF: 978-1-7867-3357-3
ePub: 978-1-7867-2357-4

Series: New Directions in Medieval Studies 1

Typeset by OKS Prepress Services, Chennai, India

To find out more about our authors and books visit
www.bloomsbury.com and sign up for our newsletters

For Betty, who has seen this through from its very beginning.

CONTENTS

LIST OF FIGURES

ACKNOWLEDGEMENTS

This book has had a long gestation, with several iterations; as such, in writing it I have had the assistance of a wide range of people. First and foremost, I would like to thank the nineteen participants from the student body of the University of Leeds for their thoughtfulness, their insight, and their willingness to subject themselves to hours of gentle interrogations by a curious medievalist. Without them, this simply would not exist.

In its first form, this book was my PhD thesis, written at the University of Leeds in the Institute for Medieval Studies and the Centre for World Cinemas. The Hyde Park Picture House helpfully provided free movie passes for the focus-group participants. On the days of the focus groups that form the core of this book, I had excellent assistance from Cassie and Nicholas Dupras, Michael Garcia, Steve Werronen and Joanna Phillips. I worked under the supervision of Lúcia Nagib, Andrew Wawn, David Morrison, and, especially, Richard K. Morris. It was their forward-thinking approach that encouraged me to undertake research as novel and interdisciplinary as this. I greatly appreciate their expert guidance and infinite patience. The examiners of my PhD were Alaric Hall and Jeffrey Richards, and they were the first both to demand that this be turned into a book, and also to show me the path to accomplish that goal.

I'd also like to thank Masahiro Mori, Sara Frazetta, and Boris Vallejo for permitting me to reproduce their images in this book.

In the years intervening, this manuscript has been read and commented on, in whole or in part, by a wide range of colleagues, family and friends. A (no doubt incomplete) list of them are Andrew Elliott, Axel Müller, Betty Sturtevant, Kate Hammond, Geoffrey Humble, Meg O'Brien, Peter Seixas, Tamsin Badcoe, and Victoria Cooper.

I also greatly appreciate the comprehensive comments offered by my anonymous peer reviewers, as well as the work of my editor, Thomas Stottor of I.B.Tauris. This is not just for his prompt and helpful suggestions on every aspect of my manuscript, but for truly believing in the project in the first place. And thanks to my copy editors, Martin Locker and Parker Low, for valiantly rooting out all of the manuscript's remaining goblins.

Finally, I appreciate immensely the assistance and support of my partner, Arielle Gingold, who saw this through its final stages and provided just the sort of critical eye it needed. Hopefully this is just the beginning.

TRANSCRIPTION CONVENTIONS

This book contains, at its core, many quotations from participants in a focus group study. The following transcription conventions have been used in order to represent the ideas accurately while retaining the clarity of their meaning, and indicate the flow of conversation:

(1) The statements of the study participants have been lightly edited, only for clarity and to remove filler words and sounds. The filler words that were removed included sounds like 'erm' and 'uh', the phrases 'like', 'and stuff', and 'sort of', as well as repeated words or phrases.

(2) Removals of non-filler words are indicated by an ellipsis in square brackets [...]. Additions by the author for clarity are surrounded by square brackets [such as these].

(3) Most of the participants were from the north of England. In many northern English dialects, plural pronouns (e.g. 'they') are often combined with a verb in the third person singular (e.g. 'was'). In written English, this may seem like a grammatical error. But in the conversational English of these participants, it was not. Therefore, those instances have been reported verbatim.

(4) Ellipses without square brackets are used to indicate that a participant's speech trailed off.

(5) Square brackets across two lines indicate that two or more participants were talking over each other at the same time. For example:

Justin: I think Orlando Bloom's character might not have been
            real.
Sean: [Yeah I thought he was just a smith, and then became
            this amazing warrior
Justin: Yeah he was just used as a kind of]
Stephen: It was kind of a stylised, I suppose like Shakespeare did
            with Henry the Fifth.

(6)   Two equal signs across two lines indicate that one participant
       interrupted another. For example:

Catherine: I think by watching, when you're little, you get
             shown Disney films, so that's what sets an
             impression, and as you go through school you get
             taught more =
Emma: = Yeah you learn, you see it all and then you put it
             together.

INTRODUCTION

It is the medieval world. Marauders, pilgrims, and wandering
gleemen go about in it. The knight stands at his garden pale, the
lady sits at her bower window, and the little foot page carries
messages over moss and moor. Marchmen are riding through the
Bateable Land 'by the hie light o' the moon'. Monks are chanting
in St. Mary's Kirk, trumpets are blowing in Carlisle town,
castles are burning; down in the glen there is an ambush and
swords are flashing; bows are twanging in the greenwood; four
and twenty ladies are playing at the ball, and four and twenty
milk-white calves are in the woods of Glentanner – all ready to
be stolen. About Yule the round tables begin; the queen looks
over the castle-wall, the palmer returns from the Holy Land,
Young Waters lies deep in Stirling dungeon, but Child Maurice
is in the silver wood, combing his yellow locks with a silver
comb.[1]

Henry Beers, *A History of English Romanticism in the
Eighteenth Century* (1899)

What now? Let me tell you what now. [. . .] I'ma get medieval on
your ass.[2]

Marcellus Wallace, *Pulp Fiction* (1994)

The Middle Ages are open to interpretation. The simple fact that the
word 'medieval' can evoke such wildly disparate ideas in the mind, and
can be used in such remarkably different contexts, seems to show that

there is something peculiar about the Middle Ages that gives it a remarkable malleability within the popular imagination.

Or perhaps the peculiarity lies with us. The events that occurred during the Middle Ages have not changed; our interpretations and understandings of them have. Reinventing the Middle Ages is hardly a new phenomenon. They have been articulated and rearticulated by academic, political, and popular cultures ever since the idea of 'Middle Ages' was popularised by the humanists and historians of the fifteenth century.[3] Each new generation has the potential to shift what the Middle Ages are understood to have been. Regarded as both a backwards-seeming ancestor *and* a source of inspiration, passion, and beauty, they are seen as opulent *and* filthy, sage *and* barbarian, playful *and* sombre. They are the point of origin for many of Europe's national histories, identities, myths, and legends. And they also are the setting of a bevy of contemporary more-or-less pulp adventure stories in every medium available. They are both real history and fantasy playground. These post-medieval articulations of the Middle Ages, whether they are academic or popular, serious or playful, are called 'medievalism'.[4]

Leslie Workman, widely regarded as one of the foundational voices in medievalism studies, provided an elegant definition: 'Medievalism is the continuing process of creating the Middle Ages'.[5] Elizabeth Emery then expands on this definition, calling medievalism: 'a constantly evolving and self-referential process of defining an always fictional Middle Ages'.[6] Integral to their ideas is that medievalism is not the process of *re*-creating the Middle Ages as they were, but continually creating them anew. The Middle Ages are lost; every attempt to explore or restore them by academics, antiquaries, or artists renders up a *new, fictional* version of the Middle Ages, *not* the Middle Ages themselves. Workman and Emery's definitions imply that those who strap on armour and spend their weekends replaying the Battle of Agincourt are not, as they are commonly known, *re-enactors*. They are *enactors* of their own Middle Ages, and participate in a tradition which pervades academic, political and popular cultures – a tradition which entices us and entertains us in every medium.

This tradition can be considered an expression of what has been termed 'collective memory' or 'historical consciousness'. Maurice Halbwachs was the first sociologist to use the term *mémoire collective* to describe how a group – rather than an individual – remembers events.[7] His work, and that of his successors (such as Pierre Nora, Eric Hobsbawm, David

Lowenthal and many others) in the ever-growing field of memory studies, explores how those memories of the past are constructed, taught, and used.[8] These collective memories are crucial for the development of individual identities, social bonds, and larger institutions, and are at the heart of cultures large and small. Subsequently, Peter Seixas and others have productively linked collective memory with the field of history education, coining the term 'historical consciousness'.[9] Historical consciousness is, to Seixas, 'the intersection among public memory, citizenship and history education'.[10] In other words, it is an expansive view of collective memory, one that integrates popular and academic histories, as well as the interaction between political and personal identities. This field of study attempts to understand the individual's perception of the collective memory and how the collective is rendered for the individual.

The subject of this volume lies at a crossroads between contemporary medievalisms and historical consciousness. People in the contemporary world enact and create their own medieval worlds each day, whether they be in a film studio, on the internet, in casual conversation, at a museum, in the classroom, or purely in their own imaginations. Where this book differs from much of the other scholarship on medievalism (a vigorously growing field of study), is that it does not focus on instances or categories of medievalism in culture. Instead, it concentrates on the broader medieval worlds that exist in the historical consciousness: what I call 'public medievalism'.[11] It is the historical consciousness of the medieval world that is the origin of instances of medievalism. And it is upon the historical consciousness that medievalisms have their impact.

This ever-changing public medievalism is a major influence upon individual expressions of medievalism. Audiences are drawn to yet-another depiction of Robin Hood or King Arthur, at least in part, because of their memories of those stories. Similarly, journalists and politicians can only describe policies or people as 'practically medieval' because of a more-or-less common understanding of what that means – regardless of whether that understanding is based in fact. And creators of culture – even academic creators of culture – are members of the public too. The *Pulp Fiction* quote at the top of this chapter helped redefine 'medieval' as part of an active verb (to *get* medieval rather than to *be* medieval) to such a degree that the *Oxford English Dictionary* now cites the film in its entry for 'medieval'.[12]

However, this redefinition of the word would never have taken root if it was not an expression – a crystallisation, perhaps – of an *already existing idea*. The public understanding of the Middle Ages is constantly under revision; individuals' ideas about the Middle Ages are neither static nor monolithic, but change as they encounter new iterations of the medieval. New visions of the Middle Ages inevitably change public views. Changing public views induce a new generation of visions.

With all of that having been said, what does the public understand about the Middle Ages? Anyone who works with the public on questions of history, including public historians, history educators, academics, and history enthusiasts, has collected anecdotes about the state of public knowledge about the past. Yet, it is insufficient to discuss the topic solely from conjecture or anecdote. In spite of this, there have been very few rigorous academic attempts to explore the public's perception of the medieval past, and serious questions remain completely unexplored.

When discussing public ideas about the past, it is first crucial to note that the public's understanding of the Middle Ages – similar to the popular understanding of anything – is culturally specific, having been shaped by education and upbringing, as well as popular and political cultures. The understanding of the period amongst Italians surely is different than amongst Americans, Britons, or Bengalis. Similarly, ideas about the past may differ based upon age group, religion, ethnicity, class, or gender. Suddenly, the question takes on a sociological dimension, and the permutations for study become nearly infinite. It is no longer a question of seeking public opinion, but asking 'which public?'

This book will describe one sociological approach to studying the public understanding of the medieval past. To demonstrate this approach, it will also report the results from one such study conducted by the author over the course of six months in 2008 and 2009. This study explored how groups of British young adults understood the Middle Ages, what experiences influenced their understandings, and how their ideas about the past shaped their world views. Furthermore, the study sought to understand the influence that films in particular have on their understandings of the medieval worlds.

Films, due to their enduring popularity, compelling narratives, and infinite reproducibility, can act as powerful disseminators of knowledge. Alison Landsberg, has termed the mass media a 'prosthetic memory' – meaning that the media allows people to experience and even 'remember' events in which they did not participate.[13] Images of history in the media can grant similar 'memories'; while I was not alive to face the armies of Saladin in 1193, *Kingdom of Heaven* gives anyone else who has seen the film specific 'memories' of that event. It is perhaps little wonder then that, as Robert Rosenstone asserts, 'A century after the invention of motion pictures, the visual media have become arguably the chief carrier of historical messages in our culture'.[14] Expanding upon Landsberg's framework, then, films about the distant medieval past (or medievalesque fantasies) may therefore act as a 'prosthetic imagination'. We no longer are required to imagine the medieval world, Narnia or Middle Earth. They can be served to us, fully rendered, on Blu-Ray.

However, this brings up a worrying point: where do prosthetic memory and prosthetic imagination intersect and blur? Am I remembering the real Agincourt through Laurence Olivier's eyes, or imagining it through the film's interpretation? To what degree does Olivier's imagination of Agincourt – or Kenneth Brannagh's, or Bernard Cornwell's – *invisibly* supplement and supplant mine? The power of film to create historical narratives – no matter how fictionalised – have made them objects of particular concern among educators and scholars, lest film-goers absorb anachronism as truth. But relatively little empirical research has been done to demonstrate how audiences *actually* interact with historical films – whether they learn from them or not. To what degree do audiences take 'Based on a True Story' as truth?

This book tackles this question head on. There has been a spate of recent scholarship on 'medieval films'. These films are typically examined as *objets du cinema*; their aesthetics are examined, their genres diagrammed, and their provenance, modes of production, and ideological positioning discussed. This strand of scholarship has been both productive and useful. However, this book focuses less on what these films are, where they come from, or how they work, and more on what they do to our historical consciousness. In so doing, this book is closest in approach to those scholars of medievalism, like Helen Young and Andrew B.R. Elliott, who have recently blended their examinations of instances of medievalism with reception theory.[15]

In order to accomplish the goal of exploring film's impact on historical consciousness, this book reports and discusses the results of a study that represents a different methodological approach. This approach is sociological in nature, and produces empirical data about public medievalism and medieval film. However, importantly, this approach can be adapted and deployed by an enterprising scholar wishing to study any of a wide array of topics relating to historical consciousness.

First, this book begins with an exploration of how to (and how not to) go about studying the public understanding of the past. This, by necessity, engages with theories and research methods developed by the interrelated fields of memory studies, public history, psychology, and sociology – and shows just how under-studied this field has been. The second chapter presents the first set of results of the qualitative study at the heart of this book. It begins with a discussion and analysis of the research participants' understanding of the Middle Ages, and then pivots to where they reported having learned about the period: in school, through pop-culture, and by consuming products of the heritage industry.

The third chapter examines closely theories drawn from sociology and education – particularly the sociology of knowledge and schema theories – which offer insights into how individuals learn history from films. The fourth introduces the medieval film as a topic of particular study, outlining the wealth of scholarship that has been produced in recent years on the topic – and how the focus on what films *do* rather than what they *are* necessitates a different approach to this field. Chapter 5 focuses on how the study participants viewed the films shown in the study, addressing a range of topics: from *Beowulf*'s use of CGI and medieval languages, to medieval masculinities in *Kingdom of Heaven*, to the perception of 'medievalness' in *Lord of the Rings: The Return of the King*. Finally, Chapter 6 considers how the participants learned from the films they saw. It examines the common themes they identified across the three films, and how the visions of the Middle Ages seen in the films corresponded to, or differed from, their preconceptions. Even though each film was very different, the study participants saw many similarities in the way they approached topics of class, race, religion, material culture, gender, and sexuality. The final chapter presents the overall conclusions and implications of the study for the fields to which it speaks: public history, medieval studies, and media studies. It addresses how understandings of medieval history develop through childhood and are influenced by pop-cultural depictions of the period. It also proposes some steps that medievalists might take in order to better interact with the public: via educational curricula, public history institutions, or popular culture.

Finally, it discusses the evolutionary and regenerative process whereby films (and other elements of culture) influence the public, which then demands and produces new, slightly different, iterations of the same popular culture.

This book is intended to be useful for a few overlapping audiences. Firstly, it is part of a growing body of work produced by scholars of medievalisms. Explorations of the depictions and adaptations of the Middle Ages are becoming more and more frequent as this discipline continues to establish itself. However, this volume represents a reversal of the usual approach; most studies of medievalisms address the objects of their study from the perspective of their production, theoretical underpinnings, impact on or representation of broader cultural shifts. This book, instead, examines medievalisms from the perspective of their reception within society, and offers empirical evidence of their impact.

This book should also be useful for those who work in and study the presentation of the past to the public. In the US (and increasingly internationally) this is commonly called 'public history'; in the UK, 'heritage' or 'public archaeology'. This includes those working in galleries, libraries, historic sites, and museums. And also, increasingly, the tent of 'public history' is expanding to include creators of popular culture in both traditional forms and online. Like language interpreters, who must be familiar both with the language they are hearing and the one into which they are translating, historical interpreters are at their best when well-versed not just in the history they are presenting, but also in their audience's preconceived ideas of the past.

This book also offers insights for anyone interested in the depiction of history (especially medieval history) in popular culture. There has been a growing interest in the study of media depictions of history, and this book seeks to contribute productively to the discussions in this field. Similarly, since the 1960s there has been a vigorous academic exploration of media audiences among media and communications scholars – some utilising methods similar to the sociological ones deployed here. This book contributes to that field of scholarship.

Finally, this book is intended to be useful for educators who teach the Middle Ages – whether at the primary-school or university level. Knowing the pervasive ideas present in the public imagination is useful when engaging with students. Having this knowledge can help educators frame discussions and highlight differences between what a student might think they already know and the (often wildly divergent) historical realities. Having a keen understanding of common pre-existing cultural ideas about one's subject is arguably just as important as being an expert on the subject itself, since teaching is often an exercise in revising pre-existing ideas as much as cultivating new ones.

So, as Marcellus Wallace said: 'What now? Let me tell you what now ...'. From Beers' 'Marauders, pilgrims, and wandering gleemen' to Tarantino's 'pair of pliers and a blow torch', 'medieval' is not just a part of our heritage. It is not just consigned to manuscripts, castles and history books. It is an active and vibrant part of our culture today. We imagine, create, and consume the Middle Ages. By doing so, we enter into a more-or-less serious, more-or-less playful dialogue about what our past was, and what we want our past to have been. When we enact our own Middle Ages, we inevitably bring ourselves into it and reshape it in our own image. Whether this is good or bad, it is an inevitable by-product of the public's understanding of the past and worthy of vigorous study.

CHAPTER 1

THE PUBLIC UNDERSTANDING OF THE PAST

The past is important for contemporary society. Leaving aside history's (or, more accurately, the heritage industry's) literal economic value,[1] the foundations of how individuals within a society understand themselves and others are formed by their perceptions of the past. There is an ongoing struggle among politicians, historians, and history educators around history and social-studies curricula. The crux of the argument centres on the purpose of history education – whether its role is for the socialisation, identity formation, and patriotism-building of a populace (on the one hand), or for the establishment of critical- and historical-thinking skills and mentalities (on the other).[2] Driving this struggle over the purpose of history is a simple idea: how the public understands – and makes use of – the past is crucial. It has a profound impact on the worldviews of a citizenry: their perceptions of themselves and of others, of the present and the future, and of the way the world is and how it should be.

Despite its importance, there has been relatively little good evidence-based scholarship on what, and how, the public thinks about the past. This gap in scholarship is perhaps due to the interdisciplinary nature of the topic; it requires a theoretical grounding that crosses disciplines and research methodologies. Researchers approaching this topic need a foundation in history and historiography, and also in social-sciences theories and methods. The question 'What does the public know about the past?' has been asked before, but more often by journalists and politicians than academics. Invariably, the results of their 'studies' are simply not scientifically valid, leaving the field open for future research.

This chapter will separate the useful, scientifically valid studies from those that are not. Along the way, it will provide an introduction to the research methods used by the scholars working in this field. This is meant to be practical as well as informative; the interested scholar should be able not only to productively pursue this largely untapped line of research (the 'how's of which explained more fully in Appendix A), but also more critically evaluate other studies conducted in this vein.

How Not to Study Historical Consciousness

In the introduction to his seminal monograph *Historical Thinking and Other Unnatural Acts: Charting the Future of Teaching the Past*, Sam Wineburg identifies a trend in the empirical study of historical consciousness, that of the survey of historical ignorance.[3] In 1917, J. Carleton Bell and David F. McCollum published a study in which they tested 668 high school students from Texas on 'the simplest and most obvious facts of American history'.[4] The average grade: 33 of 100. Wineburg goes on to illustrate the various theoretical and methodological issues with this study, but, as he notes, this did not stop studies just like it from being repeated over and over. At least three were done by the *New York Times:* one in 1942 showing students were 'all too ignorant of American History', and one in 1976 with similar results.[5] Another was done in 1987 which claimed that their test scores in history made them 'at risk of being gravely handicapped'.[6]

Studies such as these, which test recall of 'basic' historical facts are methodologically and theoretically flawed. Firstly, they fundamentally misrepresent what history is, and its purpose. As Peter N. Stearns put it:

one of the reasons history holds its place in current education is because earlier leaders believed that a knowledge of certain historical facts helped distinguish the educated from the uneducated; the person who could reel off the date of the Norman conquest of England (1066) or the name of the person who came up with the theory of evolution at about the same time that Darwin did (Wallace) was deemed superior – a better candidate for law school or even a business promotion. Knowledge of historical facts has been used as a screening device in many societies, from China to the United States, and the habit is still with us to some extent. Unfortunately, this use can encourage mindless memorization – a real but not very appealing aspect of the discipline. History should be studied because it is essential to individuals and to society, and because it harbors beauty.[7]

History is more than a collection of facts, and the point of learning history is far greater than simply learning names and dates for recitation in order to seem intelligent – whether by history instructors, employers, or surveyors.

Secondly, these studies do not hold up to keen methodological scrutiny; their sample sizes are often very small, their questions worded ambiguously, and little explanation is offered for their sampling. In short, they cannot be used to judge the broad knowledge level of a generation or nation, they can only indicate how well that group of people performed on that particular test at that moment in time.

Despite this, somehow surveys of historical ignorance are *both* perennial and alarmist. Each makes fresh claims that the current generation is populated with particularly uneducated people. And they are not just an American phenomenon. One such survey was commissioned in 2001 by Osprey Publishing, publishers of popular military history books.[8] It was conducted as part of the marketing for their series: 'Osprey's Essential Histories, a new series of books designed to make the history of war accessible to all'.[9] Their study tested 200 British children aged 11–18 on basic questions of military history. They found, as the publisher describes, that:

- 4 per cent of schoolchildren believed that Hitler led Britain in World War II.[10]
- Nearly 1 in 10 schoolchildren thought that Queen Victoria ruled at the time of the Spanish Armada in 1588, whilst 6 per cent believed the reigning monarch to have been the current Queen Elizabeth II.
- 17 per cent linked Oliver Cromwell with the Battle of Hastings rather than the English Civil War, whilst 6 per cent linked him with the Battle of Britain in 1940.[11]

These results were reproduced widely in the UK press, including the *Daily Express*, *Daily Mail*, *Daily Telegraph*, *The Times*, *The Times Educational Supplement*, and *BBC History Magazine*.[12] *The Times Educational Supplement* called it 'a survey highlighting appalling gaps in pupils' knowledge'.[13] In spite of their negative framing, these figures actually indicate a remarkably high-scoring group of young people. If, for example, one in twenty misidentified the Roman Empire as existing 150 years ago (perhaps confusing it with the British Empire), that means that 95 per cent of the respondents answered correctly. This is hardly an 'appalling' lack of knowledge, and falls well within the margin of error due to its small sample size.[14] In short, this survey has significant methodological problems that render it not especially meaningful, and only 'useful' as a marketing tool.

These surveys are not limited to for-profit companies, or to school-aged children. A similar study was conducted by the BBC in 2004, in conjunction with the release of its *Battlefield Britain* TV series.[15] They reported, among other findings,

> Almost half of 16 to 34-year-olds questioned didn't know Sir Francis Drake fought in the battle against the Spanish Armada [. . .] Gandalf, the wizard from The Lord of the Rings, was the choice of more than one in twenty 16 to 24-year-olds.[16]

The *Guardian* then used these results to attack the UK education system:

> The figures, released to mark the start of BBC Two's Battlefield Britain series on landmark conflicts in British history, left education traditionalists aghast at young people's lack of knowledge of their nation's past [. . .] Nick Seaton, chairman of the Campaign for Real Education, said of the survey: 'It clearly shows that our state education system has got a lot to answer for.'[17]

Think tank Civitas also used this survey to bolster their own attacks on the education system: 'Fifteen per cent of these youngsters thought the Orangemen were celebrating victory at Helms Deep' (*sic*), and, 'Does any of this matter? Most surely it does. In fact, it matters profoundly – not only for the sake of a good education for our children but also for the future stability and coherence of our multi-racial society. To know the history of one's country is a birthright'.[18]

But the private sector is not the only source of these studies; another was done by Derek Matthews of Cardiff University, entitled: 'The Strange Death of History Teaching (Fully Explained in Seven Easy-to-Follow Lessons)'.[19] His study constituted a pop quiz of his first-year students on 'five of the easiest history questions I could think of and what I considered any well-educated (make that any) 18-year-old should know.'[20] Perhaps predictably, the students performed poorly. The author then used this as evidence to criticise governmental educational policy and primary and secondary school teachers. More problematically still, in 2011 this study was used by the then British Secretary of State for Education, Michael Gove, in his calls for a nationalistic reform to education policy. As reported in the *Guardian*:

Referring to a survey of undergraduates carried out by Professor Derek Matthews at Cardiff University, Gove said twice as many students believed Nelson commanded British forces at Waterloo as (correctly) named Wellington – while nine students thought it was Napoleon. The education secretary said after the conference that history should 'give people the chance to be proud of our past and, in particular, proud of the heroes and heroines that fought for freedom over time.'[21]

This was far from the only time Gove used surveys of historical ignorance as evidence for the need for his reactionary reform of the English National Curriculum. In 2013, Gove stated in *The Daily Mail*: 'Survey after survey has revealed disturbing historical ignorance, with one teenager in five believing Winston Churchill was a fictional character while 58 per cent think Sherlock Holmes was real.'[22] After this article was published, a local teacher and campaigner demanded the source of this information from the Department of Education via a Freedom of Information request. Through this, it was revealed that Gove's sources for these claims were from surveys commissioned by UKTV Gold (a classic comedy TV channel), Premier Inn (a motel chain), the Sea Cadet Corps (a nautical youth organisation) and by Lord Michael Ashcroft (a conservative Lord) to commemorate historical anniversaries.[23] The problem with these studies is not just that their methodologies (and thus results) are flawed, but that they are then deployed uncritically in national debates by politicians like Gove.[24]

Using such unscientific methods to study public ignorance about history results, not surprisingly, in research with serious flaws. These flaws are of particular consequence since these studies are then used to contribute to public debates on, and indeed influence, education reform.

Doing it Right: *The Presence of the Past*

Among the legion fundamental problems with the above-described studies are two issues. First, these studies assume that knowledge of isolated historical facts is the best (or only) metric by which to judge the public's understanding of the past. Secondly, they take an explicitly negative position when framing the results – choosing, for example, to trumpet that a small minority of people did not know a historical fact, instead of that a vast majority of people did. The underlying research questions for them are: 'Does the public (not) know *{Insert Historical Fact}*?' Studies which truly intended to understand how the public perceives the past would, instead, ask questions like, 'What does the public know about the past, and what do they do with that knowledge?', 'How does the public learn about the past?', or 'How and why is the past meaningful for the public?'

One study, conducted by Roy Rosenzweig and David Thelen in the United States in the 1990s, did just that. In so doing, Rosenzweig and Thelen inaugurated an entirely new field of research which explores popular perceptions of the past using empirical research methods drawn from the social sciences.[25] Their study included a national telephone-based survey of approximately 1,000 Americans of different ages, genders, and ethnic backgrounds.[26] The overall focus of this survey was a compelling counter to the usual approach to the public's understanding of the past:

> the real issue was not, as pundits were declaring, what Americans did not know about the past, but what they *did* know and think. Incredibly, since many commentators had surveyed American ignorance, no one had actually investigated how Americans understood the past. And we believed that we needed to seek out and listen to the voices of the people who were being denounced for their ignorance.[27]

Instead of focusing on what facts Americans did or did not know, Rosenzweig and Thelen set out to explore the myriad ways that the public interacts with their past in their daily lives: through conversations with relatives, trips to museums, reading books, attending classes, and/or watching films and TV programmes about history. They surveyed how often their respondents engaged in those activities, how connected they felt to the past while doing so, and how much importance they assigned to a variety of different 'pasts' (for instance, national, familial, or ethnic histories). The results were conclusive: contrary to the picture painted by the above studies, the public engages with the past frequently and vigorously. The primary focus and vehicle for this interaction is first-person history – personal and family history. As Rosenzweig relates,

> They prefer the personal and firsthand because they feel at home with that past: they live with it, relive it, interpret and reinterpret it; they use it to define themselves, their place in their families, and their families' place in the world.[28]

Furthermore, they found that individuals use the past to shape their interactions with the world:

> Individuals turn to their personal experiences to grapple with questions about where they come from and where they are heading, who they are and how they want to be remembered [...] they assemble their experiences into patterns, narratives that allow them to make sense of the past, set priorities, project what might happen next, and try to shape the future.[29]

The individuals they studied found the history that had been taught to them in classrooms – particularly nation-centric history (like that privileged in the surveys described above) – 'dull' and 'irrelevant' to their lives. However, they saw their first-person pasts within larger historical and social contexts, whether that context be the public past or the past of their specific racial/ethnic and religious groups.[30]

These results were published in a book entitled *The Presence of the Past: Popular Uses of History in American Life*, and on a sister website.[31] This study is of seminal importance. It was the first large-scale exploration of public's understanding of, and interaction with, the past. And many of

Rosenzweig and Thelen's assumptions and results are foundational to the present book. Chief amongst them is this – and it cannot be emphasised enough:

It is imperative to approach the public's understanding of the past from the perspective of the public rather than that of the historian.[32]

They developed two other theoretical positions, which are of crucial import when studying the public understanding of the past. First:

To the public, the past is much more than just history.

As they put it:

History is the word that scholars privilege to describe how they approach the past ... respondents said history was formal, analytical, official or distant. *The past* was the term that best invited people to talk about family, race, and nation, about where they had come from and what they had learned along the way.[33]

Secondly:

The topic of the public's understanding of the past is far broader and more complex than merely their comprehension of history, as a measure of facts learned or unlearned.

Further, the public's understanding of the past is more important than their comprehension and memorisation of historical facts. Rosenzweig and Thelen were incredibly insightful when saying:

some readers, perhaps professional historians in particular, will not share the capacious definition of the past used in this study, but our respondents think about the past in these elastic terms. To the charge that our instructions and questions encouraged people to talk about the past in more expansive and less professionally conventional terms, we plead guilty – by design.[34]

Lessons of *The Presence of the Past* and its Successors

Rosenzweig and Thelen's groundbreaking study did not end the discussion about the public's interaction with the past – it began it.

The *Presence of the Past* study inspired significant work in this field, but for several reasons, plenty more remains to be done. Firstly, the results of the *Presence of the Past* are specific to American interactions with the American past. Only two major studies in this vein have been accomplished since, both at the national level: one in Australia and one in Canada.

The *Australians and the Past* study, conducted in the late 1990s and early 2000s, was explicitly based on the American study and addressed how Australians similarly and differently approached issues of historical consciousness. This was published in a 2010 volume *History at the Crossroads: Australians and the Past.*[35] In the 2000s, another landmark study was completed by 'The Pasts Collective', a group of seven university researchers and nineteen public historian collaborators from across Canada. This included the largest survey yet conducted, with 3,419 responses as well as follow-up samples of First Nations people in Saskatchewan, Acadians in New Brunswick, and recent immigrants in Ontario. It was published as a collection under the title *Canadians and their Pasts.*[36]

Each subsequent study has an acknowledged debt to the others, and built upon the foundation previously laid. While each had a different approach, at their core, each survey broadly addressed four research questions:

(1)   what sort of past (familial, national, regional, religious, etc.) do the public find most important,

(2)   what past-related activities (i.e. looking at old photographs, watching historical films, going to museums, etc.) do people engage in, how often, and why,

(3)   how connected to the past they feel while engaging in those activities, and

(4)   how trustworthy do the public find various sources of historical information (i.e. college professors, historical films, museums, etc.)?

While they had these same questions at their core, each study took a different approach to answering them. This arose from a changing intellectual landscape and different research perspectives, and also came about as a result of the particular public(s) and the particular past(s) in each country. Applying the results of these studies to other national and historical contexts, such as the topic under examination here – the British interaction with the medieval past, and in particular their interaction with film depictions of it – thus demands some adaptation. While in some ways the British may interact with the medieval past similarly to the ways Americans, Australians, and Canadians interact with their history, it is important not to assume that they do.

For example, the previous studies survey closely examined interactions with personal, familial, ethnic and national histories. One question asked in *The Presence of the Past* was: 'Knowing about the past of which of the following four areas or groups is most important to you: the past of your family, the past of your racial or ethnic group, the past of the community in which you now live, or the past of the United States?' 'Your family' was rated the most important by 66 per cent of American participants. 'National past' ranked second at 22 per cent, 'racial/ethnic past' at 8 per cent, and 'community past' at 4 per cent.[37] *Canadians and their Pasts* took a different tack; they did not ask respondents to rank these pasts against each other, but instead to rate their importance individually on a scale of 'very important, somewhat important, not very important, or not at all important to you'. However the results are somewhat similar: 'family' had the highest 'very important' rating at 66 per cent, followed by 'Canada' (for Canadians-by-birth) at 42 per cent and 'Country of birth' (for those born outside of Canada) at 59 per cent. 'Province of residence' and 'Religion or spiritual tradition' followed, at 35 per cent and 32 per cent, respectively.[38]

When looking at the UK and at the Middle Ages, however, these categories do not really apply. In terms of family history, tracing one's history back to the Middle Ages is a violent act as much as it is as a recuperative one. This act involves so many genealogical threads that a person must choose which threads to follow and which to cut off from their identity; due to the 500 years between the close of the Middle Ages and the present, true genealogical inquiry (no matter what the sellers of fraudulent heraldries might protest) becomes largely meaningless because of the sheer volume of ancestors every person has. Statistician Joseph Chang has shown that *every* person of European descent is very likely to have a common ancestor as early as 'just about 32 generations ago – perhaps 500 years or so.'[39] While this may be surprising, putting this in perspective, counting the number of direct ancestors any given person has over 32 generations is relatively simple. Two (since everyone has two biological parents) multiplied by itself thirty-two times (since this is over thirty-two generations), equals 4,294,967,296 people. Even considering that many of these 4.2 billion ancestors must actually be the same person (especially since there were not 4.2 billion people alive *in the world* at that time), it means that the statistical probability that any white European is not directly descended from Charlemagne, the prophet Mohammad (through the daughter of the Emir of Seville who converted to Catholicism around AD 1200) or *anyone else* well-established in the European gene pool is infinitesimally small. For a person not to be related to this broader gene pool, it would require a staggering amount of inbreeding.[40]

Medieval history may thus be regarded, consciously or unconsciously, as history in the third person – a history of the 'them' rather than the 'us', not 'my' history, or the history of 'my family' but at best, 'our history'. Individual medieval people may not feel as much like a part of our own extended families, perhaps due to the fact that, ironically, most of them genetically are. Medieval people become so far removed from ourselves to be alien. Compounding this distance, in contemporary Britain, a significant portion of the population is descended from immigrants who originated in South Asia, the Caribbean, or China – outside the usual geographical boundaries of 'the Middle Ages'. As a result, looking at medieval history in terms of personal or familial history makes little sense even in those countries typically included under the historical aegis of 'the Middle Ages'. But even if they claim medieval ancestry, do those claims offer most Britons anything other than personal trivia – or are they elided with racial/ethnic, religious, regional, or national histories?

But even looking to the Middle Ages for racial, ethnic, regional, or national histories is almost as problematic. The Middle Ages are understood by many medievalists to be the time when the idea of nation and national identities were first being formed.[41] The English National Curriculum explicitly teaches the Middle Ages within a national context (more on this later). However, this is complicated by the fact that there are four (or five) separate national identities which comprise the UK in addition to the catch-all 'British': English, Scottish, Welsh, Northern Irish (itself a matter of multiple identities), and, for some, Cornish.[42] This complex tapestry of identity is even reflected on the 2011 UK Census questionnaire (Figure 1.1).

British identity, as a recent article by Eric Weiskott explores, has a complex, and fraught, history that stretches back to the Roman

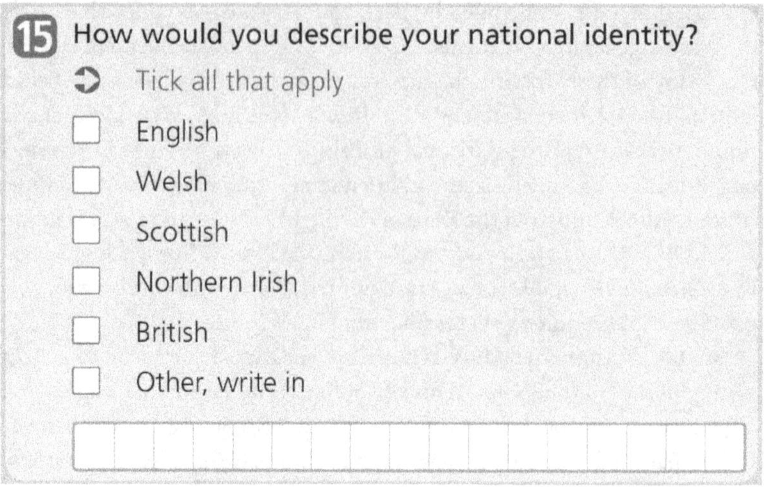

15 How would you describe your national identity?
➔ Tick all that apply

☐ English

☐ Welsh

☐ Scottish

☐ Northern Irish

☐ British

☐ Other, write in

Figure 1.1 Surveying complex national identities in the 2011 UK Census. Source: 2011 UK Census.

colonisation of the island.[43] Today, the term 'British' encompasses the histories of the smaller nations that comprise the Union, often in conflict with one another, and the even smaller kingdoms that preceded them. This tapestry makes contemporary British national identity complex, particularly when addressing how the Middle Ages contributes to British identity. Further complicating matters are the racial, ethnic, and religious histories of the UK. Would a British person of Pakistani descent engage with the medieval past as a part of 'their' history? And more, despite attempts by white nationalists in Europe and the US to claim the Middle Ages as a nostalgic place-time of ethnic purity, not only was it not so 'pure' as they hope, but the racial categories they cling to would have been meaningless to medieval people.[44]

And then, religion: perhaps a Catholic might see the Middle Ages as part of their religious heritage. But would a member of the Church of England? Would a Methodist, or a Sikh? In the UK, the Middle Ages may be considered a part of national, ethnic, or community pasts (no matter whether those connections are tenuous or not), but it is unknown to what degree the British public actively engages with its medieval past in this way.

Thus, while the Canadian, American, and Australian studies done are impressive foundational works for this discipline, the way that they conceive of and categorise history inherently excludes the Middle Ages (as well as any histories further removed in time or space). Their research design – by focusing on personal, national, ethnic, and religious pasts, seems to imply that the public does not (or perhaps cannot) find the medieval past to be important, and does not engage with it meaningfully.[45]

But that is simply not true. If the public truly had no interest in the Middle Ages, the parade of books, films, TV shows, and video games released each year that are set in medieval or medievalesque worlds would struggle to find an audience; medieval re-enactment groups and medieval fairs would cease to exist; Medieval Studies departments in universities across the globe would close for lack of student enrolment.[46] But they do not. Something must be driving the continued voracious consumption of the Middle Ages by the public. Perhaps the discrepancy can be explained by the use of the word 'important' in the questions asked in the national surveys, for example, in this question asked in the American study: 'Knowing about the past of which of the following four areas or groups is *most important* to you'.[47] When close-read, the word 'important' in this case implies a sense of authority – perhaps for some of the respondents, this may have meant that it has relevance to contemporary issues. For some it may have meant that it is central to their sense of their identity, or was central to the creation of the world they see around them. Read this way, perhaps the Middle Ages were not 'important' to these people – but perhaps they may have been 'exciting', 'meaningful', 'fascinating', or 'fun'.

This issue around the word 'important' reveals one of the limitations of the research methods chosen by these large-scale national surveys. Each of these surveys primarily used quantitative research methods.[48] Their reasons for doing so are implicit in the purpose of their research: they sought to capture the perceptions of their entire nation, and to compare, using statistics, different subgroups within it (by race/ethnicity, religion, region, etc.). Most of the questions on these surveys were closed-ended (e.g. multiple choice, true/false or yes/no questions). This allows for relatively quick tabulation of the results and interpretation of the findings using statistics. The statistical basis for their conclusions allows them to be generalised to broader populations, and gives these methods a mathematical validity and reproducibility that make them compelling pieces of research.

However, the chief limitation of these quantitative surveys (and all such surveys) is that these research participants were responding to questions that had been developed by the researchers. Some questions in the large national surveys permitted open-ended answers, such as: 'Can you please tell me the name or the location of the last historic site that you visited?', or 'Can you please tell us why you think [the most trustworthy source] is a very trustworthy source of information about the past?'[49] But even these are structured in such a way as to elicit relatively brief answers from clear prompts. The participants are responding to, and within, an intellectual framework – such as the idea of importance discussed above – established by the researchers. Though these national surveys are far superior in every conceivable way to surveys of historical ignorance, some of the same issues arise: the surveyors define what is important, and how to talk about the issues at hand. That focused scope may or may not reflect the full shape of the issues, and does not allow these issues to be explored with the greatest possible depth, detail, or nuance.

Another Approach: Qualitative Methods

An alternative approach is to use qualitative research methods for studying the public understanding of the past. While qualitative methods present an alternative to survey methods such as those described above, they are perhaps better understood as complementary to them: qualitative methods can answer different research questions. Qualitative research methods include interviews, observations, ethnographies, open-ended questionnaires, and focus groups. They offer depth and nuance that quantitative methods cannot. And when juxtaposed against quantitative studies, each approach can help to better contextualise the results of the other. Because far more data is gathered from each research participant in a qualitative research study, far fewer are needed for a successful study than one using quantitative methods. Instead of surveying aspects of the breadth of a large population (as quantitative methods do), qualitative methods work in great depth with a smaller population chosen carefully. Qualitative methods are well-equipped to explore difficult, ambiguous questions, or topics where there is little previous research. They are useful or in those instances where it is best to have the intellectual framing of the issue determined by the participants themselves. In other words, these methods are perfect for exploring questions of historical consciousness and the public understanding of the past.[50]

So what questions might qualitative studies be better able to answer about the public understanding of the past? These methods are well-equipped to explore the basic question 'What does the public understand about the past', especially if 'the public' is defined in a meaningful way. For example a study exploring how survivors of the Blitz interpret the past (both their own and other pasts), or how historical re-enactors view the period they create could be compelling. Well-designed qualitative studies could also explore and add nuance to a myriad aspects of historical consciousness. How do people relate history – both the recent and distant past – to their gender, racial, national, or religious identity? Why do people participate in modern-day pilgrimages to historic sites? How does consuming popular-cultural escapist historical fantasies affect an individual's understanding of the past? How might historical narratives contribute to prejudice and hatred in the contemporary world? Qualitative methods could also be used to explore how primary, secondary, or post-secondary history education influences interpretations of present events. In sum, studies of this type could help us to begin to answer the question: *why* is the past important, exciting, meaningful, fascinating, or fun?

The Middle Ages in Popular Imagination and its Methodology

As mentioned in the introduction, this book reports the complex findings of a qualitative study that I conducted from 2008–9, which I called *The Middle Ages in Popular Imagination*. Detailed descriptions of the research methods and sampling strategies used in the study, as well as the rationales behind them, are available in Appendix B. That being said, it is important to introduce, in short form, what was done in order for the results that follow this chapter to be fully understood.

As mentioned, qualitative research methods allow researchers to ask and answer a wide range of research questions about historical consciousness and public medievalism. The focus of this study was on two overarching topics:

(1) What does the public know about the Middle Ages?
(2) How do films shape that public knowledge?

Those two questions are far too broad to fully explore with only one study. So 'the public' was further narrowed to 'British young people', and 'films' was defined as 'Big-budget Hollywood medieval films from 2000–9'.

The Study Participants

Nineteen British young people (Figure 1.2) attending the University of Leeds were recruited for the study, and split into four groups. One group began in November 2008, and the others began in April, May, and June of 2009 (I will refer to each as the 'November', 'April', 'May', or 'June' group, respectively). The only restrictions on participation were that these young people:

(1) Must have been educated exclusively in England (meaning all were subject to the English National Curriculum),
(2) Could not have studied the Middle Ages academically beyond GCSE level (meaning that they were not unduly influenced by academic ideas of the period),[51] and
(3) Must have seen at least three medieval films in the past (meaning all had at least a basic familiarity with and interest level in cinematic medievalism).

They were recruited from the general populace at the University of Leeds in after-hours non-curricular sessions.

The participants recruited represented a diversity of age, gender, and course of study (Figure 1.2). Eleven women and eight men participated. Eight were studying arts subjects and twelve the sciences (one participant is counted in both categories as he was studying both music and mathematics). Participants were between nineteen and twenty-four years old at the time. Each participant was given a pseudonym for purposes of anonymity.

Each group had a different social makeup. The June group was a group of friends (which resulted in a more freewheeling discussion), whereas the other three groups consisted of strangers. Though some participants were more forthcoming with their opinions than others, I have attempted to ensure that the analysis in the coming chapters captures the opinions of all participants, no matter how talkative or reticent.

Pseudonym	Group	Gender	YOB	Course of Study
Catherine	November	F	1989	Fashion Design
Eleanor	November	F	1988	Pharmacology
Elizabeth	November	F	1988	Mathematics
Emma	November	F	1989	Psychology
Jane	November	F	1989	Law
Carin	April	F	1988	Theology and Religious Studies
Chloe	April	F	1985	Medicine
Erica	April	F	1985	Zoology
Rob	April	M	1988	Philosophy
Dan	May	M	1990	Mathematics
Jake	May	M	1988	Product Design
Jess	May	F	1986	Physics
John	May	M	1988	Physics
Laura	May	F	1990	Linguistics and Phonetics
Mark	May	M	1990	Mathematics
Justin	June	M	1989	Biology
Katy	June	F	1988	English and History
Sean	June	M	1988	Biology
Stephen	June	M	1989	Music and Mathematics

Figure 1.2   Demographic details of the research participants.

The Films

This study was concerned, first and foremost, with the impact cinema has on the broad historical consciousness. As such, the three films chosen for this study were selected because they had the largest public impact. Cultural impact is difficult to quantify. So, though it is an imperfect gauge of popular impact, the three films were chosen based upon being the three cinematic medievalisms with the highest UK box-office receipts. The particular films with the highest-grossing UK box-office receipts from the period 2000–9 were: *Beowulf*, *Kingdom of Heaven*, and *The Lord of the Rings: The Return of the King.*[52]

Choosing these three films for study has important implications. One is an adaptation of medieval history, another an adaptation of medieval literature, and the third an adaptation of a foundational work of medievalist epic high fantasy. The two set in the real world take place seven hundred years apart, and each presents a very distinctly different vision of the Middle Ages that represent some common 'visions' of the Middle Ages – Vikings and crusades. In short, while these three films do not represent all the ways the Middle Ages are represented in film, they are a sampling of that diversity.

Each participant-group met three times. In the first and second sessions, participants were first led in a discussion of their perceptions of the medieval past, beginning with a word-association game to help break the ice. They were then shown a film – in the first session, *Beowulf*, in the second, *Kingdom of Heaven*. Afterwards, an open-ended discussion was held about their reactions to the film, how it related to their perceptions of the Middle Ages, and what they thought should be done to make it 'more medieval'. The third session was run similarly, though because of the long running time of *The Lord of the Rings: Return of the King*, the session began with the film screening and ended with a longer plenary discussion, which addressed both their reactions to *Return of the King* and a comparison of the three different films along thematic lines.

The Data

The data for this study were derived from the transcripts of these interviews. This was done using standard qualitative coding and sorting methods – in other words, tagging sections of the transcripts with themes that emerged from their discussions (for example 'role of women', 'knighthood', or 'film realism'), and then grouping and comparing how those themes were expressed in order to understand their nuances. The participants' ideas are reproduced in the following chapters verbatim and in sometimes lengthy quotations or complex back-and-forth conversations. This was done in order to communicate the nuances of their ideas as fully as possible as they emerged (or in some cases, erupted) over the course of the interviews. These complex ideas, when compared and contrasted across the different individuals and groups, begin to reveal the broad outlines around the question of what the public understands about the Middle Ages and the role of medieval films. This nuanced comparison of the ideas – coupled with the rigorous data-gathering methods – elevates these data beyond the level of mere anecdote, revealing wider implications about the historical consciousness of these people and, arguably, those like them.

The study results are broken down broadly into three sections. The first section was, simply, what participants' knowledge about the Middle Ages was prior to influence from the films. The second part examined how they reacted to the films individually, and responded to the various aspects unique to each film (such as whether the CGI of *Beowulf* made it more, or less, believable as a medieval film). The final part involved participants' perceptions of the medieval world related to what they had seen in the films. This involved a complex comparison of the images, icons, and ideas presented in the films with their expectations of reality and their previous knowledge.

Conclusion

In summary, the contemporary public's understanding of the past is a topic worthy of concerted study with the best available research methods. The results of such study – especially when done well – can have wide-ranging implications, not just within the academic world, but informing such diverse fields as the heritage sector, political debates, and educational practices. And even more, at the risk of overstatement, it can open a unique window into how the people within a particular culture at a particular moment understand themselves, their origins, their place in the world, and their future.

The field of the contemporary public understanding of the past has been opened by a series of landmark, wide-reaching, quantitative survey-based research projects. Their research leaves plenty of room for other topics to be explored by using different methodologies (such as the qualitative methods used in this book) and by asking different questions. *The Middle Ages in Popular Imagination* study hopes to break ground on an intellectual terrain rich for exploration. The next chapter will begin that effort by delving into the study participants' complex, nuanced, and even self-contradictory perceptions of the medieval past.

CHAPTER 2

THEIR UNDERSTANDING OF
THE MIDDLE AGES

We do not see things as they are, we see things as we are.[1]

Anaïs Nin, *Seduction of the Minotaur*

This chapter explores the ideas about the Middle Ages voiced by the *Middle Ages in Popular Imagination* study participants prior to their having been shown the three films. It explores their complex, often contradictory ideas about the medieval past without any other influences.[2] Their perceptions (and misperceptions) often point to deeper cultural myths and commonly held beliefs. They can indicate where popular culture and academic culture may work in concert, or come into conflict; they can also indicate how history is understood 'in the wild', so to speak, where academic knowledge is put in unconscious conversation with knowledge acquired from myriad other sources.

Choosing Words Carefully: 'Medieval' or 'Middle Ages'?[3]

At the beginning of the session, participants were given a word-association exercise. This was intended both to get the participants thinking about the subject and to give them something to which they could refer back if the later conversations flagged. The exercise also provided another source of data, which would be based upon their individual opinions and pre-existing understandings alone rather than influenced by any emergent groupthink. For this exercise, they were given five minutes to write every word they associated with the Middle Ages on a blank piece of paper. However, when planning this project, a question arose: should the page be labelled with the word 'medieval', or the words 'Middle Ages'? And how should the moderator refer to the period when asking questions?

At first thought, the two terms may seem synonymous. And, technically, they are; 'medieval' was a mid-nineteenth-century neologism derived from the Latin *medium aevum*, meaning 'Middle Ages'.[4] But, are these terms synonyms for these participants, or do they play upon the historical consciousness in different ways? Considering that the specific methodology used for these interviews[5] was intended to allow participants the freest rein possible not only in deciding what to say but how to define their terms, if they were to be asked only about one term, how could that choice steer or frame the conversation? Even such a minute methodological point reveals how little is known about popular perceptions of this period.

In order to explore this possible fundamental knowledge gap, it was decided to do both. So, the word-association exercise was done twice with each group. First, half the group was given a sheet with 'medieval' at the top and the other half was given one with 'Middle Ages' at the top. At the end of the five minutes, they were given another sheet bearing the other term and asked to repeat the exercise. The group then discussed what they wrote on their sheets, the relative importance of the words they wrote to their perception of what these terms meant to them, and whether they felt there were differences between the terms.

The sheets were collected after the focus group, and the frequency of the responses counted.[6] Figures 2.1 and 2.2 provide a list of the terms which were mentioned by more than three people across all the groups for the terms medieval and Middle Ages.

Some categories and patterns emerge when reading these lists: for both, warfare (knights, castles, armour, swords, crusades) dominated. Figures associated with social classes (kings, queens, peasants) are also found in both. Social inequality (poverty, divide between rich and poor) feature as well, though more so for 'Middle Ages'. Each features dirt and unpleasantness, either in the environment (mud), in people (bad hygiene), or in social conditions (poverty, war, torture). Legendary people (King Arthur, Robin Hood) and creatures (dragons) were

'Medieval'	#
Castles	10
Knights	10
Armour	7
Disease (incl. Plague, Black Death)	6
Battles	5
Crusades	5
Kings	4
Queens	4
Peasants	4
Clothes	4
Swords	4
Feasts (incl. Banquets)	4
Dirty (incl. Mud, Bad Hygiene)	4
Religion (incl. the Church, Christianity)	3
Dragons	3
Jesters	3
Torture	3
Jousting	3
War	3
King Arthur	3
History	3
Horses	3

Figure 2.1   Responses to 'Medieval' word-association exercises and frequency (3+).

mentioned more often than historical ones. The only real person on either list is Henry VIII – perhaps surprising since he is more often associated by scholars with the Early Modern period.[7] But for some reason he is more a notable part of the 'Middle Ages' than any actually

'Middle Ages'	#
Disease	10
Knights	8
Castles	8
Jousting	5
Poverty	5
Battles	5
Dirty (incl. Mud)	5
Religion (incl. the Church, Christianity)	5
Armour	4
War	4
Peasants	4
Crusades	4
King Arthur	4
Robin Hood	4
Swords	4
Farming	4
Henry VIII	4
Vikings	3
Kings	3
Dark Ages	3
Horses	3
Divide between Rich and Poor	3

Figure 2.2   Responses to 'Middle Ages' word-association exercises and frequency (3+).

medieval person. The Church gets some mention, but only in general terms or in the specific context of crusade. Some differences are seen in the frequency of responses across the two sheets, but with such a small sample size, the conclusions that can be drawn from this exercise are limited. But when the participants were asked to explain their ideas beyond simple word association, a much fuller picture began to emerge.

The 'Medieval' 'Middle Ages'

At first, two participants had difficulty seeing any distinction at all between the two terms. When first asked to write a word-association sheet for the term 'Middle Ages', having already completed one for 'medieval', Emma hesitated: 'I don't really know the difference'. Sean also had difficulties: 'I didn't really find any sort of difference between medieval and Middle Ages.'

Most of the others did not share their hesitation. Each of the four participant-groups independently developed discrete definitions of 'medieval' and 'Middle Ages'. Interestingly, these definitions were remarkably similar across the four groups.

History and Fantasy

The participants' primary distinction between the terms 'medieval' and 'Middle Ages' rested along the – admittedly blurry – line between fantasy and history. Almost all participants said the term 'Middle Ages' refers to a period of real history, whereas 'medieval' refers to a setting for fantasy and legend. John said:

> I feel like 'medieval' refers to something which is more existing today. So more like a retrospective view. And, it also links to a bit more fantasy, which people built up to more fantasy medieval stuff. But 'Middle Ages', to me, is a much more official term given to a period, the actual period of time.[8]

Participants in other groups echoed John's assessment, saying, 'medieval I associate [with] legends rather than true history', and 'Middle Ages I've thought more along the lines of the Royal Armouries and history stuff, whereas medieval ones I've thought of fairy tales, and legends, and King Arthur.' This broad association of 'medieval' with fantasy and 'Middle Ages' with history had a number of resultant effects upon the participants' understandings and interpretations of these terms.

Many participants also limited the term 'medieval', in geographical terms, to Great Britain alone, whereas they applied 'Middle Ages' to a wider geography. They often did this based on a sense that, being more historical, 'Middle Ages' was more geographically diverse, whereas their familiarity with British legends – having been raised in the UK – caused them to be more closely associated with 'medieval'.

Some also added a moral dimension to their definitions. They commonly described the Middle Ages as seeming worse than medieval. 'Middle Ages', to them, carried connotations of poverty, filth, barbarism and oppression. Chloe called the era evoked by the words 'Middle Ages' 'more primitive' than the one evoked by 'medieval'. When describing their word associations with 'Middle Ages', Stephen and Justin said:

Stephen: Well, at the top [rank of their sheet for 'Middle Ages'] we have disease, basically. We just associate it with disease, general unpleasantness. And then we've got unrest and punishment underneath that, so pretty usual.

Justin: Yeah, 'medieval' is essentially more focused on the glamorous type things where this ['Middle Ages'] is more on the streets and it being kind of horrible and mangy basically.

The fact that Stephen calls his focus on disease, unrest, and punishment 'pretty usual' emphasises the degree to which he feels this is a commonly understood idea. And, at least among these groups, he was not wrong; there were many other responses from all of the groups in this vein: 'For 'Middle Ages' we had [...] all the nasty kind of things', '[when] I thought [about] the Middle Ages, I think of dirtier, smellier people than medieval', 'Middle Ages I just thought was really backwards and dirty'.

By contrast, the word 'medieval' more commonly attracted romantic connotations. Jess thought 'medieval' referred to a time where 'it's all sort of party-ish and they're having feasts and have got decent clothes'. Elizabeth, Emma, and Catherine also had an animated exchange about medieval clothing:

Catherine: [When I think of medieval costume
   Emma: Medieval, yeah.][9]
Catherine: It's like the big flowing dresses of the rich people and
   the big headdresses = [10]
Elizabeth: = But with the Middle Ages I put down mud and dirt
   first.

Other examples from these three include: 'for medieval' we had more, romanticised, monsters, and banquets, fighting, jousting, that kind of area', '[medieval] was all about knights and castles', and 'medieval was more grand'. This sense of 'medieval', indicating a bright, cheery vision of the Middle Ages, directly contrasts with the definition of the word in the *OED* – which ascribes barbarity and backwardness to the term. It also contrasts with the popular idea of something described as 'practically medieval', or the *Pulp Fiction* 'get medieval on your ass'.[11] 'Medieval', to study participants, bore romantic connotations of aristocratic adventure, grand feasts, and lavish costume. Instead, it was 'Middle Ages' that evoked barbarism, dirt, poverty, and disease. Though contradictory, both definitions exist simultaneously in participants' minds without any seeming cognitive dissonance.

Two Visions of the Middle Ages

Several scholars have identified the two images mentioned by the participants (of the jolly-fantastical and dark-historical) when constructing taxonomies of popular medievalisms. However, each scholar describes these images somewhat differently, and none corresponds precisely with the definitions put forward by the participants. For example, regarding the dark vision, Umberto Eco describes one of his famous 'ten little Middle Ages' as:

The Middle Ages as a *barbaric* age, a land of elementary and outlaw feelings [...] they are also the Middle Ages of early Bergman. The same elementary passions could exist equally on the Phoenician coasts or in the desert of Gilgamesh. These ages are Dark par excellence [...]. With only a slight distortion, one is asked to celebrate, on this earth of virile, brute force, the glories of a new Aryanism. It is a shaggy medievalism, and the shaggier its heroes, the more profoundly ideological its superficial naïveté.[12]

This also appears in the second entry of David Williams' taxonomy of popular depictions of the period:

Whatever the purported date, these Ages are dark, dirty, violent, politically unstable or threatening. Here are *The War Lord*, *Conan the Barbarian*, and Lang's Nibelungs and Huns. These are the ages of Bergman, and of Richard Fleischer's *Vikings* despite the hearty jollity of its heroic violence.[13]

Andrew B.R. Elliott calls it:

the world of barbarity and squalor in which dark forces sweep unchecked through defenseless villages, storm monasteries and ransack their way into the annals of history. It is the world of superstition and religious zeal, too [...] and we know – thanks to years of conditioning – what to expect from the dark primitivism of the Middle Ages.[14]

Elliott is particularly astute in highlighting the social-cognitive element of these understandings and expectations of the Middle Ages. Generation after generation has been conditioned on what to expect when they encounter the Middle Ages – a process that begins in early childhood. Most of the participants in this study had been conditioned to expect exactly that: they felt the term 'Middle Ages' *specifically* referred to the unpleasant vision of the period. They focused on a handful of interrelated key aspects of this. To them, the Middle Ages denoted a time rife with war, violence, poverty, and social inequity; people of this time were unclean, they were unhealthy, and their governments were autocratic and oppressive.

Williams and Elliott also address the imagery attributed to the word 'medieval': romantic adventure and opulence, the location of Sherwood Forest, Camelot, and Disney's medievalisms. This vision is the ancestor of the medievalisms of the Romantic period, of *Ivanhoe* and the Eglinton Tournament of 1839.[15] Eco does not have a ready category for this in his 'Ten Little Middle Ages', but Williams describes this as: 'These Middle Ages are bright, clean, noble, sporting and merry. This is Hollywood and often Sherwood. It is Douglas Fairbanks and Robert Taylor. Despite the outlaws, the politics are of the establishment.'[16] Elliott describes the iconic:

> procession of knights in glistening armour and bright, spotless raiments [...] the colourful flags adorning the castles flutter playfully in the breeze. A princess emerges from a turret on the castle walls [...]. We have seen its tournaments, its loud declamations of loyalty to the king and obeisance to the beautiful queen; its honour and its chivalry ....[17]

Many participants reported that they had a sense that the word 'medieval' was connected with myth, legend, fairy tale, and fantasy.[18] Jane made this clear: 'medieval ones [words on her word-association exercise] I've thought of fairy tales and legends like King Arthur.' For Elizabeth, 'medieval' evoked associations with a time period that she termed 'legendary-old'. 'Legendary-old' meant, for her, not just myth and legend but a specific genre of fairy-tale myth and legend: one containing wizards, dragons, witches, and larger-than-life kings and queens. When the group was asked what sort of legends fit within this category, Jane listed, 'King Arthur and Merlin, Chaucer, Heath Ledger'.[19] Other figures mentioned by others in the group included 'knights', 'Robin Hood', and 'Shrek'. Shrek, at first glance, might seem an odd inclusion in this list of noble heroes (and the men who play them). However, it is an illuminating difference; though Shrek is the muddy, dirty, and smelly Middle Ages *par excellence*, in his world he is an outsider. In his adventures, he breaches the wall between the medieval and the Middle Ages for comic effect. He represents an exception that proves the rule.

Beyond this emerging binary of a 'light-fantastical' medieval and 'dark-historical' Middle Ages, the participants also developed a variety of ways of defining and discussing the period. Scholars generally understand the 'Middle Ages' to be defined in two ways: temporally and geographically. While many scholars limit the period to the European region from approximately the years 500–1500 CE (though with significant variation as will be discussed below), the participants of the study had very different ways of understanding the question of 'when' and 'where' the medieval world existed.

When Were the Middle Ages?

I think of 'medieval' as a very, very, very, very, very long time ago.

Catherine, *November Focus Group*

The participants themselves had difficulty expressing exactly when the Middle Ages occurred. While this might seem to be a staggering knowledge gap (considering it is perhaps the most basic question about any historical period), this is not entirely surprising, since scholars have the same problem. There is an ongoing scholarly debate about where the temporal boundaries of 'the Middle Ages' should be drawn, and on what basis. The relative merits of these academic delineations of the period are not important here. However, it is important to understand the major academic periodisations (at least in Anglophonic scholarship) so that they can be compared with those voiced by the participants.

The lower boundary of the Middle Ages is relatively simple. Fifteenth-century Italian historian Leonardo Bruni was one of the first to divide history into the tripartite framework of 'ancient' (or 'classical'), 'middle', and 'modern'.[20] He placed the end of the 'ancient' period (and the beginning of the Middle Ages) at the deposition of the last Emperor of the Western Roman Empire in 476 CE. While the start point in 476 CE is admittedly arbitrary, it is a bracket which has been used commonly by subsequent historians as a marker for the end of the Western Roman Empire – and thus the beginning of the medieval – with relatively little shift until the present day.[21]

The end point, on the other hand, is more controversial, and depends largely on the perspective of the scholar. Each differing scholarly perspective is rooted in an idea of a fundamental change that occurred between 'medieval' and 'modern'. This is key to their perspective on the defining characteristics of the Middle Ages. Bruni ended the medieval period in the middle of the thirteenth century, with the downfall of the Holy Roman Empire as a major influence in Italian politics. This was clearly because he was a scholar of Italian political history.[22] The *Oxford English Dictionary*, however, places the end at 1453 when the Ottoman Empire conquered Constantinople, extinguishing the last vestigial possibilities of crusade, thus seeing crusade as a central unifying concept.[23] Many recent historians are less willing to make such a clear break between medieval and modern. Some historians of England see the end of the medieval as the ascension of the Tudor Dynasty, or the dissolution of the monasteries. Others point instead to broad cultural trends: the Protestant Reformation, the flowering of the Renaissance, the advent of print culture, or the voyages across the Atlantic which began the colonisation of the Americas.[24] Some do not see one crucial moment at all, but prefer to view the fifteenth and sixteenth centuries as a time of gradual but profound cultural change which brought the Middle Ages to a close. This fluidity calls into question just what made the Middle Ages distinct, and makes it easy to understand why non-specialists may find it difficult to clearly define the period.

Subdividing the Middle Ages: Early, High, Late, Dark

Complicating the idea even further, scholars subdivide the Middle Ages in a variety of ways. The most-commonly used paradigm divides the thousand years into three parts: the 'early' (c.500–c.1000 CE), 'high' (c.1000–c.1300 CE), and 'late' (c.1300–c.1500 CE) Middle Ages. Confusingly, there are also some national variants; British archaeologists (and some historians) sometimes call the period c.500–c.1050 'Anglo-Saxon', reserving 'medieval' for the years between c.1050–c.1500. The chief break is the Norman Conquest which, while certainly consequential to the history of the British Isles, is much less so outside of them. Scholars of the Scandinavian Middle Ages sometimes use the 'Viking Age' (late-eighth–mid-eleventh centuries CE).[25] Scholars of the Early Middle Ages have developed the term 'late antiquity' (mid-third to eighth centuries CE) as a way of emblematising the continuity (especially in the East) rather than utter collapse of the Roman way of life. Each of these academic terms have trickled into the popular historical consciousness. But they have done so slowly and unevenly – even if, for example, the heritage industry, education sector, or film industry were to read the latest academic scholarship and accept these new paradigms, it takes time to rewrite signs at historic sites. It takes significant effort to rewrite textbooks and retrain teachers. Moreover, old and beloved books and films never die. This muddies even the most basic waters of medieval chronology and terminology considerably.

Take, for example, 'the Dark Ages'. Even though the term has been abandoned by contemporary historians, the phrase remains common in public parlance. The term was re-invented by Petrarch (previously it had been used to refer to a time before the coming of Christ) and popularised by Italian Humanists in the fifteenth century.[26] This was done as a way of distinguishing themselves from what they saw as a period of religious fanaticism and 'barbaric darkness' from which they saw themselves as attempting to emerge.[27] The term 'Dark Ages' then changed meaning, even over the course of the twentieth century. As Fred C. Robinson argues,

> In popular encyclopaedias and in many of the older dictionaries *Dark Ages* is defined as simply a synonym of *Middle Ages*. In 1904, however, W. P. Ker in his book *The Dark Ages* said that the two terms 'have come to be distinguished, and the Dark Ages are now no more than the first part of the Middle Age, while the term medieval is often restricted to the later centuries, about 1100 to 1500 ...'. This is a distinction which was for a time carefully observed by some historians.[28]

Robinson goes on to conclude that the term 'Dark Ages' has fallen out of academic parlance due to its connotations of 'intellectual stagnation'. He proposes rehabilitating the term by associating 'dark' instead with 'our dim perception of the period (owing to limited documentary evidence about it)'.[29] So, 'the Dark Ages' is an unusually loaded term, meaning either:

- the Middle Ages in its entirety,
- the Early Middle Ages only,
- a period of intellectual darkness, and/or
- a period about which little is known or knowable.

Examining these various competing terms and their definitions illustrates just how muddied these waters can be. But even more importantly, every one of these terms and definitions were used by the participants when describing the period. It is little wonder they were confused.

When Did They Think The Middle Ages Were?

The research participants were never flatly asked 'When do you think the Middle Ages occurred?', since the underlying research methodology dictated that they be permitted to define the period in whatever way they saw fit. However, perhaps unsurprisingly, many discussed chronology when defining the period. That said, few had a confident idea when the Middle Ages were. Many only had a sense of it being 'a long time ago'. Some defined it within a range of a few hundred years, or more commonly, defined its dates by anchoring it against significant historical events.

Elizabeth was unsure about specific chronology: 'Four hundred years ago I wouldn't associate with medieval; I would associate [it with], maybe, a thousand years ago or something like that. [. . .] That's just what I think of in my mind. I don't know whether it's right.' She was correct, though it is difficult to know why she chose these numbers, and she had difficulty explaining her answer. Jess was somewhat more confident. 'I thought Middle Ages was, I don't know, 800 AD to somewhere in the middle of the thousands [...] In the middle of what we've been through.' Again, Jess was (more or less) correct. But, that is the least interesting aspect of her statement. She posited the Middle Ages as *a literal middle-period* in the history of human civilisation, which indicates that she fundamentally agrees with the tripartite division of civilisation into 'classical', 'middle', and 'modern'. Prehistory is outside the scope of history and thus outside her sense of human experience. Furthermore, her use of the first-person pronoun – 'what *we've* been through' – seems to imply that she intuitively identifies with her historical forebears. She sees a sense of continuity with past peoples – at least those a part of 'civilisation'. Later in the group, she limited her definition of the term 'Middle Ages' specifically to Britain after 1066: 'I tend to think of Norman people in Britain, after the Norman invasion. That's what I tend to think of as the Middle Ages'. By contrast, she defined the word 'medieval' as the end of the period, 'just before Elizabethan times'.

Mark defined the beginning of the period not by calendrical dates but by a sense of the dominant cultures in England coupled with a pejorative view of the culture of the Early Middle Ages:

Well, medieval for me, I would say, it started pretty soon after the Romans moved out and we had all the Anglo-Saxons [and] Vikings. There's a lot of fighting, a lot of oppression. There wasn't a lot of creativity allowed. And people, generally, stagnated for however many hundreds of years.

On view here is the idea of intellectual and cultural regression in the Early Middle Ages, despite recent scholarly attempts to banish it.[30] Echoing what Jess said in another group, Mark also differentiated between 'medieval' and 'Middle Ages', but in the opposite direction. To him,

> Middle Ages, I would say, is when it all, when [...] people start to think more freely. There's a bit more technological advances. You've got catapults; you've got proper castles being built instead of just chopping down trees and sticking them in the way of your opponent.

Mark was a technologically minded mathematics student with an affinity for computer games that feature medieval warfare (as will be discussed later). So it is perhaps unsurprising that he equates progress not just with technology, but specifically with *military* technology. Mark also (without prompting) identified himself as a strict Evangelical Christian (more on this later, as well). This likely frames Mark's world view, wherein the Middle Ages is an era before what he believes is a freedom of thought only present after the Reformation.

The term 'the Dark Ages' was reserved for their (perhaps more informal) conversations about the films they were shown (as discussed in Chapters 5 and 6). In fact, in their expansive later discussions, the participants used all four meanings of the term: as synonymous with Middle Ages, as referring only to the Early Middle Ages, as a period of 'intellectual stagnation', and as a scantly documented period of history. To these participants, 'the Dark Ages' is not an outmoded term at all. If anything, it is overloaded with meanings.

Where Were the Middle Ages?

There is also a broad disagreement among scholars about the other ways in which to delineate the Middle Ages. In popular parlance – and among some academics – 'The Middle Ages' is used to describe a period of time (c.500– c.1500 CE) no matter where on the globe: whether Paris, Machu Picchu, or Antarctica. However, latent in the definitions described above is the idea that 'the Middle Ages' are a period of time in a particular place. Unlike 'the seventeenth century', which is a descriptor of time alone, 'the Middle Ages' (like 'the Victorian Age' or 'the Meji period') describes a time, place, and culture. This is the reason why the difficulty in defining the period's end exists among scholars; if it is seen as a cultural movement, the Middle Ages ended at different times in different countries for different reasons.

All of the varying definitions of the Middle Ages, whether in terms of empire, crusade, religion, colonialism, or technology, roughly define the Middle Ages geographically as edged by: Iceland, England, Scotland, Ireland, and Scandinavia in the north; Lithuania and the western reaches of Russia in the North-East; the Middle East, the Holy Land, Egypt, and, arguably, Ethiopia and Nubia in the southeast; and stretching across North Africa to Morocco in the southwest.

It is for this reason that the travels of Marco Polo, Leif Ericson, and Christopher Columbus (or the alleged journeys of John de Mandeville), were, and still are, considered extraordinary – they were voyages from the known into the unknown, crossing theretofore uncrossed geographical and cultural boundaries out of the Middle Ages and into somewhere and, to some degree, 'somewhen' else. That having been said, there has been significant work among medievalists to broaden the idea of where the Middle Ages were or, at the very least, where medieval people were. This is being done by illuminating the beginnings of a global network of trading and knowledge exchange centred in the Islamic and Buddhist Empires of Asia.[31]

Where Did They Think the Middle Ages Were?

Perhaps surprisingly, the participants were much more confident and more specific in naming *where* the Middle Ages were than *when*. But contrary to the typical definitions of the Middle Ages, with only a few exceptions, they projected their own English upbringings upon their understandings of the Middle Ages, locating them only in Western Europe, Britain, or England.

John and Dan noted that the idea of historical periodisation did imply geographical boundaries – even to a single country or region. John began: 'when you talk "ages", they never refer to the whole world. Each, not necessarily country, but they all have their own timelines.' Dan agreed: '"Middle Ages" is reflective only of [one] country at the same time. Time is still going on in other countries.' Others drew those boundaries very tightly: Jane said simply of her word association page: 'I wrote down England.' Similarly, Chloe, as part of an explanation of a broader idea (wherein she felt 'medieval' referred to the legendary whereas 'Middle Ages' referred only to the historical) Chloe felt 'the big one [difference in her definitions from the other participants] is that we thought 'medieval' was Britain, British, and English, whereas 'Middle Ages' was a bit more widespread'. Later, she defined 'a bit more widespread' as 'Western Europe'. Robert, acting as spokesman for his group, agreed, 'When we'd said medieval, we associate it with Britain.'

Elizabeth said: 'I didn't write down England, but I was just thinking of England. I didn't think of, well, I put Crusades, but English Knights ... I wasn't thinking of anywhere else.' Here the Crusades are mentioned as an exception to the rule rather than central to it – the rule standing only because of English participation. This was common. In the June group, Justin and Stephen echoed it:

Justin: When I think of the Middle Ages, it's probably set in Britain to be fair. I would say.
Stephen: Or it involves Britain.
Justin: Or involves Britain some way, yeah.
Stephen: It kind of, the war in Jerusalem and stuff.
Justin: I mean, I know that there must be something, you know =
Stephen: = there's other stuff =
Justin: = there's other stuff going on and there must be other types of places, but
Moderator: So the war in Jerusalem involves Britain how?
Stephen: Um, because they sent people to crusade.

Their idea that England was central to the crusades is a misconception which pervades Anglo-American popular culture, likely a result of the centrality of the Third Crusade in the English popular imagination of the Crusades. English participation in the history of the Crusades as a whole was minor as compared to the French or German contributions, especially in the early crusading period. Christopher Tyerman writes, 'On the face of it, English involvement in the First Crusade was minimal and peripheral.'[32] The clashes of Richard the Lionheart and Saladin gained huge popularity during the nineteenth century as a part of the cultural fascination with the Middle Ages that spawned medievalisms like Sir Walter Scott's novel *The Talisman*.[33] That fascination remains to this day: all of the five films released to date which depict the Crusades in the Holy Land as central to their plot include Saladin as a character. All but one include Richard I.[34]

This geographical definition that limited the Middle Ages to England even influenced participants' perceptions of medievalesque fantasies. For example, Jane regarded the 1992 film *Aladdin*'s setting as exceptional among Disney cartoon films because it is *not* set in England.

Jane:	I was just thinking. You have exceptions, something like *Aladdin*. [...] obviously that's [not been] set in, ... England, forest and that sort of setting, it's been moved across to ...
Moderator:	Oh, you mean it's not set in [England and forest
Jane:	Yeah it's] got a completely different setting =
Moderator:	= So are the other ones set in England and forests and stuff?
Jane:	Or France, I suppose, technically.

Wooded landscape is here identified both with the Middle Ages generally and with England specifically. France is mentioned but only hesitantly, as an aside and technicality – likely in reference to *Beauty and the Beast*. France was cited in this way numerous times by this group, and also by Jess in the May group. Eleanor went on to explain her rationale for including France in the Middle Ages: 'I had France as well, but that was because of the guillotine and Marie Antoinette sort of things.' There are several fascinating issues with this statement: first, the fact that she needed to explain, unprompted, why her Middle Ages included France shows how entrenched the idea of Middle-Ages-as-England is in her historical consciousness. Also, her misconception that the period of the guillotine and Marie Antoinette was within the Middle Ages is perhaps surprising. It can be explained by its parallel associations. Marie Antoinette is an icon of royal opulence and wealth, of absolute monarchy and of the grisly results of such excesses of wealth and power. This image fits neatly with many schematic associations Jess – and the other participants – had with the Middle Ages. The guillotine, as well as being an object symbolically tied to the fate of Antoinette, is also symbol of capital punishment and public execution.[35] This coincides neatly with the strong popular associations between torture and public execution and the Middle Ages. Henry VIII's presence in the word association exercises may be the result of similar associations. Like Marie, Henry is also commonly associated with absolute monarchy, opulence, and execution. Henry VIII is perennially popular in British popular culture, and these focus groups were also held while the popular TV series *The Tudors* was on the air, which may have led to his immediate presence in their minds.[36] So, while Eleanor's statement is obviously wildly anachronistic, it sheds significant light on the picture of the Middle Ages which is beginning to emerge. Though Marie did not die in the Middle Ages, her death may have been 'medieval'. Though Henry did not live in the Middle Ages, he led a 'medieval' life.

John said films were at least partially responsible for his sense that the Middle Ages were limited to a few locales in Western Europe:

> in terms of film anyway, there doesn't seem to be anything set in this sort of time, outside some parts of Europe. [. . .] I can't picture what Italy would have been like in these periods, because it's never ever been discussed really [. . .] and obviously any other continent as well. Obviously there's other stuff going on, but it doesn't come to mind at all.

Jess immediately followed with a rather extreme delineation:

> I just assumed the rest of the world doesn't exist. [. . .] I didn't think of anything in Africa, I only think of England. And not going to say Scotland, just literally England is all I think of when I think of this period [. . .] and a bit of Wales.

This is an important distinction – John and Jess do not *necessarily* exclusively associate the period with Britain; however, they struggle to associate it with anything else due to a lack of knowledge. Beyond their own borders, the world disappears into obscurity.

Perceptions of Medieval Religion and Crusade

Over the course of the study many participants also discussed their view of the iconic elements of the Middle Ages (i.e. gender, kingship, warfare, class, knighthood). However, they did so in far greater detail when discussing the three films they viewed – and thus these will be discussed as part of Chapters 5 and 6. However, since they were so central to the second film, *Kingdom of Heaven*, on the second day the participants were led on a pre-film discussion on their perceptions of two particular elements of the Middle Ages: religion and crusade.

Despite being one of the defining characteristics of the period, very few participants spontaneously discussed medieval religion on the first day. The notable exceptions to this were those few participants who held pointed views about medieval religion which seemed rooted in their personal faith and specific religious affiliations. For example, Mark had a particular focus on religious issues. As a self-described 'Charismatic Baptist', Mark found little to redeem medieval religion.[37] On their word association exercises, both he and Dan (who did not volunteer his religious identity/background) focused on religion. Mark described the results of his and Dan's word associations: 'papists, pre-Reformation, we've got the Crusades, we've got witch-burning again, schisms, but we've also got things like cathedrals, [...] monks, and nuns'. He and Dan also frequently used the anti-Catholic epithet 'papist' to refer to medieval religion. To Mark, the most significant differences between the Middle Ages and the present day were the reforms of Martin Luther: '[the] Middle Ages ended [in] Luther's era, Reformations, when there was a lot more free-thinking [...] we've moved on to the Enlightenment Age where science was allowed to flourish'. He also said 'freedom of thought' was absent in the Middle Ages. With these statements, Mark planted himself in opposition to the Middle Ages, both as a Protestant and also as a scientifically-minded mathematics student. To Mark, the border between medieval and modern is a religious, intellectual, and scientific one. Medieval culture was defined primarily by its 'backwards' religion and repressed intellectual culture. Though the other participants did not express views similar to Mark's in the pre-film discussions, several did so after having seen the *Kingdom of Heaven*.

That religion was largely ignored in the initial discussions may be a product of the increasingly secular outlook of British society in 2008 and 2009. Annual studies conducted by British Social Attitudes, the primary social research survey in Britain, found that in 2009, 51 per cent of Britons identified as having 'no religion', following a rising trend from 34 per cent in 1989 and 44 per cent in 1999 (Figure 2.3).[38]

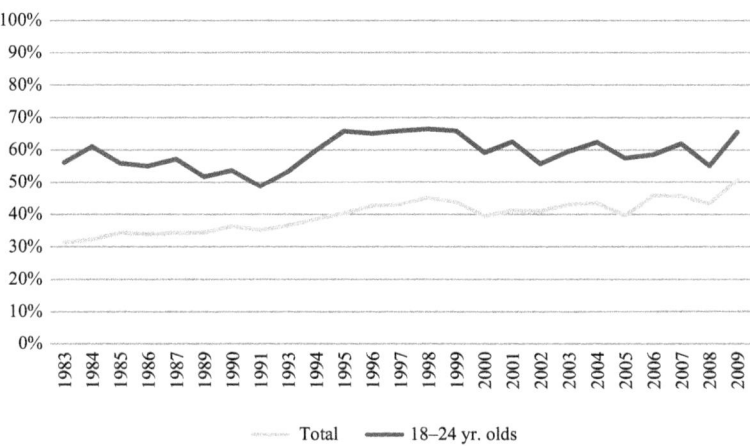

Total   ━━━ 18–24 yr. olds

Figure 2.3   British People Identifying with 'No Religion', 1983–2009.

That said, the age demographic of the participants of the present study, 18 to 24-year-olds, has oscillated between 50 per cent and 65 per cent over the same period with no particular trend.

What effect personal religious views may have on individuals' historical consciousness and perceptions of the medieval past warrants further study.

What Does 'Crusade' Mean?

Another word-association exercise was done at the beginning of the second meeting – this time using the word 'crusade' (Figure 2.4).

For 'crusade', the overall pattern which emerges is of Christian knights making a journey to Jerusalem at the behest of the Pope to do battle with Muslims: in other words, the Crusades to the Holy Land. A sense emerges as well that this was not just a war of Christians against Muslims, but of Christianity against Islam – a conflict of religions rather than individuals or nations. Unsurprisingly, given their perennial popularity in popular fiction (e.g. *The Da Vinci Code*), the Knights Templar were also mentioned, as was Saladin.

As on the previous day, the participants were then asked to define what the word meant to them. Overall, the participants reported

Knights	7
Jerusalem	6
War	6
Journey	5
The Pope	5
Christianity vs Islam	5
Battle	4
Muslims	4
Holy Orders (esp. 'Templars')	4
The Holy Land	4
Holy War	3
Armour	3
Religion	3
Christians	3
Saladin	3

Figure 2.4 Responses to 'Crusade' word-association exercises and frequency (3+).

holding two coexisting but contradictory definitions. One definition was rooted in the historical Crusades – the specific conflict between Christians and Muslims during the Middle Ages. The other was the more general sense of crusade, often used metaphorically to describe people or political movements in the modern day. Interestingly, some participants fused these two ideas, claiming that the historical Crusades were a non-violent enterprise, and some projected contemporary politics and conflicts onto the historical Crusades.

Historical Crusade

Their historically orientated definitions of 'crusade' – encompassing the series of conflicts between Western European Christendom and the Middle East during the Middle Ages – also carried additional connotations. Firstly, almost all who defined crusade in this way referred only to the Crusades in the Holy Land. The vast majority of specific examples they offered referred to the Third Crusade, highlighting its pre-eminence in their historical consciousness. Only Chloe made reference to any other crusades: 'I think of them [the Crusades] more as Christians marching to defend their religion against – it's mainly Muslim, but it can be other sects.'

Like 'the Middle Ages', scholars have disagreed on a range of even basic definitional issues around 'crusade' (e.g. how many crusades there were, what constitutes a crusade, why they began and ended, etc.).[39] Many of these complex issues have not yet trickled into the popular historical consciousness, as evidenced by the focus on the Third Crusade amongst most participants. But Chloe's statement took two contrary positions:

(1) 'crusades' were not limited to the Middle-Eastern theatre, and
(2) they were defensive.

It is unknown where she learned these ideas, but including sectarian conflict in the definition of crusade betrays a fairly sophisticated understanding of the Crusades. Perhaps without realising, Chloe's idea comes from the 'pluralist' or 'generalist' school of thought amongst Crusade historians. In contrast with 'traditionalist' historians of the Crusades, pluralists argue that a crusade need not necessarily be directed to the East, and thus can include the later crusades called against heretics and Protestants.[40] These later crusades have featured in a few recent popular medievalisms, such as Kate Mosse's popular Languedoc Trilogy of novels (*Labyrinth*, *Sepulchre*, and *Citadel*).[41] However, these later crusades still remain fairly obscure – at least by contrast with those in the Holy Land.

Additionally, though the idea of a crusade as defensive may seem bizarre today, this is one of the oldest concepts in Crusading ideology. This was the very position that Pope Urban II himself reportedly took; in calling for the First Crusade, he urged knights to 'rush as quickly as you can *to the defence* of the Eastern Church' (my emphasis), who were, for Urban, under threat from the Turks.[42] This idea is in direct contrast with contemporary cultural perceptions which typically view the Crusades as aggressive (and thus morally indefensible) rather than defensive. Chloe did not remember where she learned those things, and it is entirely possible she may have misremembered or conflated ideas of other conflicts. But by whatever method, Chloe seems to have come to a more scholarly understanding of the Crusades than it might first seem.

Aside from Chloe, the participants' specific understandings of the Crusades were almost entirely drawn from the Third Crusade. These participants all said that the goal of the Crusades was the acquisition or defence of Jerusalem by Christians, and the only specific historical figures mentioned were Richard the Lionheart and Saladin. Some said that their familiarity with the Crusades stemmed from Robin Hood stories, like Jess who mentioned, 'They've always got Richard the Lionheart coming back at the end, because he's been off fighting in the Crusades.'

Incidentally, Robin Hood's association with King Richard I (and by proxy, crusade) is itself post-medieval. It was the invention of Anthony Munday, playwright of two Robin Hood plays: *The Downfall* and *The Death of Robert, Earl of Huntington*, which he wrote at the close of the sixteenth century. In addition to creating Robin's typical role as a dispossessed nobleman, A.J. Pollard relates that 'Munday was responsible also for [. . .] transposing the plot to the reign of Richard I while he is absent on crusade, leaving his realm in the care of his wicked brother John.'[43] This has become the standard; all Hollywood films that depict Robin Hood places him during the reigns of Richard or John, and many (from *Robin Hood* starring Douglas Fairbanks to the more recent *Robin Hood: Prince of Thieves*, *Robin Hood: Men in Tights* and *Robin Hood* starring Russell Crowe) include narratives wherein Robin undertakes, escapes, or laments participation in the Crusades.[44]

Participants also described the crusader knight as central to their idea of crusade. They held a relatively specific view of what a crusader knight would have looked like. Chloe thought of 'lots of people in big cloaks'. Robert then expanded, 'knights on horseback and those capes [. . .] horses in, I don't know what the word is, but the coat kind of thing'. Here they are probably referring to the surcoat developed for wear by European knights over their armour during the Crusades, and the similar caparison for the horse – a common feature in the depiction of crusaders in contemporary medievalisms.

Because of this outfit, Justin incorrectly identified Saint George as a crusader: 'Saint George, because I envision him wearing the suit of armour with the red cross style, and beards and stuff and chain mail.' He said he learned this image of George as the typical crusader from the climactic scene of *Indiana Jones and the Last Crusade*, when Indy finds 'the Holy Grail, when he goes in, and it's Saint George', who has 'got his little Saint George armour on and the beard and [. . .] the chain mail on his head'. Justin has misremembered; the crusader in this scene in *The Last Crusade* is not Saint George. The cross worn by that character seems to be a stylised image of a cup superimposed upon a version of the Templar cross. He has conflated this grail knight and Saint George perhaps because they both are often depicted dressed in coif, mail and surcoat (usually adorned with a cross). Saint George was not a crusader, nor is he associated with crusading. The red cross on a white field is only coincidentally used by both the Knights Templar and Saint George (and thus the flag of England). This conflation of crusading and the patron saint of England may reinforce the incorrect idea that the Crusades were a predominantly English endeavour.

'Moral' Crusade

The second definition of crusade that participants discussed was the metaphorical sense of the word: a struggle (often a political one) in order to achieve a goal, often with the adjective 'moral' preceding. This second definition was used almost exclusively to discuss modern struggles, individuals, or grass-roots political movements. Erica defined the word as a journey of self-discovery: 'a long journey of getting to know yourself, getting to spread your message, but not war [. . .] a big journey to spread your message, and you always know yourself afterwards'. Chloe agreed, saying she felt that crusade 'was quite peaceful and about a journey rather than a conflict' and that it was about 'fighting for your religion, but in a non-violent way'.

Laura's definition focused instead on group effort: 'a group of people who have [a] one-purpose mind [. . .] on a journey towards it, towards achieving it'. The June focus group agreed in their assessment that the politics of modern-day 'crusading' was 'very conservative', and were engaged in by – in Stephen's words – 'little Englanders' and 'church-going folk who [. . .] are likely to get outraged'.[45] They then linked moral crusading with the politics of the right-wing *Daily Mail* and *Daily Express* newspapers. Stephen reiterated the conflation of Saint George – as he appears on the masthead of the *Daily Express* – with crusading, because 'their logo is Saint George, isn't it? [. . .] with the shield and the red cross. So it's got a crusade symbol on its letterhead of every paper every day.' Though Saint George appears on the paper as a

British nationalistic icon rather than a crusading one, it may be interesting for future research to investigate how widespread the false association of George (and by proxy English nationalism) with crusading is, and what implications this may have in the English historical consciousness.

Some referred to 'crusade', without the 'moral' adjective, to apply to liberal politics as well, for example, 'Al Gore going on his environmental crusade.' To Jess, the modern idea of crusade could have positive connotations: 'there is more sort of [a] good thing, crusades. Whereas if you look back on history and the legacy of the actual medieval crusades, it has more negative connotations to it.' Modern people fighting for their beliefs had a sort of nobility to it, whereas medieval people doing the same was a tainted endeavour.

Merged Definitions: A Moral, Historical Crusade? Modern Violent Crusades?

A few participants merged these two definitions in their minds. They projected the modern idea of a peaceful, moral crusade onto the Middle Ages – believing that the medieval Crusades were not centred on war, but were primarily cultural struggles. Erica felt that the Crusades (and, to her, 'holy war' in general) were primarily for the purpose of evangelisation, being to 'defend your religion and spread the word of your religion'. Chloe agreed: 'I thought it was quite peaceful and about a journey rather than a conflict [...] its intent in the first place is to be peaceful.' Justin felt that the conflict was primarily cultural rather than violent: 'I mean there's a certain amount of warfare probably, but more as in destroying certain things of the opposition rather than actually destroying them [...] trying to break down their culture in a way.' Stephen felt that the conflict of ideologies was key: 'it seems about a clash of ideologies, and it's just going to go backwards and forwards and it's not going to resolve itself'. Even though Stephen was referring to the historical Crusades at this point, he used the present tense to describe them, drawing, perhaps, unconscious links between crusaders past and present. This perception of the medieval Crusades as a primarily peaceful, cultural, religious, or ideological struggle is puzzling. Some seemed to conflate the idea of 'pilgrimage' and 'crusade'. Others seemed to see 'crusade' as an early iteration of the extremely problematic 'clash of civilisations' paradigm promoted by conservative thinkers like Samuel

P. Huntington, or neoconservatives such as Niall Ferguson, which pits the 'West' in contradistinction to the rest of the world.[46]

Hand-in-hand with this idea, the June focus group projected their understanding of recent conflicts in the Middle East onto the medieval Crusades. Katy felt that implicit in the word 'crusade' was an idea of asymmetric warfare: 'I always associate it with one side being a lot stronger than the other.' Justin was more explicit, 'I'm not sure I see it as an actual war'. Instead he called it a 'historical guerrilla' war. Sean felt that crusade is 'more of an overwhelming thing [. . .] in my mind, [the overwhelming side] it's Christianity'. For Justin, Muslim opposition to the Crusades was an insurgency or resistance: 'you get Christians coming in, and then everyone else in their houses. It's more a force against people [. . .] having a certain amount of resistance because people are so set in their beliefs' – resistance being, to him, a result of cultural obstinacy rather than something nobler. These participants seemed to fill in their knowledge-gaps about the Crusades with what felt, to them, like an appropriate analogue: the contemporary wars in the Middle East.

The Crusades were not a historical guerrilla war or an occupation by an overwhelming force. That said, there may be several reasons they feel that this is an appropriate analogue. Perhaps it is based upon the rhetoric used by those engaged in these contemporary wars (like George W. Bush, Osama bin Laden, Saddam Hussein, or Muammar Gadaffi) that compared modern conflicts to the Crusades. As Finke and Shichtman argue, the use of 'crusade' as a rhetorical device by these figures to link present conflicts with the Crusades 'raises important questions about how we justify the decision to go to war but answers them, disturbingly, almost exclusively through Huntington's "clash of civilizations" thesis. The crusades analogy suggests "nothing less than an apocalyptic conflict between irreconcilable cultures".'[47] Perhaps it is the 'clash of civilisations' paradigm the participants see in both: East versus West, Christendom versus the Dar al-Islam – or perhaps instead, Christianity versus Islam. Perhaps it springs from their perception (discussed more below) that the Muslim world during the Middle Ages was not really 'civilised', and therefore was unable to mount an effective defence. Or, perhaps, they simply have a presentist perspective – where their default intellectual position is to believe that the past is just like the present.

This idea of the Crusades as analogous to contemporary conflicts is doubly curious when compared with the typical image of the Crusades held by the participants: that of the clash between Richard I and Saladin during the Third Crusade. Participants never described Saladin as the leader of an insurgency or a guerrilla warrior, but as a king equal in status to Richard. Despite this contradiction, the participants projected their view of the present onto the past as a way of justifying or rationalising their worldviews. Projecting the present onto the past permitted them to believe that the present is logical, even inevitable, because the conflicts that exist now have always existed in a similar form. By extension, this past and present will be perpetuated into an infinitely repeating future that is both comforting and disconcerting in its stability.

As seen above, even the most basic questions about the Middle Ages – what it was, when and where it occurred – and some of its major features are up for debate. Scholars have debated these questions for decades – it seems, understandably, that the public has a similar lack of clarity about even these basic ideas. That is not to say, as popular perception might suggest, that they know nothing. If anything, they know too much – or perhaps more specifically, their knowledge includes an array of fragmented and sometimes self-contradictory information. Their minds suture the gaps in their knowledge in the way minds do: by applying paradigms about which they have more knowledge (such as the current wars in the Middle East) to areas about which they have less (i.e. The Crusades). Much of this ambiguity within the popular historical consciousness arises from the fact that there are a wide range of sources of differing quality. Academics ceased using 'The Dark Ages' years ago, however academic knowledge is only one source among many.

Learning the Middle Ages

A key component to better understanding the participants' historical consciousness lies in better understanding the sources of their knowledge. In essence, if academics or educators are interested in shaping the popular historical consciousness, it is crucial to understand which disseminators of historical knowledge have the most impact. All participants were asked where they felt they got their knowledge about the Middle Ages.[48] In a discussion on the second day, Stephen and Sean had difficulty answering to their own satisfaction:

Stephen: I don't know. On the one hand it would be interesting
           to know where all our preconceptions come from. But
           on the other, we can't. Whenever you've asked that
           question, we just don't [know], it just comes from
           somewhere.

Sean: It just comes from loads and loads of things.

Stephen: So I don't [know]. It could have just been at a very, very
           young age that we got these ideas in our head and that,
           like we said yesterday about gut reactions, that you
           know that something is true.

It is impossible for even the most introspective person to know every
source for their knowledge on a given topic. Our historical consciousness
is never set in stone, rather, it is constantly under construction, and the
sources of information are often forgotten or misremembered over time.[49]
Therefore, the statements of the participants cannot be considered
definitive or complete; however, they remain a useful window into their
memories of learning about the Middle Ages and what they judge, *post
hoc*, to be important sources of historical knowledge. The following
section will accordingly explore the ideas about the Middle Ages
acquired within the classroom and outside it, as children and as adults.

Childhood Medievalisms

When asked where they felt they gained their knowledge of the Middle
Ages, most participants initially responded by recounting experiences
learning about the period in school during their childhood. Since the
sample excluded anyone who had learned about the Middle Ages at
GCSE level or above, their school learning about the Middle Ages was
only at the primary and secondary levels (approximately ages 5–16).
Some participants (such as John and Mark) felt they could not separate
their memories of learning from school from their informal learning
from popular culture. But many others reported negative experiences of
learning history in school. For example, Dan argued that 'I felt like I can
separate it [learning from pop culture and from school] in this case
because I felt like I learned nothing about this from school.' Emma
echoed Dan's complaint: 'I remember doing it [the Middle Ages] in
school, but [only] a tiny bit and I'm sure that I didn't really learn
anything.' Participants also criticised the emphasis on certain aspects of

history over others in school. For example, Dan said 'history, we'll learn about the Nazis. Anything before that we're going to forget [...] it seems like this topic [the Middle Ages] and other topics, Romans for example, or Saxons, or most history – it seems like we were taught that at primary school level as if to demean it.'

This is a serious allegation – though it is perhaps understandable if he felt the only education he received on an important topic was given to him at the primary or secondary school level. It is also possible that participants may have been performing a casual dislike of their previous schooling for their peers in the focus group in an attempt to promote their current intellectual superiority, or increase their status with the group or the moderator. That said, it would be improper to dismiss their criticisms of the curriculum without first interrogating the way the English National Curriculum currently addresses medieval history.

In reflecting on their schooling, most participants reported that their understanding of history had been compartmentalised into strict periods. For example, Stephen listed 'You have: the Anglo-Saxons and the Vikings, and then the Middle Ages, and then the Tudors.' I followed up by asking what other periods they had learned in school. The only other historical periods mentioned – either in response to this question or mentioned in other contexts – were 'Baroque', 'the Reformation', 'the Restoration', 'the Victorians' and 'the Second World War' (sometimes referred to by participants as 'The Nazis'). Any periods between these or any sense of transition from one era to another were not mentioned. Also, here again lay the distinction between the early-medieval Anglo-Saxons and Vikings and 'the Middle Ages'. Dan found this strict periodisation into easily named segments useful: 'I can fit other things that I know happened around that time into a box of when it happened. And if I can't accurately know that these other things are happening, then I can't really picture what's happening.'

Despite the casual disregard many had for their schooling, several of the ideas they developed about chronology and geography, previously detailed, can be traced, at least in part, to the English National Curriculum. Due to the fact that the English National Curriculum is applied to the whole country, it offers a useful common baseline from which to discuss participants' schooling.[50] The English National Curriculum as taught to these students was established in 1991 and revised in 1999 (though without significant revision to its medieval history requirements).[51] In its history guidelines, history is divided into modules with titles like 'Tudor and Stuart times', 'Victorian Britain', 'The Roman Empire' and 'The Era of the Second World War'.[52] Medieval history is required to be taught on two separate occasions: once during Key Stage Two (ages 7−11) and once in Key Stage Three (ages 11−14). In Key Stage Two (KS2), students are taught Iron Age through early medieval British history in: 'Invaders and settlers: Romans, Anglo-Saxons and Vikings in Britain.' After this, in KS2, students do not proceed chronologically to learn about the later Middle Ages, but skip ahead to 'Tudor and Stuart Times'. Students return to the Middle Ages at Key Stage Three (KS3), in a module entitled 'Medieval Realms: Britain 1066 to 1500'. This may explain the idea the participants held that the Early Middle Ages were not part of the Middle Ages. Firstly, it is understandable that students might not associate Anglo-Saxons and Vikings with the Middle Ages since they were taught in tandem with the Romans rather than the later period. Furthermore, by calling their latter module 'medieval', it implicitly dictates that anything outside these boundaries is not. In fairness, if forced to choose, grouping the Anglo-Saxons with the Romans (on the one hand) or with the Normans (on the other) could offer equally rich pedagogical opportunities. But, it is hardly surprising that, since they are taught in tandem with Roman Britain, these participants held either the outmoded idea that the Anglo-Saxons were not medieval, or a general confusion about what is, and what is not, medieval.

Another feature of the history provision of the English National Curriculum is how clearly it focuses on the national history of the British Isles to the exclusion of the rest of the world. The Middle Ages outside Britain are rarely addressed and, when they are, it is only in relation to how the wider world is relevant to Britain. For example, in the 'Britain and the wider world' subsection of the KS3 module 'Medieval Realms: Britain 1066 to 1500' it is explained: 'pupils should be taught about [. . .] the idea of Christendom and the extent to which the British Isles were part of a wider European world'.[53] In the *National Curriculum Council Consultation Report* of 1990, this focus is made even clearer. It reads: 'pupils should be taught about the major feature in Britain's medieval past and the legacy of the Middle Ages to the modern world. The focus should be on the development of the medieval monarchy, and the way of life of the people of the British Isles.'[54]

Additionally, the very structure of the curriculum units may have influenced participants' perceptions of the time period of the Middle Ages. Optional 'supplementary study units' in the curriculum include 'Castles and Cathedrals: 1066–1500', 'Relations between England and Scotland from the Norman Conquest to the Treaty of Union', and 'The Crusades'. This unit structure (as well as the required 'Medieval Realms' module) may help to explain why some participants felt the Middle Ages was post-1066; it is less likely that such specific ideas about periodisation would have been established by popular culture. That said, the curriculum also follows underlying cultural currents. Though it has the power to influence future ideas, it is as much a reflection of the British historical consciousness as the statements of the participants were.

Overall, the modularisation and periodisation presented by the curriculum does not seem to help students to understand wider historical movements or phenomena, or to see the transition between periods as anything other than a complete cognitive break. This is exacerbated by the fact that history was not taught to them sequentially, instead skipping through the centuries. As a result, the transitions between historical eras are lost. This educational paradigm makes 1066 and 1500 centrally important dates in British medieval history. And, since medieval history outside Britain is not taught, it implies that these dates are centrally important beyond British shores, and that Britain was the centre of the medieval world. Even though most participants did not hold very high opinions of the education in medieval history that they received in primary and secondary school, the paradigms established by the curriculum of their schooling were often repeated in their discussions and seemed to form a foundation of their historical consciousness. And this educational paradigm has clearly influenced the broader public; Siobhan Brownlie's 2010 survey of the British public, reported in her *Memory and Myths of the Norman Conquest*, found that an overwhelming majority of Britons see the Norman Conquest as an important event in their history.[55]

Learning Outside the Classroom

In the final report of the National Curriculum History Working Group in 1990, the group made a positive estimation of the value of experiential learning as a way to engender children's interest in history:

It is important that field trips, and museum and site visits form an integral part of the school curriculum for history [. . .] The use of all the senses can convey an image of living in the past in a way that a narrative account may fail to do.[56]

The participants agreed. They consistently stated that experiential learning of this kind was more memorable than their classroom learning. Some cited the impact of living-history-type experiences or trips to historical sites, while others reported learning outside the classroom with their families.

For example, Katy said that a major source of her knowledge about the Crusades was gleaning from paintings that her grandfather had hung on his wall, and about which he would tell stories; she said, 'whenever I think of Crusade I think of that picture'. Chloe cited a visit to Winchester Castle where she saw 'the round table'.[57] Elizabeth said that some of her associations with the Middle Ages came from a trip 'to Warwick Castle and they had jousting on and [. . .] blacksmithing! And stuff like that. I thought that was really, medieval/Middle Ages. So I think every time I see a castle, I see it with that kind of history.' Carin and Jane also each cited trips to the local Royal Armouries museum as a memorable influence.

Participants were most enthusiastic when describing memories of living-history lessons, especially those in which they wore medieval clothes or ate medieval food. Jane gave an animated recount of when 'our level went to Westminster Abbey and [we were] dressing up like a monk and being forced to like eat some weird porridge stuff' which she positively contrasted with 'sitting in the classroom being told something read from a textbook that just went straight . . . [gesturing over her head]'. Eleanor also recounted how in class 'we used to dress up and make our own costumes and . . . make the old food that they used to have'. Jane and Elizabeth fondly recalled similar experiences, where 'it was fun, we dressed up like Vikings', and 'we went to a castle; dressed up'. They recounted these experiences with an intensely animated passion – difficult to convey here only in text. The passion that these memories inspired – even after several intervening years – illustrates just how memorable and impactful these experiences were.

Furthermore, the focus in these living-history experiences upon their experiences with medieval dress and food may have contributed to an understanding voiced by several that differences in dress and food are among the most significant differences between the Middle Ages and today (explored further below). Alternately, this may reflect how people engage with history in general. Living history and social history are particularly compelling to the public because they illustrate the differences between our personal experiences and those of past people – they create historicising moments where the differences between the past and present are made intimately personal and relatable. In so doing, they paradoxically close the gap between the present and the past. By using 'role play' elements where students adopt the dress or food of the Middle Ages, they allow the students to imaginatively experience the Middle Ages on a personal level. Living and experiential history is not only a popular way to present the Middle Ages to the public, but has become an important way that the heritage industry engages with its audience. Since these experiences seem to be so memorable, evoking excitement and interest years or even decades afterwards, this would seem to give credence to the importance of history presented in this way in terms of its potential to influence historical consciousness. Activities such as these could hold a powerful place in any school curriculum.[58]

In summary, most participants claimed not to trust the history they were taught in school. On the other hand, they were most enthusiastic when describing memories of participating in their learning experiences, whether by learning with family, visiting historical sites and museums, or engaging in living-history-style lessons. They felt that history, medieval history in particular, was not treated in depth (although it is debatable whether this can be realistically expected of primary or secondary schooling). Most also recalled a sense of discomfort at the modularisation of history. Despite participants' disregard for some aspects of their formal education, many of the paradigms for understanding the period learned in school seem to have remained with them into adulthood. This implies that classroom experience, no matter how dismissed after the fact, should not be discounted in terms of its effect on individuals' historical consciousness.

Popular Culture

The other major source of learning described by the participants was popular culture: novels, films, and video games. For example, some had fond childhood memories of reading about the Middle Ages in *Ladybird* and *Horrible Histories* books. Sean also cited the novel *Eclipse of the Crescent Moon* as something which gave him an insight into 'the Islamic point of view' of the Crusades (though considering that *Eclipse of the Crescent Moon* is neither told from the Islamic point of view nor set during the Crusades, this seems odd).[59] Jess said the medievalist novels of Bernard Cornwell were one of her preferred sources for knowledge about the Middle Ages: 'I read historical romance books, I love them.' She said that they helped her learn about the 'clothes' and 'how to run a castle and a household'. She went on to say 'they go into relationships so you remember that people are real people, even in the Middle Ages. It wasn't all just wars and boring-boring, you know?' Even though Cornwell's novels often do feature war, Jess used these books to open a window into her specific historical interests which trend towards social history and material cultures. And even more importantly, this helps feed her historical empathy – reinforcing the sense that historical people are, despite their historical distance, like her.

In addition to schooling and reading, participants said that much of their historical consciousness of the Middle Ages was found in the popular culture they consumed as children, citing television, film, and popular fiction as sources. Erica felt that an early exposure to the Mel Brooks' lampoon comedy *Robin Hood: Men in Tights* established an expectation of cinematic medievalism: 'being little and watching *Robin Hood [Men in Tights]* with my parents [...] I've always associated medieval films with tackiness, and [being] just a bit crappily made. But it [that] makes it more believable.' This experience seems to have been formative for Erica; her judgement of subsequent films takes this film seen in childhood as a baseline, which, considering it is a farcical parody film, may have led to some unusual expectations. To her, the expectation of reality effects (described more below) and historical authenticity are inverted. She equates 'poorly made' with 'believable' – but only for medieval films. This contributed, in part, to her (and others') negative estimation of the CGI-heavy *Beowulf* (discussed in Chapter 5).

Disney's Medievalisms[60]

In their discussions of the popular culture they consumed as children, several participants' cited Disney films as a major influence on their understandings of the Middle Ages. Of all the groups, the November group had the longest and most animated discussion of Disney films. This was possibly influenced by the composition of the group; all five of the participants in this group were women. Since many of Disney's films (especially the 'princess'-oriented fairy tales) are aggressively marketed to girls, these women may have had more experience growing up with Disney's films than the men.

The November focus group felt that they learned from Disney films, but in a subtle way:

> Catherine: I think by watching, when you're little, you get shown Disney films. So that's what sets an impression. And as you go through school you get taught more =
>
> Emma: = Yeah you learn, you see it all, and then you put it together that it =
>
> Catherine: = You learn a bit about that =
>
> Emma: = Is with medieval and all that, but you already have seen, have got a picture of it in your head. Then you come to school and it goes together.
>
> Elizabeth: Yeah.
>
> Emma: You don't learn it deliberately, but you just know it from what you['ve] seen and then what they tell you.
>
> Jane: I suppose you go to school and they say 'They have knights in the medieval times.' Without being told, you immediately see a guy on a horse with the sword and the shield. And without them having to say, 'This is what they wore.'

Their expectations of the Middle Ages had been established by Disney, then reinforced and validated by school – or perhaps vice-versa – in a process that is neither entirely voluntary or conscious.[61] This clearly illustrates Piaget's theories of the unconscious mechanisms of learning (which will be explored more fully in the next chapter).

It is difficult to know an origin point as, especially to a child, any sense that school has more authority than a film may not yet have been established (and may remain problematic even in adulthood). Due to the commonality of medievalism in popular culture, many, if not most, children are exposed the Middle Ages and medievalist fantasies before they can differentiate between fantasy and reality. Adolescent cognitive psychologists W. George Scarlett and Dennie Wolf describe the 'transition from the pretense of symbolic play to that of storytelling occurring between the ages of three and five'.[62] To them, before the age of five, children have not fully developed the cognitive distinction between story and reality. 'Between three and five, consciousness of the boundary [between fantastical pretence and practical action] develops, making possible a new and precise understanding of pretense which permits both the internal organisation and social sharing of make-believe.'[63] As children are exposed to the Middle Ages through children's popular culture, they become accustomed to seeing elements of the fantastical Middle Ages (like wizards and dragons) alongside elements of the historical Middle Ages (such as knights and castles). This forms a foundation of their historical consciousness. As they age, these fantastical elements eventually become understood as not existing in reality (or having existed in history), but the sense that these fantastical creatures are located within the context of the Middle Ages remains. In short, though they become understood to be not real, they remain understood to be medieval.

TV and Films for Adults

Participants reported that their learning from popular culture did not stop at childhood. Even prior to the film screenings, many participants cited films and TV programmes which they viewed as adults as knowledge sources. The films and TV programmes included *Monty Python and the Quest for the Holy Grail*, *A Knight's Tale*, *Shrek*, *Robin Hood: Prince of Thieves*, *Robin Hood: Men in Tights*, and the BBC TV series *Merlin*. A common feature of all these is that none of them purport to depict true events; none of them is 'historical' in the strictest sense. The closest is *A Knight's Tale*, which, while featuring historical figures like Geoffrey Chaucer as characters, invents a fictional story around them. The others are iterations of Robin Hood and King Arthur or, in the case of *Shrek*, *Men in Tights*, and *Monty Python*, comedic subversions of the type.

For each, the participants were asked: 'Was there anything about [the film] that was particularly medieval?' The most common response was the inclusion of a variety of icons of the period, rather than the depiction of historical people or events. The November group listed: 'The clothing in *Shrek*', 'the horses', 'the set in *Merlin*', 'castles', the 'dragon', 'noblemen and peasants', 'queens, kings', and a 'divide between rich and poor' – all present in their word-association exercises. It seems possible that if a film were to include some of these elements, some viewers would consider it medieval no matter what other anachronisms it had. This raises a question: do medievalesque fantasies, which feature so many of the same icons of the Middle Ages, influence the understanding of real events? Where does the cognitive divide between history and fantasy occur? Is there even such a clear divide?

On the other hand, a few participants were more critical in their approach. Jane criticised the BBC TV series *Merlin* for what she felt was a historically inaccurate plot device. In it, she believes the filmmakers applied modern ideals of egalitarianism and democracy anachronistically to the story of Arthur:

> history's deliberately being taken out of it. [. . .] in the last episode, King Arthur went to go and help Merlin defeat somebody ravaging his village. [. . .] But, without – it was against his father's permission, who was the king. And he [. . .] was asleep on the floor next to his servant and with all the poor people. I don't think that really would have happened, because as the prince he just wouldn't have done that. And, I don't think he'd have gone against the king's wishes for [to save] a servant. [. . .] the historian watching it would be like, 'It's not right, they've deliberately twisted it to, for people watching it who aren't historians, [in order for] the majority of people to just enjoy it.'

She balked at what she considered pandering on the part of the creators to 'people watching it who aren't historians', including presumably herself, to create a 'nice story'. To her, the legend of Arthur is explicitly and exclusively medieval, and, as such, even a modern retelling of the story must retain the socio-cultural expectations she has of the period. Never mind that the series features magic and fantastical creatures every week. The historical inaccuracies which mattered most to Jane were the subtler deviations from her expectations of medieval society and culture.

Playing the Middle Ages: Video games

Many male participants cited video games as sources of knowledge. The video game industry has grown exponentially over its past thirty years of existence. It is at currently at the point where the earnings on a single game can eclipse that of even the biggest Hollywood blockbusters.[64] Video games also require more of their users than films do. Their defining trait is their interactivity, and players spend orders of magnitude more time with a game than viewers do with a film. While the average film lasts between two and three hours, video games typically can take ten or more times that to complete – if they even can be completed at all. Dan, Mark, John, and Jake from the May group all referred to medieval-themed strategy games as trusted sources of information. Three titles were mentioned: *Medieval: Total War*, *Age of Empires*, and *Sid Meier's Civilization 4*.[65]

Jake said a source of his knowledge about the Crusades was: '*Age of Empires* games and one of the campaigns, he's [Saladin] in one of the campaigns on that, so that's where I get that.' When asked what the word 'medieval' meant to him, Dan responded: '"Medieval", I thought a lot more in terms of war because I base my knowledge on a game that's about warfare [. . .] *Medieval: Total War*. So medieval, I knew a lot of stuff about how they killed people.' The impact of this game upon his idea of the medieval is clear. When examining Dan's word-association exercise (Figure 2.5), each of the elements he reported for 'medieval' are elements of this game. Even number 2, which describes classical-era Germanic groups, are playable factions in *Medieval: Total War*'s sister series, *Rome: Total War*.

Mark also trusted the historical information presented in his game of choice:

> I suppose *Sid Meier's Civilization 4* would have been a source because that is, that also has a very large amount of information in it. And I can't help but think that they'd probably gone and done their homework, probably, before they spend that much effort on anything.

So to him, the overall effort put into the game by the designers implies that the history in it is trustworthy. He also used the video game as an underpinning for his cynical view of humanity: 'I look outside and I think, has much changed really? No, we've just worked out better ways to chop each other to bits. But maybe that's just because I play a lot of *Civilization*.' Though Mark may have been

Total War!
Longbows
Huns / Vandals / Goths
Holy Roman empire
Saxons
Cavalry
Yeomen
Fortresses/citadels
Post-Roman
Crusades
Papist Europe
Early gunpowder
Khan!
Low pop's [populations]

Figure 2.5   Dan's word-association exercise for 'Medieval'.

making a joke, the underlying idea that history is defined by military progress coincides neatly with the version of history presented by these war games.

These remarks by the participants affirm the research done over the past decade on the topic of learning through video games. Conservative cultural commentators have viewed video games as, at best a worthless frivolity, and at worst as 'murder simulators'.[66] By contrast, scholarship, such as James Paul Gee's *What Video Games Have to Teach Us about Learning and Literacy*, or Richard E. Mayer's *Computer Games for Learning: An Evidence-Based Approach*, has found that video games – even ones not necessarily designed for educational purposes – can be a powerful tool for learning a variety of skills and subjects.[67] This includes historical subjects as well, as explored in the recent *Playing with the Past: Digital Games and the Simulation of History*.[68] The statements of the participants indicate that they learned a significant amount from video games, which clearly shaped their historical consciousness. Further studies of this process using empirical methods could be very fruitful.

Conclusion

The participants held a wide variety of ideas on each medieval topic that they raised, sometimes with broad agreement, but more often only provisionally and with exceptions. Overall, it is remarkable to see both how little and how much they seem to know about the Middle Ages. On the one hand, they often struggled to define the period, and espoused a very insular viewpoint. On the other hand, they occasionally evinced a remarkable amount of knowledge in those specific subjects which interested them, or with which they had experience. All of them seemed to *care* about the Middle Ages, to a greater or lesser degree. Though possibly a product of the focus group environment, none of them were apathetic in their opinions about the period or about history in general – there were no murmurs of 'I don't know', 'I don't care', or 'it doesn't matter'. None of the word associations were left blank. There seemed to be not just a genuine interest but an enthusiasm for discussing the period. Each held a vivid (if not always detailed or strictly accurate) imagination of the period which they had drawn from an amalgamation of their previous experiences, whether educational, personal, or popular-cultural. It seems inappropriate to dismiss or to overemphasise the importance of any one of these categories of previous experience; each contributes to a generative, evolutionary process from which their historical conscious-ness emerged, and through which it was constantly under revision.

In summary, the participants held a number of discrete and often contradictory images of the Middle Ages in their minds. This resulted in, for example, the above-detailed different characteristics applied to the terms 'medieval' and 'Middle Ages' where 'Middle Ages' is strictly historical, and 'medieval' a fantastical playground. Further defining the period showed the breadth of ideas about it; participants had difficulty defining the Middle Ages in time and space, which is perhaps understandable considering their experience with the shifting ways in which the Middle Ages has been defined both by academics, by popular culture and within the National Curriculum. They were able to define the period chronologically with more confidence only when anchoring it with the various peoples of Britain (Anglo-Saxons, Normans, Vikings). Their geographical definitions took a similarly insular view.

'Crusade' had a similar dual definition, split between the historical and the metaphorical. On the one hand lay the crusades in the holy land,

and the other the 'moral crusading' of twentieth-century culture warriors. But most interesting was the intellectual cross-pollination that was observed between these two definitions, where the medieval conflicts were read as peaceful or defensive.

Learning about the Middle Ages comes from a range of sources both within the classroom and outside it. Despite deriding their classroom knowledge, it seems to have bestowed enduring overarching paradigms, a few technical terms (e.g., 'serfs' rather than 'peasants'), and some specific facts. They likely learned more from school than even they realise or wish to admit. That having been said, the heritage industry seems to have no such problem, being both memorable and enjoyable, and offering powerful learning opportunities. Putting on historical clothing and eating historical food – if only temporarily – offers the illusion of peering into another's experience through a naturally pleasurable activity. And more, this demands little of us; the monk's habit and rule is easily cast aside.

Many of the concepts established by these sources of knowledge – whether it be the strict periodisation in the National Curriculum or the focus on technology and warfare of video games – were reflected in the participants' general commentaries. The sources not only gave rise to participants' specific ideas but also seemed to shape their broader historical consciousness.

However, a few of their comments showed a rather concerning trend. When discussing the Crusades prior to the film on the second day of the focus groups, the participants cited three films as their source material for their understandings of the Crusades: *Kingdom of Heaven, Robin Hood: Prince of Thieves*, and *Indiana Jones and the Last Crusade*. Interestingly, some of the participants misremembered 'the last crusade' as a historical event rather than just as a film title. Jess included it on her word association, and later explained: 'the last crusade, I don't know what the first one was or anything but I just wrote the last crusade'. Justin associated the word crusade with a quest to recover 'the holy grail' and 'religious artefacts, almost like the shroud of Turin' because of its association with 'the last crusade'. Speaking semiotically, these participants remembered the sign 'the last crusade' but forgot the signified was the Indiana Jones film rather than any historical event. The association with crusade was meaningful only because the source was forgotten.

This is a prime example of one of the most insidiously powerful processes observed in this study: forgetting. When the source of knowledge is forgotten, its validity can no longer be interrogated. Facts can be misremembered, knowledge that is only used infrequently can slip, become confused, or be conflated with other information. As Stephen and Sean asserted, most of our sources of knowledge on any topic have been forgotten: 'it just comes from somewhere'. This phenomenon can elevate popular culture to the level of an unassailable source of knowledge, as valid as the best academic research. Once the source is forgotten, who can tell the difference?

Participants seemed to misremember or forget the sources of quite a lot of their knowledge, which led to some anachronistic thinking or projecting the present onto the past. This exposes the power of popular culture to set images that cannot be reliably criticised; though participants may initially disbelieve information seen in a Disney or fantasy film, if they forget that their historical knowledge came from that film, there is no way to differentiate the reliable from the unreliable.

One of the chief purposes of studying the participants' existing knowledge of the Middle Ages was to have a 'base line' against which to compare their reactions to the films they viewed. However, in this initial study of participants' knowledge, no one singular image of the Middle Ages was found, even within one participant. Instead, each person held a variety of coexisting images and paradigms about the medieval past. Many of these were in discord with each other, which provoked little or no cognitive dissonance among the participants. As a result, the historical consciousness of the Middle Ages is not a single image but a series of images that change when approached from a different angle. There are not an infinite number of Middle Ages, but there are certainly more than one. This is why medievalisms can be so diverse; they use or subvert any number of competing images of the past. Furthermore, audiences can interpret what they see in a film through different frameworks depending upon the way it is presented to them, through genre, medium, or subject. The next chapters will examine how this process takes place, and the theories that have been developed to explain how individuals learn from films.

CHAPTER 3

LEARNING HISTORY FROM FILM

Movies are particularly well suited to translate social values into felt needs that seem as authentic as the memories of childhood. Although we may not always agree with them, or even recognize that they are courting our consent, we tend to accept the frames of references that they supply.

Peter Biskind, *Seeing is Believing*[1]

Having established the initial outlines of the participants' historical consciousness about the Middle Ages and their initial reactions to each film, we can now turn to the question of how they viewed the three films. What did they learn about the Middle Ages from having watched them? And, perhaps most importantly, what does the medieval world look like to them after having viewed these films? Some elements of the films surely must have shaped their perceptions of the past while others were discarded. What specific elements that they saw led them to see the films they were viewing as 'medieval', and did their definitions of that idea shift over time?

This chapter will address first the ways in which the large, national surveys of perceptions and engagement with the past (first introduced in Chapter 1) explore popular perceptions and consumption of historical films. It then goes on to outline some of the theories fundamental to our understanding of how we learn, before finally using those theories to explore the other studies which have grappled with questions about how individuals learn from historical films.

How the Public Views Historical Films

The American, Canadian, and Australian national survey studies discussed in Chapter 1 all addressed the impact of viewing historical fiction film and television in their surveys. Each one asked their respondents whether they had viewed a film that depicted the past at some point the last year. The results are remarkably similar to one another: 81 per cent had in the US, 84 per cent in Australia, and 78 per cent in Canada.[2] Despite the commonality of historical film viewing, their participants also treated filmed history with intense scepticism. The participants of the *The Presence of the Past* study rated historical films and TV programmes very low in two areas. They were found not to be believable versions of history, and they did not offer profound connections to the past.[3] Participants were asked to rate 'how connected to the past' they felt when engaging in a range of past-related activities (i.e. visiting a history museum or historic site, celebrating holidays, studying history in school); films and TV programmes were ranked second-to-last with a mean score of 6.0 of 10.[4] The only activity that scored lower was 'studying history in school'. On how trustworthy films and TV were as a source of information, they were ranked dead last at 5.0 of 10.[5] When these numbers are compared to the responses for other past-related activities, especially in the qualitative portions of the survey, the differences are clear. The respondents emphasised the importance of being able to actively interrogate a historical source when assessing its trustworthiness. This is difficult to achieve with a film, which may explain why relatives, personal acquaintances, and college professors consistently ranked higher than films in terms of trustworthiness.

Some historians fear that, when viewing an historical film, the images on screen wash over the passive viewer who blankly accepts them as factual. But media reception studies have found since the 1970s that audiences actively engage with the media that they consume. Theorists (beginning with Stuart Hall, refined by John Fiske and others) have focused on this concept of an 'active audience'.[6] An active audience critically analyses what they see and crafts meanings from it; a passive one simply lets the media wash over them. This is consistent with the study results. None of the participants accepted everything they saw as literal truth. But neither did they reject everything as outright fantasy. The participants were clearly a very active audience, even though they came to some incorrect conclusions. While the model of the 'passive audience' is incorrect, the kernel of truth in it is that the presentation of information in watching a film *is* a one-way process. The fact that a film audience cannot interact with, interrogate or challenge that which they are seeing may be an important factor in the visual media's relatively low score as a reliable source of historical information.

But adding to this lack of interrogability is the fact that people do not like feeling deceived. In a qualitative study conducted in 2004 at Stanford University, seventh-graders (aged 12 or 13) compared their ideas about Pocahontas (which the researchers found was mostly comprised of information from the 1995 Disney film) with the historical evidence. When the film's account was compared with the historical record, researchers Sam Wineburg and Daisy Martin reported that the '7th grade students responded indignantly to the movie version of the Pocahontas tale, expressing outrage at being fed a distorted, if not patently false, story', even going as far as 'writing letters of complaint to Roy Disney'.[7] This is similar to the findings for adult participants in *Presence of the Past*: 'In explaining why they distrusted movies and television, many respondents talked about their hatred and fear of being manipulated by people who distort the past to meet their own needs.'[8] Those 'own needs' are the *raison d'être* of the film industry: creating entertaining stories that appeal to broad audiences in order to turn a profit. Rosenzweig and Thelen explain: 'Television and movies provided the most blatant arenas for distorting the past because they appealed to low common denominators that could assemble the largest possible audience.'[9] Two of their respondents held particularly pointed views about the accuracy of historical fiction film and TV. One said,

> historical accuracy is not the primary goal of movies and TV, [. . .] in order to enhance the dramatic power of film, I'm sure facts were altered and deleted, important facts were left out [. . .] Films and TV glorify incidents in the past and de-emphasize the negative effects of those events.[10]

Another respondent noted, 'Television and movies "are embroidered to suit the producer and designed to make money. They are going to have enticing things in them which probably didn't have anything to do with the truth at all".'[11]

In spite of the low regard participants held for historical films and TV programmes as trustworthy sources, in *The Presence of the Past* this activity ranked third out of the ten past-related activities in terms of how many participants had done them in the last year.[12] Thus, despite the derision seemingly held for historical films and TV programmes, viewers must get something out of the experience. Obviously films and TV programmes are easily available (which make them more accessible than, for example, most museums). But it is unlikely that participants take nothing away from the experience of watching – or else their popularity would need serious explaining. Rosenzweig and Thelen recounted several respondents who found the image and emotion provided by film important. For example, a nineteen-year-old Mexican American woman from Texas said 'I like movies like *JFK* and *Malcolm X* [...] when you read a book, you can't picture it and you can't see what is happening, but when you see it in a film, you get more emotional about it.'[13] Rosenzweig and Thelen go on to note,

> In using movies to be transported to a different time or to encounter a famous person or event from the past, [participants] were not mainly looking for the current state of historical knowledge about that subject, because they did not believe that was the strength of movies.[14]

The strength of film is instead in conjuring a vivid, emotionally affective and lasting sense of time and place. Thus, though the participants ranked historical film and TV very low in terms of its trustworthiness compared to other past-related activities, this does not mean they did not trust film and TV, nor that it does not affect them. Film and TV work more subtly upon the imagination. As Scott Alan Metzger warns in his article 'Pedagogy and the historical feature film',

> When students watch history movies without the support of sufficient content knowledge and nuanced understandings of history, a possible (or probable) outcome is for the filmic account to 'colonize' their thinking about the past – taking up residence in the mind as a kind of literal truth, as Van Sledright (2002) and Wineburg, Mosborg, and Porat (2000) found when talking with students about the historical events behind the Disney's

1995 animated musical *Pocahontas* and Robert Zemeckis's 1994 film *Forrest Gump*.[15]

This would explain how *Pocahontas* became the standard for the adolescent students in the Stanford study discussed above. And if this is true, how does this intellectual 'colonising' work within an individual or a group? What, and how, do people learn from historical films? This chapter and the next will focus on this question – how people learn from films both through the 'active' audience position already seen, and also by having their perceptions of the past 'colonised'. This draws upon theories and studies drawn from three cognate disciplines: sociology, psychology, and education.

The Sociology of Knowledge and Constructivism

Any empirical study of the public understanding of history – such as this one – places itself, intentionally or not, within the sociological subfields of the sociology of knowledge and constructivism. A 'sociology of knowledge', was coined by Max Scheler in the 1920s and the idea more fully developed and refined by Peter L. Berger and Thomas Luckmann in the 1960s. In their foundational *The Social Construction of Reality*, Berger and Luckmann propose that all knowledge is constructed socially, and that all social phenomena are a product of previous social interactions with individuals and with commonly accepted institutions.[16] From this perspective, any person's knowledge – even their most basic perceptions of reality – are defined socially and may differ based upon their social position; 'what is "real" to a Tibetan monk may not be "real" to an American businessman'.[17] The 'sociology of knowledge' is particularly relevant for the present study due to its interest in common knowledge:

> The sociology of knowledge must first of all concern itself with what people 'know' as 'reality' in their everyday, non- or pre-theoretical lives. In other words, common-sense 'knowledge' rather than 'ideas' must be the central focus for the sociology of knowledge.[18]

Their distinction between 'knowledge' and 'ideas' (which they define as higher order philosophical constructs) represents a fundamental difference between sociological and philosophical approaches to knowledge. Whereas philosophy is generally concerned with the development of valid arguments and ideas, Berger and Luckmann suggest the value of exploring how individuals and societies acquire:

> whatever passes for 'knowledge' in a society, regardless of the ultimate validity or invalidity (by whatever criteria) of such 'knowledge'. And in so far as all human 'knowledge' is developed, transmitted and maintained in social situations, the sociology of knowledge must seek to understand the process by which this is done in such a way that a taken-for-granted 'reality' congeals for the man in the street.[19]

This premise, that an individual's knowledge (including knowledge of history) is a social construct that may have little correlation to objective reality, has important implications. As mentioned previously, determining the *validity* of an individual's or group's knowledge (in our case, their historical consciousness), or its relationship to objective reality or to scholastic understandings *is not the goal of this study*. While it may be worthy of note if the knowledge the subjects express corresponds with what scholars believe, this is only incidental, and only worth full exploration if it reveals a larger socio-intellectual trend. Far more central is what that common knowledge *is* and how it is constructed. If people actually 'know' that Gandalf won the Battle of Waterloo, it is important to explore how they came to believe this, how widespread the idea is, and what larger implications the idea may have – rather than to simply point out its falsehood.

Historical knowledge is acquired through a variety of social institutions, for example school, interaction with elders, with peers, or with popular culture. Media theorist John Fiske argued in his seminal *Understanding Popular Culture* that a fundamental feature of all popular culture is its flexible interpretability – that a film's audience (for example) can come away from it with vastly different 'knowledge', depending upon their social circumstances.[20] Audiences make, and remake, the films they watch in their own images.

Personal historical knowledge – even with tenuous sources or relationship with reality – can have a profound effect upon people's lives. Berger and Luckmann explain:

I relate to my predecessors through highly anonymous typifications – 'my immigrant great-grandparents', and even more, 'the Founding Fathers', [...] the typifications of predecessors have at least some such [individualised] content, albeit of a highly mythical sort. The anonymity of both these sets of typifications, however, does not prevent their entering as elements into the reality of everyday life, sometimes in a very decisive way. After all, I may sacrifice my life in loyalty to the Founding Fathers – or, for that matter, on behalf of future generations.[21]

The academic school of thought that explores the construction (and constructed-ness) of knowledge has become known as constructivism.

Audience researcher David Morrison used constructivist theories of knowledge to develop research methodologies for studying audiences of media. Much of the theoretical basis for the research methods used in this study is based on his *The Search for a Method: Focus Groups and the Development of Mass Communication Research*, and demonstrated in his *Defining Violence: The Search for Understanding*.[22] In the late 1990s, Morrison was commissioned by several British broadcasting companies to help them define violence in the media. In his study, published in *Defining Violence*, he and his team sought to 'understand the factors at play when someone categorises an act as violent', in order to 'discover whether there is a single definition of violence'.[23] Morrison asked participants in focus groups to respond to a range of media clips and judge what in them was 'serious violence and what was, although violent, not serious violence'.[24] This allowed the participants to judge violence subjectively rather than defining it according to predetermined criteria. Allowing the participants to construct their own idea of what 'violence' is in their own terms and with nuance was an important model for the design of the study in this book.

'Violence' and 'medievalness'[25] are both subjectively defined concepts that have multiple meanings and complex nuances. Each can be applied to a wide range of things for multiple reasons. Each person's definitions of what they are differs, based upon their experiences. Rigid-thinkers might be inclined to define something as either 'medieval' or 'not medieval' on a binary (since it would either be something from the Middle Ages or not). On the other hand, some may understand 'medievalness' to be a relative quality, where something can be 'more' or 'less' medieval. If this is true, defining the elements that make something subjectively (more or less) medieval is of far greater import than simply generating a list of those things which are or are not considered to be medieval. Morrison's theoretical way of exploring violence is thus applicable to this study.

For this reason, a primary research question of this study is: what, specifically, makes a film seem more or less medieval? By exploring the films in question in this way, a basic picture of what qualities, characters, images or icons are used to define the period emerges. This picture can illuminate the core essence of 'medievalness' for these people.

How We Learn: Schema Theory

'Medievalness' – the quality that makes something recognisably medieval – is a complex abstract concept. Though rich in connotations and associations, no one can point to a single object (as one could, for example, with a 'ball' or a 'cat') and say 'that *is* the Middle Ages'. As explored earlier in Chapter 2, 'The Middle Ages' and 'medieval' evoke ideas that are abstract, intangible and amorphous. As a result, the best way to understand the idea of the Middle Ages – and thus, the study participants' ideas of the Middle Ages – is as a schema. In short, *schema* are how educational theorists describe all of our cognitive structures. They are fundamental to how we understand and organise information, and they are the mechanism through which we incorporate new knowledge into the old. The schema 'the Middle Ages' and its component parts represent knowledge in many forms and at a variety of levels of abstraction. This knowledge can employ different senses, for example sight ('what a knight looks like'), or sound ('what medieval music sounds like'). The knowledge can be intellectual ('when were the Middle Ages?'), archetypal ('what a medieval king is'), empathetic ('what it was like to live in the Middle Ages'), or moral ('were the Middle Ages good or bad?'). The research participants applied each of these aspects of schema to their interpretation of the medieval films.

The word schemata (sing. schema) was first used in the modern sense by Kant in his *Critique of Pure Reason*:

Indeed it is schemata, not images of objects, which underlie our pure sensible concepts. No image could ever be adequate to the concept of a triangle in general. It would never attain that universality of the concept which renders it valid of all triangles [. . .] The concept 'dog' signifies a rule according to which my imagination can delineate the figure of a four-footed animal in a general manner, without limitation to any single determinate figure such as experience, or any possible image that I can represent *in concreto*, actually presents.[26]

Schema theory was first developed by Sir Frederic C. Bartlett in his book *Remembering*,[27] and has since been greatly expanded by the work of Richard A. Anderson and others.[28] As a short summary of the theory, David Rumelhart and Andrew Ortony outline what they call the 'four essential characteristics of schemata':

(1)   'Schemata have variables.'[29]

For example, a 'ball' can be red, or blue, large or small, soft or hard.

(2)   'Schemata can embed one within the other.'[30]

This means that the schema 'football' is nested conceptually in the 'ball' or 'sporting equipment' super-schema.

(3)   'Schemata represent generic concepts which, taken all together, vary in their levels of abstraction.'[31]

This means that, as stated above, there are schemata for all concepts whether abstract or concrete.

(4)   'Schemata represent knowledge, rather than definitions.'[32]

This means that everyone has schemata about all aspects of life, some concrete: 'how to operate a toaster', some abstract: 'the past'. 'The Middle Ages' (and 'medieval') are abstract schemata.

These four characteristics make schemata conceptually flexible; they can be adapted according to context in a way that a purely definitional model could not. Though schemata exist at all levels of abstraction, according to Rumelhart and Ortony, 'previous works have concentrated on representing the internal structure of, at most, lexical terms. Not until very recently [in 1977] have attempts been made to represent conceptualisations at more abstract levels.'[33] Brewer and Nakamura explored these more abstract levels, defining schemata as:

higher-order cognitive structures that have been hypothesized to underlie many aspects of human knowledge and skill. They serve a crucial role in providing an account of how old knowledge interacts with new knowledge in perception, language, thought and memory.[34]

To them, schemata can represent the conceptual scaffolding formed by conclusions drawn from previous experience and through which future experiences are understood. In short, an individual's schemata comprise the collection of tacit knowledge and experience they have acquired, be it practical, theoretical, or historical.[35]

Schema also often have other schemata embedded within them, the component schemata being called *subschemata*. Each subschema works as a building component of its *dominating schema* – subschema define what a dominating schema is (and is not). Rumelhart and Ortony explain: 'In much the same way as the entries for lexical items in a dictionary consist of other lexical items, so the structure of the schema is given in terms of relationships amongst other schemata.'[36] For example, 'Robin Hood' is one subschema of 'the Middle Ages'. Some subschemata integral to the 'Robin Hood' schema may be 'longbow' and 'Sherwood Forest'. Some subschemata are required (like perhaps 'robs from the rich and gives to the poor'), some optional ('green hat'), and some counter ('machine gun') to the dominating schema. As Rumelhart explains, 'A schema contains, as part of its specification, the network of interrelations that is believed to generally hold among the constituents of the concept in question. Schemata, in some sense, represent stereotypes of these concepts.'[37] This illustrates why prejudices – about the Middle Ages or anything else – can be so difficult to revise, since doing so requires not just an alteration to one concept, but entire intellectual super- and sub-structures.

The process of learning is one of conflict, comparison and compromise. As Robert Axelrod asserts, 'When new information becomes available, a person tries to fit the information into the pattern which he has used in the past [...] If the new information does not fit very well, something has to give.'[38] Jean Piaget, the father of the constructivist school of learning, described two mechanisms that illustrate how this 'something' gives. Sometimes, an individual's mental frameworks are revised to accommodate the new data they encounter. This is done through a mechanism that

Piaget appropriately called *accommodation*.[39] As Piaget explained 'experience is never simply passive receptiveness: it is active accommodation'.[40] To Piaget, another process went hand-in-hand with this. Often the old system does not give way. Sometimes it does not need to, and new information can be readily incorporated into already existing frameworks. But sometimes, when conflict occurs between the old and new, the new information is itself changed; it can be regarded as an 'exception to the rule' or discredited due to previous experience. Most insidiously, over time new information can be misremembered to fit already established patterns, or forgotten entirely. Piaget called the process by which this is done *assimilation*.[41] Established schemata have an intellectual inertia which can only be overcome by repeated conflict and gradual revision, with multiple rounds of assimilation and accommodation making way for a truly new intellectual paradigm – which Piaget called *adaptation*. Adaptation – representing true learning – inevitably takes time and repeated exposure to new information.

As individuals gain experience, their schemata develop to include more variables and specificity. To most, learning about the Middle Ages comes from children's books, family trips to historical sites, school, fantasy novels, advertisements, popular culture, or any number of other personal experiences through repeated accommodation and assimilation. Film plays its part – in the complex manner explored above. Its messages act in concert or in conflict with prior experience, and are accommodated or assimilated into this broader schematic soup over time.

Leaning History from Film

Several scholars in the field of education have focused on the impact that historical films have on those who view them: what, and how, people learn about history by consuming films. This has taken the form of both theoretical work and, perhaps more relevant here, through empirical studies. Almost all of the empirical research was done with adolescents, with most focusing on students' interpretation of film in classroom educational contexts. While there are several methodological and contextual differences between their studies and the *Middle Ages in Popular Imagination* study, each previously completed study highlights some of the issues that will be explored with the students' responses in Chapters 5 and 6.

Educational Benefits – and Pitfalls – of Historical Film
Historical fiction film can be a powerful educational tool. Firstly, and perhaps most importantly, it can inspire students to learn more about a subject. As Ron Briley writes, 'the historical engagement of film texts should encourage students to pursue more background reading and research into the topics depicted on movie and video screens'.[42] But more than simply inspiring students towards further learning, or teaching them historical content, historical films can also be used, as Scott Alan Metzger argues, to teach several important aspects of historical literacy. Metzger argues that films can help teach:

(1) Narrative analysis: 'Film-based lessons have great potential to help students see the past as constructed narratives supported (or unsupported) by evidence and interpretation';[43]
(2) Historical cultural positioning: 'how a film's themes and images conform to or contrast with the broader culture of its time relates to the deeper nature of films as texts';[44]
(3) Historical empathy: 'an emotional and psychological competency that requires the viewer to recognize and respect potentially foreign perspectives [...] the clarity and connection students can achieve through history films become even more critical when dealing with representations of race and the treatment of historically exploited social groups';[45] and
(4) Discernment of presentism: 'Presentism is a problem that history feature films typically exhibit [wherein] Filmmakers often use a historic event as a metaphor for current concerns, attitudes, and values that are easier to sell to contemporary audiences.'[46]

Perhaps more ephemerally, Metzger argues that historical films can also make history – even long-buried history (such as the Middle Ages) – seem 'real and meaningful'.[47] A reason for this drives at the heart of history education: film offers a different type of learning experience altogether. While learning history is often an intellectual – and, if taught well, empathetic – endeavour, film makes history into a deeply aesthetic experience. This should not be undervalued. An historical film's viewers can be not just moved by the character's story, but by the emotionally affective images. Film can encourage students not just to be interested in the past, but to care about it and find intense beauty in it.

However, as Metzger rightly pointed out, using films to teach these important historical competencies requires an active teacher who guides students through engaging critically with the film as a text. As Briley writes, 'it is essential that students be urged to question what is presented on the screen and to always ask what is missing from the frame'.[48] If a teacher does not provide contextualisation and scaffolding to an historical film, it can lead students to learn a wide array of misinformation – a phenomenon only compounded if those films are shown in class. For example, in 2009 a project that involved students watching historical films while studying associated primary source texts was undertaken in the memory lab at the department of Psychology at Washington University, St. Louis.[49] As project leader Andrew Butler notes,

> Watching a film clip increased correct recall of consistent information relative to recall of the same information when subjects did not see the clip. However, when the information in the film contradicted the text, subjects often (falsely) recalled misinformation from the film.[50]

The rate of misinformation recalled reached 50 per cent on some questions. It was most prevalent when students were either not warned about the historical inaccuracies, or only given a general warning that the film was historically inaccurate. However, students consistently fared better when the teacher specifically pointed out those sections of the film that were inaccurate, highlighting the importance of guidance by an educator.[51]

Unfortunately, most teachers who use films to teach history do not typically offer much critical scaffolding. Alan Marcus and Jeremy Stoddard conducted a survey-based study of educators who used historical films in their classrooms.[52] They found that a surprisingly large number of teachers were using films in their classrooms. These teachers were predominantly using films to supplement their teaching of historical content, and as a way of better representing groups that have been marginalised historically (e.g. in films like *Glory, Amistad*, or *Dances with Wolves*).[53] However, these teachers were often not going the critical step beyond that into examining films as culturally positioned texts often rife with presentism.[54] They were using films to build historical empathy, but not encouraging their students to engage with the films critically.

And more, when approached 'in the wild', away from classroom and teacher interference, historical films typically militate against critical reading. Their cultural positioning is designed to be invisible, their presentism offered as natural. It is for this reason that Pope John Paul II said (perhaps apocryphally) of *The Passion of the Christ* that 'It is as it was.'[55] President Woodrow Wilson infamously (and also likely apocryphally) proclaimed of Klan-promoting film *The Birth of a Nation* 'It is like writing history with lightning. And my only regret is that it is all so terribly true.'[56] *The Passion of the Christ* is not 'as it was'; *The Birth of the Nation* is not 'terribly true'; but, both go to great pains to present themselves as such.

In the 1990s Peter Seixas conducted a qualitative study intended to understand better how students critically interpret films' cultural positioning on their own, without the scaffolding provided by a teacher. In this study, Seixas showed Canadian tenth graders the films *Dances with Wolves* (1990) and *The Searchers* (1956).[57] The students were then interviewed to better understand how they negotiated the vastly different representations of Native-/White-American conflicts in the late 1800s. Seixas found that the students had a wide range of interpretations of the contradictory way these two films presented similar historical events. Some simply failed to acknowledge the differences between them. Some uncritically accepted the more recent interpretation of the past that they saw in *Dances with Wolves*. Others engaged in a complex negotiation of the historiographical changes evident in the films, seeing the earlier as a product of its time (though none seeing the then-current *Dances with Wolves* as one). While those students who had more aptitude and interest in social studies were inclined to have a more complex interpretation of the film, Seixas found that there was insufficient evidence to imply that one caused the other. But, the conclusion remains that there were a diverse range of interpretive strategies on display, implying that when encountered casually, some engage critically with historical films (especially if they are already interested in the subject matter) while others may simply passively accept them. *The Middle Ages in Popular Imagination* study, though conducted with older students, has some similarities with Seixas'. That said, none of the students in the present study had studied the Middle Ages at an advanced level, so it has yet to be seen whether these relative amateurs also displayed the same complexity of interpretation that Seixas' participants did when comparing films.

Conclusion

In exploring how school children acquire historical understandings from the media, educational researchers Alan Marcus, Richard Paxton, and Peter Myerson postulated that: 'While the written word predominates in how adult historians think about the past, the same may not be the case for K-12 students.'[58] Their claim deserves to be emboldened. Some *historians* may think about history primarily in terms of written text, as textual inquiry has been the mainstay of the discipline since it began – but adult non-historians may not think similarly. There is no evidence that the written word dominates how adult non-historians think about the past any more than it does in children. The present study accordingly uses adults as its focus rather than children, and mass media rather than the written word.

Most of the education scholars discussed above focused on the effects of watching films in the classroom. The present study differs by examining the consumption of historical films by relative novices to the subject without the influence of a teacher. Medieval films are most often viewed by the public in the cinema or at home, not only well removed from a teacher's influence, but also in free time away from formal learning. As a result, the present research has broader implications for the study of the power of historical film in the public sphere. Finally, these studies almost exclusively used Canadians or Americans as their subjects, and focused on films depicting American history. The current study broadens that focus not only by testing with subjects outside of the Americas, but engaging with a much more distant history, where questions of cultural positioning, presentism and marginalised groups are complicated by their removal from the immediacy latent in more recent pasts.

While most previous studies have focused on the question of whether students learn from films and how this learning compares with what they are taught in class, this study takes a broader look, similar to Seixas' work, asking: how do they interpret what they have seen? When presented with conflicting information, either between the film and their prior knowledge, or between two films, how do they negotiate that difference? Does a film's cultural positioning and its presentism remain invisible, or do even relatively casual visitors critically engage with films not just as representations of the past, but as texts? In short, what do they learn?

CHAPTER 4

THE MEDIEVAL FILM

The film and television industries have been among the foremost influencers of the historical consciousness over the twentieth and twenty-first centuries. This is particularly true of the Middle Ages – which has been a consistent favourite setting for films and TV shows. These industries have been incredibly productive; moving-image depictions of medieval histories, tales, or legends – including fantasies set in recognisably 'medievalesque' worlds – are commonplace. Perhaps more importantly for the purposes of this study, they are popular as well. The number of films on medieval subjects is impressive and, as a result, their potential to impact the historical consciousness is far-reaching. Kevin Harty's book *The Reel Middle Ages* catalogues over nine hundred films made before 1999 which depict the Middle Ages.[1] This list stretches back to the earliest days of the medium: *Jeanne d'Arc* was directed by Georges Méliès in 1897. Perhaps more impressively, Harty's nine hundred does not even include any TV series, documentaries, or medievalesque fantasy films.[2] Nor does it include the twenty-first century renaissance in medieval and fantasy epic films spurred in large part by the successes of *The Lord of the Rings*.[3]

Despite this popularity, it is notoriously difficult to define and circumscribe the category of 'the medieval film', and to define precisely what makes this grouping recognisably 'medieval'. This core problem of defining this 'medieval flavour' – that which makes something recognisably medieval – is of primary concern here. Those very elements which make a piece of popular culture recognisably medieval surely must be a core part of public medievalisms. David Williams defined the corpus of medieval films as, 'in the narrative cinema *a medieval world whose images are familiar* and from whose power and excitement perhaps not even professional medievalists are quite immune' (my emphasis).[4] Here, Williams sets out one of the core points of interest when approaching films about the Middle Ages: many of these films show us similar medieval worlds with familiar images. These worlds, and images, construct a more-or-less universally recognisable amalgamated Middle Ages. While each medieval-ish world presented in a film inherits its ideas from previous medievalisms (and may borrow from other media or time periods), this amalgamated, 'moving-image Middle Ages' is distinct both from those representing other time periods, and in other media.

Approaching Medieval Films

Partially as a result of the number and diversity of medieval films, there have been a few different academic approaches used in their study. The particular theoretical and methodological approach taken usually depends upon the academic discipline of the scholar. Each of the disciplines which has addressed filmed versions of the Middle Ages – film studies, history, and literary studies – utilises its own approaches and asks its own questions. For example, a fundamental split between the studies of these films by medievalists and those by film studies scholars often centres on the question of genre and corpus. Scholars of film studies do not usually consider films which depict the Middle Ages to be a distinct genre (unlike, for example, the epic, the noir, or the musical). Nor do they typically study medieval films as a corpus (or view them as part of an identifiable, distinct group). Medievalists generally do. As a result, film versions of the Middle Ages have largely been assessed by film scholars either individually, as part of a genre recognised by their field, or as part of the output of an *auteur*.[5]

The reason film scholars do not regard 'medieval films' as a genre is that, by most definitions, the medieval film is not one. For example, Rick Altman sets out four 'meanings' of genre in film. He defines them as:

- genre as *blueprint*, as a formula that precedes, programmes and patterns industry production;

- genre as *structure*, as the formal framework on which individual films are founded;
- genre as *label*, as the name of a category central to the decisions and communications of distributors and exhibitors;
- genre as *contract*, as the viewing position required by each genre film of its audience.[6]

The category 'medieval film' does not operate according to any of these definitions. In terms of genre, a medieval epic like *Braveheart* (1995) has more in common with a Greco-Roman epic like *300* (2007) than with a medieval noir like *The Name of the Rose* (1986) or medieval comedy like *Black Knight* (2001).[7] The medieval setting can bring with it many stock characters, memes, and tropes, but that is not enough to comprise a coherent genre by any of Altman's definitions. Instead, it can be considered a genre modifier.

What is a Medieval Film?

It is understandable that medievalists would examine medieval films as a group. However, thus far there has not been a conclusive definition of what makes a medieval film 'medieval'. The boundaries, or even the defining features of what is called a 'medieval film' remain very much under discussion among scholars. The definitions generally fall into one of two camps, largely divided among scholars with backgrounds in history and those with a background in literature.

Historian medievalists tend to examine medieval films in one of three ways:

(1) as a cultural artefact which can reflect a certain cultural moment;
(2) as a teaching tool to help students learn about the period; and/or
(3) as an attempt by filmmakers to adapt or create a history on screen.

A notable example which uses all three of these is John Aberth's book *A Knight at the Movies*, which analyses a large number of films as cultural artefacts and for their historical accuracy.[8] Similarly, historians like Robert Rosenstone and Robert Brent Toplin have occasionally engaged with the depiction of the Middle Ages in film as part of their larger project of defining what a historical film is, analysing how historical films work, and considering whether historical films should be considered 'histories'.[9]

The other academic camp which has discussed medieval films draws on literary studies. These examine the medieval film in one of two ways. One branch approaches them thematically, as new adaptations of medieval tales (most commonly by scholars of Arthuriana).[10] The other branch approaches them with critical theory-based methodologies. Their works usually address a single film or small handful under a particular theoretical lens (i.e. queer theory, psychoanalytic theory, or postcolonial theory); this school of thought has been the most dominant of any voices in the sub-discipline in recent years.[11]

Some of these literary/theoretical studies do not restrict the label 'medieval' only to films which depict the Middle Ages (or fictionalised versions thereof), but include films which have a medieval 'flavour', or use medieval themes and tropes in non-medieval settings.[12] But this quest to explore any and all medieval resonances risks generalising 'medieval film' (or medievalism) too far. Some of the 'medieval' themes or resonances found may be as much a product of the scholar's perspective as a result of the creator(s)'s intent or the audience's interpretation. Maslow's 'Law of the Instrument', that 'It is tempting, if the only tool you have is a hammer, to treat everything as if it were a nail' may apply here.[13] This can give rise to problematic assumptions – for example, labelling film tropes as specific to medieval films (when they are not). The fundamental problem that remains is the assumption raised earlier: are 'medieval' films actually special in some way? Is the scholarly attention given to them really justified?

In the introduction to their collection *Medieval Film*, Bettina Bildhauer and Anke Bernau explore the idea that trying to approach 'medieval film' either in terms of its genre or its themes results in equally unsatisfactory conclusions. They argue:

Both the generic and the thematic definitions have obvious limitations and undermine each other, raising the question of the usefulness of such a free-floating term as medieval film. Medieval films have not developed coherent genre conventions: unlike western or horror films, they can share the characteristics of these genres and others. Yet defining medieval films solely by their setting, as those whose plot takes place at a time between, say, AD

500 and 1500, would result in the exclusion of a large number of films which are based on medieval stories; set in a fantastic Middle Ages; or set in a time before 500 or after 1500, but none the less consistently identified as medieval by film-makers, promoters, critics and audiences. The latter observation might imply the usefulness of classifying medieval films as those which are *perceived* to be medieval films by individual recipients or producers, but this still would leave the question open as to which features of the films lead to such perceptions.[14]

This is an excellent analysis of the core issue.[15] Films which depict the Middle Ages (or fantasy visions of it) are certainly worthy of study. But what makes them unique objects of study for medievalists is latent in their argument: because people see these films as medieval, and as a result they contribute to the historical consciousness of the Middle Ages. Bildhauer and Bernau elegantly lay out the need for the study at the centre of this book when they argue for 'the usefulness of classifying medieval films as those which are *perceived* to be medieval films by individual recipients or producers' and that this line of inquiry raises 'the question [. . .] as to which features of the films lead to such perceptions'.[16]

I agree. The best way to classify medieval film is as those which are perceived by their producers and/or audiences as recognisably 'medieval'. And, the best way to understand why is to identify which features lead to those perceptions.[17] Doing so requires active and vigorous engagement with audiences and filmmakers, as well as the adoption of a broader interdisciplinary approach.

Medievalness in Film

Bernau and Bildhauer's call-to-arms deserves to be broadened. They ask: 'Which features of the films lead to such perceptions [of 'medievalness']?' The answer surely rests in the culturally defined popular understandings of what the Middle Ages were. Rather than limiting the focus only to film, their statement raises the question: 'what do individuals identify as "medieval" in general?' Only when that question has been answered can we then proceed to ask 'what causes them to apply the label "medieval" to a film?' and 'what features of a film cause it to be recognisably "medieval" to its audience?'.

The goal of the study presented in this book was thus to explore three questions. The first was explored in Chapter 2:

(1) What do individuals understand 'medieval' or 'Middle Ages' to mean?

The second and third questions are central to exploring how the audiences of the medieval film understand, and learn, from what they are viewing.

(2) What features of a film cause it to be understood as 'medieval' by its viewers?
(3) What effects does watching a film understood to be 'medieval' have on what they understand 'medieval' to mean?

Any film which is perceived to be medieval by its viewers has the potential to contribute to the public understanding of the Middle Ages. That makes it, for better or for worse, a medieval history. If a film is not understood by its consumers to be 'medieval', then no matter what sources, analogues, or resonances it may have with the Middle Ages, it is not a medieval history and thus irrelevant to the above questions.

The contemporary reception of medievalisms is one of the central questions in both medievalism studies and medieval studies today – and is of course central to determining the factors that would lead a viewer to classify a film as 'medieval'. This monograph opens two new lines of inquiry in that topic by investigating what the public understanding of the Middle Ages actually entails and by focusing on the audiences of medieval films, rather than either the films themselves or their producers (though the makers of medieval films warrant future study). This approach focuses on the effect that films have upon those who watch them – and the implications of those effects.

Examining the Corpus and Audience of Medieval Films

So, proceeding with an eye firmly fixed upon audiences and films as an influence on historical consciousness, what can be said about the 'medieval film' as a whole? Firstly, it is important to put to rest the quest for perfect historical accuracy. No matter how compelling it may seem, the cinematic Middle Ages is *a* Middle Ages rather than *the* Middle Ages. Contemporary representations are not the thing itself; representations inherently cannot be totally accurate.

But that is hardly the end of the story. As Rosenstone explained (and as quoted in the introduction of this volume), film has become, arguably the chief carrier of cultural messages.[18] Though today, interactive media and television should be added to that sentiment, the moving Middle Ages – a group that includes film, TV, and games – is arguably the dominant cultural version of the Middle Ages. Furthermore, the moving Middle Ages, with its familiar tropes, images, and icons has been used to depict legendary, fairy tale and fantasy worlds that are more-or-less similar to more realistic ones. This has been done so often that ideas of the 'medieval' and the 'Middle Ages' may be a blur of history and outright fantasy – a prosthetic memory mixing with a prosthetic imagination. If both historical and fantasy films draw from the same groundwater, it is inevitable that the two will become mixed in the popular historical consciousness.

Figure 4.1   *Ceci n'est pas un moyen âge.* Laurence Olivier in *Henry V* (Eagle-Lion Distributors Limited, 1944).

The Dominant Modes of Depicting the Middle Ages in Film
As explored by historians like Aberth, films that depict the Middle Ages
are a product – and thus a reflection – of the historical consciousness of
the Middle Ages at a specific cultural moment. Each medieval film
becomes part of a long evolutionary process, wherein filmmakers are
influenced by their culture and influence it in turn.

In the nineteenth century, certain norms for interpreting the Middle
Ages in popular culture were established during the explosions of interest
in the medieval.[19] At the close of the nineteenth century, film was
invented. Early film depictions of the Middle Ages thus deployed the ways
the Middle Ages had been interpreted – both visually, narratologically,
and politically – throughout the nineteenth century. This, in turn, became
the baseline for how the Middle Ages were to be presented in subsequent
films. Filmmakers may draw from previous successful films (and
medievalisms in other media) as often, or more, than they draw from the
actual Middle Ages. The filmmakers working in the early years of cinema
created depictions similar to the Middle Ages with which they were
familiar. As a result, in the early years of film, British, German, and Eastern
European filmmakers (and American immigrants from those countries)
depicted their national medievalisms in their films. Thus, romantic and
pre-Raphaelite art, the operas of Verdi, Gounod, and Wagner, and Gothic
Revival architecture found their way into early films.[20] As a result,
nineteenth-century modes of depicting the Middle Ages became the
original cinematic image of the period: frozen and infinitely reproducible
in celluloid, a source of endless borrowings and *homages*.

The mixture of authentically medieval works with eighteenth- and
nineteenth-century visions of the period created an opulent, idealised
image of the period. This 'light medieval' is especially apparent in
adventure films such as *The Adventures of Robin Hood* (1938), *Prince
Valiant* (1954), *The Court Jester* (1956), or *Camelot* (1967).[21] Three of
the four Disney animated films that depict the Middle Ages – *Sleeping
Beauty* (1959), *The Sword in the Stone* (1963), and *Robin Hood* (1973) –
follow this formula.[22] However, over the course of the 1960s, the
dominance of this idealised image of the Middle Ages was supplanted by
a darker, grittier, and more pessimistic vision of the period. This 'dark
Middle Ages' was spattered with mud and blood, and full of war
and plague. It came into vogue in *Becket* (1964), *The War Lord* (1965),
and *The Lion in Winter* (1968).[23] The trend was then exaggerated and

entrenched in subsequent decades by films such as *Lancelot du Lac* (1974), *Excalibur* (1981), *Henry V* (1989), *Army of Darkness* (1992), *Braveheart* (1995), *The Thirteenth Warrior* (1999), and even Disney's *The Hunchback of Notre Dame* (1996).[24] Not long after this image came into vogue, it was aptly parodied by *Monty Python and the Holy Grail* in 1974:

Peasant: Who's that then?
The Dead Collector: I dunno, must be a king.
Peasant: Why?
The Dead Collector: He hasn't got shit all over him.[25]

In the twenty-first century, comedies or adventures set in the Middle Ages have become self-aware and steeped in irony and iconoclasm, skewering the light vision of the medieval as 'unrealistic'. In *A Knight's Tale* (2001) we first encounter the great English poet Geoffrey Chaucer as a naked wastrel shuffling down a dusty lane.[26] Postmodern cynicism – which leads one to question idealistic revisions of the past (like the aforementioned technicolour adventures from the 1930s to the 1960s) – may cause one instinctually to label the darker, ironic, or iconoclastic revisions 'more realistic' than its predecessors.

However, they are not. They are no closer to the actual *zeitgeist* of the Middle Ages – if such a thing even exists – than the merry images. Instead, the dark and light visions conform to the culturally determined and culturally specific popular images and ideas in vogue at their time. The Middle Ages were never as good or as bad as we desire, imagine, or perhaps even require them to have been. Though the ideal of total historical accuracy has been (more or less) successfully assaulted by successive waves of academic critics, it is important to reiterate that cinematic constructions of history are just that. Their past is not *the* past, no matter how sophisticated or new.

Neither of these two dominant modes of depicting the Middle Ages – bright and cheery or muddy and bloody – arose spontaneously. They did so as a result of a phenomenon whereby the Middle Ages are brought to heel in service of peculiar cultural trend. In all media, there has been a tendency for the authentically medieval to be – consciously or unconsciously – deemed 'not medieval enough'. In order for it to conform to the *idea* of the Middle Ages, it must be altered, exaggerated, and re-imagined. The medieval is altered in an attempt to fix or improve

Figure 4.2   Two very different cinematic Middle Ages. John Boorman, *Excalibur* (Warner Brothers, 1981); Mel Gibson, *Braveheart* (Paramount, 1995).

it, to make it more awful or more awesome. It becomes the Middle Ages not as they were, but as they *should have been*.

This phenomenon can be called 'hypermedievalism'. Hypermedievalism is the tendency to push historical ideologies, material cultures, landscapes, and even the human body to grotesque extremes. This process of exaggeration is not unique to depictions of the Middle Ages (for example, see the rendering of the classical world in Zack Snyder's *300*).[27] But the fact that the Middle Ages has been appropriated as a fantasy playground as often as it has makes these 'hyper' versions of the

Middle Ages very common. This can have the side-effect of making the 'hyper' seem real.[28] Iterations of hypermedieval fantasy and depictions of medieval reality often borrow from one another and share similar aesthetic bases. For example, the fantastical medievalist art of Frank Frazetta and Boris Vallejo (Figures 4.3 and 4.4) has, over the course of the twentieth century, spawned a genre of art replete with bulging barbarians and barely armoured medieval warrior women.[29] In these, the aspect of the historical consciousness of the Middle Ages that is exaggerated is the 'savagery' and 'barbarity' often attributed to the period. This results in grotesque exaggerations of the sexual characteristics of the male and female body as well as what covers it: armour is adorned with spikes, patches of fur or sharp gothic fluting. Swords grow to giant proportions, are given serrated edges, and drip gore. Everything is painted black, including the sky, the castles, and the land.[30]

Figure 4.3 Boris Vallejo, 'Dragon slayer', 1989. Reproduced with kind permission from the artist.

This genre of art commonly adorns pulp fantasy novel covers, illustrations, calendars, posters, and comic books. Subsequently, it has been borrowed for use in other visual media, like video games, TV and film, especially when they depict people considered 'barbaric' like the Norse, Anglo-Saxons, or other early medieval peoples.[31] This is particularly problematic when this aesthetic is used in films that mix fantasy and reality, such as depictions of medieval legends or more realistic low-magic fantasy films. Some examples of these include *Robin Hood: Prince of Thieves* (1991), *Braveheart* (1995), *The Thirteenth Warrior* (1999), and *King Arthur* (2004).[32]

The Rise and Fall of Political Hypermedievalisms

It is not just the visual aspects of the Middle Ages that have been pushed to 'hyper' extremes in film, ideological and political interpretations of the period have also been subjected to this treatment: presenting the Middle Ages not as they were, but as we may believe they 'should have been'. During the nineteenth century, the Middle Ages were routinely co-opted for political purposes both in public discourses and in the arts. Often, renderings of the Middle Ages in the arts were bent in service to the establishment of a mythological past. This mythological Middle Ages was replete with nostalgic heroism which served to establish, promote, and justify emerging ethnic and national identities. This manifested in a wide range of art forms: opera, theatre, novels, and fairy tales. For example, Wagner's medievalist operas *Lohengrin*, *Tannhäuser*, *Parsifal*, and *Der Ring des Nibelungen* (The Ring of the Nibelung) were part of a project to establish a 'national' Germanic culture that claimed its origins in medieval romance, legend, myth, and folklore.[33] Verdi's *I Lombardi alla Prima Crociata* (The Lombards on the First Crusade) is part of a similar nation-defining project in Italy. In England, the novels of Sir Walter Scott, particularly *Ivanhoe*, popularised ideas of the medieval origins of English 'Saxon' ethnic and political identity. As Clare Simmons argues, '*Ivanhoe* provided a pattern for oppositions that the nineteenth century's need to classify – and to judge – took further than the earlier myth of the Norman Yoke implied', and 'inspired popular interest in Saxons and Normans'.[34]

As a result, many films of the twentieth century have used the Middle Ages for similar nationalistic purposes. Many of the best-regarded (by critics and scholars) medieval films of all time are either pieces of state-sponsored political propaganda or have highly nationalistic

Figure 4.4   Frank Frazetta, 'Death dealer', 1973. Reproduced with kind permission from the rights holder.

overtones. This includes: for the French, *La Passion de Jeanne d'Arc* (The Passion of Joan of Arc) (1928), for the Nazis, *Das Mädchen Johanna* (Joan the Maid) (1935), for the Soviets, *Alexander Nevsky* (1938), for the Allies in World War II, *Henry V* (1944), for Franco's Spain, *El Cid* (1961), and for Gamal Nasser's Egypt, *El Naser Salah Ad Din* (The Victorious Saladin) (1963). Even when not used for overtly nationalistic purposes, the Middle Ages have often been used in film to promote, and invent historical precedent for, the political, religious, or cultural ideals of the people who produce and consume them.[35]

By contrast, more recent Hollywood-style medieval films are rarely *overtly* propagandistic, political, or moralising due to their being designed to cater to a global marketplace. Though they sometimes pay homage to American cultural meta-narratives (e.g. rote use of 'freedom', 'liberty', or 'equality' narratives transposed onto, for example, Robin Hood in Ridley Scott's 2010 *Robin Hood*), globalisation has a homogenising and blurring effect on big-budget films. In order to appeal to an international, multicultural audience, the morality and politics on display in these big-budget films are often calculatedly conventional, uncontroversial, and malleable.[36] Blandly acceptable modern morals are now often put in medieval mouths, which are intended to be adaptable (and acceptable) to a variety of worldwide audiences. But like the 'dark' and 'light' Middle Ages, neither the political nor malleable Middle Ages are reflective of medieval realities.

Conclusion: Does This Affect the Audiences of Medieval Films?

To what degree does an audience see any of these things? It is all well and good to state that medieval films may be loaded with aesthetic and political traditions that influence their current state. But are these aesthetics and politics understood to be part of the age and culture in which the film was made, rather than a part of the Middle Ages, to those who view them? Or do their audiences see everything within them as medieval? Buffeted as they are by competing interpretations of the Middle Ages in school, in their entertainment, and their daily lives, what do viewers integrate into their historical consciousness and what do they reject? If filmgoers simply dismiss all they see in medieval films as the fanciful invention of filmmakers-as-entertainers (rather than as a valid source for historical information), then the medieval film has little significance for scholars outside of the realms of film and cultural studies. However, if these films *do* have an impact upon their viewers, and by extension the broader historical consciousness of the Middle Ages, then the visions and versions of history presented in these films may be of great significance for educators and historians. In sum, do the ways in which the Middle Ages are depicted in film today (with an aesthetics and politics that freely mixes the medieval, the medievalist, and the hypermedieval) actually influence viewers' ideas about the period? The next chapter will show how the three films viewed by the participants had a significant impact upon their perceptions of the medieval world – though often in unexpected ways.

CHAPTER 5

THE MIDDLE AGES THEY WATCHED

I wouldn't have seen it if I hadn't believed it.[1]
David L. Hamilton, *Cognitive Processes in Stereotyping and Intergroup Behavior*

Having established, in Chapter 2, the initial outlines of the *Middle Ages in Popular Imagination*'s participants' historical consciousness about the Middle Ages, how did they view the three films they were shown? What did they learn? What did they find important enough to discuss? This chapter will first address the ways in which the participants reacted to each of the three films – *Beowulf*, *Kingdom of Heaven*, and *The Lord of the Rings: The Return of the King* – and then discuss the structures that emerged from their conversations. In other words, how did they respond to, and interpret, historical films which did not necessarily show them the history they expected to see?

Beowulf

Robert Zemeckis' 2007 film *Beowulf*, as the name would imply, is an adaptation of the well-known medieval poem of the same name. In many ways, it is the most faithful version of the *Beowulf* story yet told on film – for example, the Zemeckis film retains the final episode with the dragon that other versions have eschewed. But was the poem well-known enough to influence the participants' interpretation of the film? Does the film's status as an adaptation of medieval literature – with all the academic gravity that *Beowulf* brings with it – make its film adaptation seem more medieval? Or was it treated like any other fantasy?

Even though their academic study of the period was limited to primary and secondary school, some participants had had previous experience with the poem. Four of the thirteen participants mentioned that they had been taught *Beowulf* in school, and that their interpretations of the film were founded upon this experience. For example, Erica recounted:

> Erica: I read the poem, well, had the poem read to us.
> Mod: When did you have the poem read to you?
> Erica: Primary school, I think. So, I kind of knew what it was about.
> Mod: Okay.
> Erica: So it [the film] was pretty well done.

For Erica, her perception that the film adhered closely to the original poem was the basis for her positive judgement of the film. However, she did not stop there:

> I always remember the poem from primary school as being quite, not violent but kind of *raw* [. . .] I remember doing at primary school how nasty the Vikings were and that was one of the poems they read to us. And we had to study how nasty it all was and how barbaric and all that kind of stuff. But then in the film, it wasn't like that at all. It was kind of like the hero coming to save the day. It was [. . .] a bit too much [of a] general hero, villain, princess kind of thing. Whereas in the poem [. . .] it was read out to be like, look how barbaric the Vikings were, look how horrible they were [. . .] they're really vicious

The impact of her previous experience on her ideas about the film was not as simple as critiquing the film's adherence to the original poem. Her memory of learning about the poem *Beowulf* in primary school centred on an interpretation of the Vikings' barbarity – probably in KS2 in its module on the Vikings. She criticised the film for adhering to

Hollywood adventure movie tropes at the expense of her memory of her classroom's interpretation of the original. However, her memory that the poem was interpreted in terms of 'look how barbaric the Vikings were [. . .] they're really vicious', seems a bit odd. At the very least it is out of date. Recent academic discussion of the medieval Norse no longer focuses on their traditional image as voracious pillagers, but views them instead as extraordinary seafarers, explorers, traders, and settlers. Popular culture (such as the recent TV series *The Vikings* and *The Last Kingdom*), however, continues to portray the medieval Norse as hypermedieval savage raiders as it has done since the Middle Ages, when they were considered by some, as Kevin Harty has argued, 'the global terrorists of their day'.[2]

But in even more basic terms, the poem *Beowulf* does not even depict Vikings. Though it is set in Denmark and Geatland (now Götaland in southern Sweden), the story takes place, and was probably first composed, well before the Viking Age (considered to be from the eighth to eleventh centuries).[3] If we look back to the geographical definition of the Middle Ages, it is arguable that it was during the Viking Age that Scandinavia joined the Middle Ages. That said, it is a common misconception that all pre-modern Norse were 'Vikings' – that 'Viking' is a durable ethnic label rather than a specific cultural moment. The Vikings are now a concept with such mass that any related culture gets pulled into its gravity well – as such, *Beowulf*, with its meditation on Iron Age Scandinavian warrior culture, gets lumped in with the Vikings.

Considering her statement about Vikings and *Beowulf*, it might be tempting to lay the blame for Erica's enduring misperception at the feet of her teacher. But without knowing more about the specific lessons about the poem, judgement should be reserved. Erica's memories may or may not be accurate – and any learning she did in school has surely been supplemented by and conflated with a multitude of depictions of the Vikings as vicious raiders with horned helmets. A false memory of a school lesson, or even a shift in apparent focus, is certainly possible.

Erica's assessment of the film was that it was too conventional – 'was a bit too much general hero, villain, princess kind of thing' – to be historically accurate. But the original poem is, if reduced to its basic plot points, a remarkably conventional action/adventure story. It features a larger-than-life male hero vanquishing monsters in a vaguely three-act structure. The only element of a Hollywood film missing from the poem is a love interest (which the Zemeckis film provides, more or less). Erica's condemnation of its conventionality revealed an idea that the use of film conventions make a story, by definition, neither historically accurate nor a faithful adaptation of literature.

Stephen and Justin (who attended school together) also covered *Beowulf* in class. But their teacher had a very different interpretation:

Stephen: I remember covering *Beowulf* to some extent, but I think the story kind of stopped with 'And he killed the mother and that was it.' Instead, he had sex with the mother, fathered a dragon child, and [it] killed him and his wife and his mistress. Yeah, they kind of stopped it at 'yeah, killed Grendel's mother, happily ever after'. [laugh] I remember trying to draw a cartoon strip of it. You remember Mrs Baldwin's class?

Justin: Yeah.

Mod: Okay. So, so, the seedy bits, the raw bits, the extra sex bits you thought [they] were a bit ... they fit all together as one?

Stephen: Yeah, I think that, yeah it's more representative than the stuff at school.

To Stephen, the film diverged from his expectations of the poem because it included 'seediness' and sex. But this conflict – between the film and his memory of the poem – caused him to reject his childhood memory and accept the sexual narrative in the film as authentic to the original. This happened despite that narrative being an invention of the filmmakers. This is not to say he accepted the film as a completely faithful adaptation; he later said 'It is always interesting to see how much of the story had been changed', to which Justin replied, 'Probably quite a lot I would have thought.' Justin is tentative in his assessment, but seems, nevertheless, to default towards an assumption that a film adaptation requires deviations from the original. But, the sexual narrative of the film was one piece he incorrectly accepted as authentic.

These statements echoed a broader suspicion of filmmakers-as-adaptors of literature. Many participants felt that the filmmakers would be more driven by economic or aesthetic concerns than the desire to make a faithful adaptation of *Beowulf*. For example, Erica said that the filmmakers

> water some stuff down to try to get as [many] viewers as possible. I don't think they've really taken into account the historical value of it. [They've] just thought, 'if we do it this way, more people will come' [. . .] [they] try to make it as mainstream as possible and [the film] was not keeping to the true story really, the poem and stuff. Yeah, [that] ruined it a bit.

To her, the story of *Beowulf* has value because of its history, and that perceived attempts to make the film more broadly appealing 'ruined' the film for her. Even though her knowledge of the 'true story' of *Beowulf* was sketchy, this film was *not* it. Similarly, when asked how the fantastical elements in the film related to the historical elements in the film, three of the June group related this to conventionality:

Sean: Was there a dragon in the original poem?
Stephen: I'm not sure.
Justin: I can't remember there being a dragon.
Stephen: No, well, I can say we stopped at Grendel's mother [in school], I didn't realise he fathered a =
Justin: = yeah, I didn't realise there was a dragon there. But the dragon kind of keys into it when you think of a medieval tale.
Sean: It does.
Stephen: I think it would be very interesting if there isn't a dragon in the original poem, because that suggests that Hollywood has added a dragon. Because [for Hollywood] it's a medieval film and therefore it has to have a dragon in it.

They admit that their memory of the poem is incomplete; it is possible that they were never taught the final episode of the poem in school (omissions from school teaching already being present in their minds after their assessment of the supposed omissions of the sexual material). But this is also unsurprising due to the general disregard for the final episode of the poem in popular culture. As previously mentioned, no other film or TV adaptation of *Beowulf* includes the final episode with the dragon. Beowulf is most often thought of in his battle with Grendel (hence the title of the 2005 film *Beowulf and Grendel*). Dragons have appeared in popular culture more often in high- or late-medieval styled worlds than in depictions referencing the Early Middle Ages; Saint George is the prime example but this is also evident in films like *DragonHeart* (1996), *Dragonslayer* (1981), or even *Shrek* (2001). That said, since *Beowulf*'s release, there have been at least two major popular cultural depictions of dragons existing in Viking-esque fantasy worlds: the DreamWorks animated film series *How to Train Your Dragon* (2010, 2014), and the bestselling computer game *Skyrim* (2011). It is unknown whether this signals a lasting shift in how dragons are presented in popular culture.

The study participants supported the idea that the film is medieval because the presence of a dragon is almost a prerequisite for medieval fantasy. Yet this explanation seemed too simple for them. So, they went through a complex decision-making process, trying to deduce whether what they saw was believable.[4] On the one hand, a dragon is *the* archetypal medieval monster – as such it may have been in the original. On the other, this very universality makes it suspiciously conventional. Stephen later added, 'Either this story is where the idea of a dragon in every fantasy comes from, or, Hollywood has thought "It's a medieval fantasy, therefore it needs a dragon".' Stephen does not know that both are, at least partially, true.

Starting with *Beowulf* as an origin for the trope of the dragon: *Beowulf* is certainly not the oldest tale to include a dragon (which were present, albeit in a somewhat different form, in classical literature), though it stands as part of a tradition that offers the oldest surviving dragon stories from the Middle Ages – and certainly is the oldest extant in any form of English.[5] As Christine Rauer argues, for the dragon in *Beowulf* 'no literary sources have been established consensually but [the episode] is surrounded by large numbers of analogues'.[6] Scholars have explored dozens of analogues in the Germanic and Scandinavian traditions, including the dragon that Sigmund fights in the *Nibelungenlied*, or Thor's battle with Jörmungandr during Ragnarök in the *Edda*. But Stephen was not referring to *Beowulf*'s age, but rather its place in the foundational canon for modern-day medievalesque fantasy dragons. Though no scholar has traced the sources and evolution of the dragon in modern medievalisms completely, it could be argued that J.R.R. Tolkien, standing as one of the foundational authors for the modern pulp-medievalism genre, played a significant role in the current cultural ubiquity of the dragon. Tolkien modelled the dragon Smaug in *The Hobbit*, in part, after the Germanic/Scandinavian tradition of which he was so fond. Considering Tolkien's scholarly interests, it could be argued that Smaug – and thus the prototypical modern fantasy dragon – was perhaps most influenced by the dragons he found in these tales, including *Beowulf*.

But, back to Stephen's statements: Stephen and the other participants seemed to view Hollywood's influence as corrupting by default. Their interpretation of the film was that the tropes of Hollywood are inherently antithetical to fidelity to the original poem. As a result, at any point when the filmmakers' presence became apparent, the film was not to be trusted. What they do not know is that a few of these film tropes may, in fact, have had their origins in medieval literature.

Beowulf *as History and/or Fantasy*

Zemeckis' version of *Beowulf* occupies an uncomfortable middle ground between history and fantasy. The film is ostensibly set in a real place and time: the opening subtitle declares it to be set in 'Denmark, A.D. 507' (Figure 5.1).

And yet, it is a world replete with fantastical monsters and magic. Thus the film is set both in our world and not. Might *Beowulf*'s medieval

Figure 5.1   Setting the historical scene in Zemeckis' *Beowulf* (Paramount Pictures, 2007).

provenance and setting cause viewers to think of it as more historical than a straightforward fantasy like *The Return of the King*? How did they cope with this blending of the historical and fantastical?

As would be expected of adults, none of the participants felt *Beowulf* presented a true story. For this reason, some also refused to identify the film as medieval. Erica said that *Beowulf* was 'trying to be more of a fantasy than the historical' because of 'the different types of monsters and the whole [. . .] mythology about them'.[7] Jess also rejected the film as a depiction of the Middle Ages, 'because it was a fairy-story, you know what I mean? The Middle Ages were a real time period, so they didn't actually have dragons.' To both, the inclusion of fantasy elements excluded the film from consideration as a depiction of the period – fantasy and history are simply mutually exclusive.

Some saw the film as a hybrid. Robert said, 'It seems that it's jumping on the *Lord of the Rings* bandwagon [. . .] I didn't really get what he's [the Director] aiming at, because there's parts of it where I think it's aiming at historical accuracy, but other times it's ridiculous.' Justin had seen fantasy films before, but he identified *Beowulf* as special because 'it was quite original in the sense that it showed you . . . I mean, I hadn't really seen too many movies that showed the Middle Ages quite in that same kind of complete[ly] mystical way like that did.' To him, the film was not a fantasy, but a film set in the real medieval world but with a layer of magic added. This approach is relatively common among film adaptations of medieval literature, such as *Excalibur* (1981) or *Robin Hood: Prince of Thieves* (1991).

Although none believed *Beowulf* was completely true, and some rejected it as an historical film, many found specific scenes or elements to be medieval. Chloe said 'I thought it was a really medieval movie', to which Erica then expanded, 'In my medieval [word association] sheet, basically everything that I'd written down was in the film.' When pressed for specifics, she listed, 'Battles, kings, swords, armour, monsters, dragons, knights, religion, division between rich and poor, hog roasts, medieval harpy music [. . .] Everything I'd written down was in that film.' The opening scene – depicting a feast interrupted by Grendel's assault – was singled out as particularly medieval. Erica related,

I thought the first scene, the banquety scene, that was typical, what I would assume from what I'd seen. [That] stuff that was pretty much typical, and I thought that [it] was really well done and it captured quite a lot of glimpses of medieval life in one scene [. . .] Most everything on my sheet was pictured in that first scene. There was banquets, lovey music [. . .] the drunken people; there was people in armour, and it had a little bit of fight[ing], and the hog roast and then the king sat on his throne. And everything, basically, that you saw of being medieval was in that scene.

This corresponds with how historian Martha Carlin identifies feasts, such as the one that opens *Beowulf*, as a key component of medievalisms in our culture:

From Victorian novels to Hollywood films, and from Gary Larson's *Far Side* cartoons to themed restaurants featuring 'medieval banquets' complete with jousting, the medieval feast has served as a lens through which people could view the past either as a symbol of lost aristocratic splendour, or as a barbarous but entertaining spectacle.[8]

For Erica, the opening scene of *Beowulf* presented very much the latter – a barbarous spectacle that fit soundly within her expectations of the Middle Ages, and helped her see the film as authentically medieval.

The opening scene in any film is a particularly important one. It establishes the tone, often introduces the main characters, and presents the world of the film. While the first scene of Zemeckis' *Beowulf* can be criticised for presenting a stereotyped vision of a barbaric drunk-and-dirty Early Middle Ages, that vision clearly resonated with these viewers. To them, it practically shouted 'medieval!', and so by that metric it could be considered a success.

However, some participants resisted thinking of the scenes of *Beowulf* in terms of the Middle Ages. Justin said 'it didn't fit in with the archetypal image that I had of medieval'. Dan saw it more in terms of fantasy than history, 'I didn't think it was especially middle-agesy – that wasn't what struck me. [It] was more [of a] fantasy realm where other things were happening, [though it] featured [. . .] the Middle Ages a bit more.' Jess hated the film. This manifested in a variety of ways; she particularly took issue with the film's medievalness both as a result of her negative reaction to the film's lack of realism, and also to its setting:

I don't know. When I think Middle Ages, fair enough, maybe feasts and stuff are what I think of it. But the rest of it, the entire storyline just felt so ... I mean just so ridiculous, you know what I mean? And I thought, 'maybe in Denmark', but I wasn't thinking 'oh that could easily happen here'.

She first gives a nod to the opening scene as an effective one but quickly labels the remainder of the film as absurd. She relates this to her overarching insular idea of a specifically British Middle Ages; it isn't possible in Britain because Britain is not so ridiculous. Medieval Denmark is a place so liminal in her mind that it *literally* can be labelled with 'here be dragons'. This seems to contradict her previous statement that in the film 'there was loads of monsters and stuff which, fair enough, you associate with Middle Ages'. She intuitively understood the received image of the Middle Ages as a location for fantasy and monsters, but in this instance rejected it in favour of a more rigid definition, possibly due to her frequently expressed dislike of the film overall. She disliked the film so much she was willing to contradict herself in order to find weapons with which to cudgel it – perhaps because she may have found difficulty in explaining the exact reason for her disdain.

Beowulf's Dark, Middle, or Universal Ages

In further discussion, some of the participants who identified *Beowulf* as 'very medieval' later expressed discomfort with that label. Much of this uneasiness centred around some participants' perception that this film was set in the 'Dark Ages' and was about 'Vikings', which placed the film in a different time or place than the Middle Ages. Erica said, 'I do class medieval as being British, that kind of vibe, whereas Vikings I didn't really class as medieval [. . .] It would be before medieval.' Justin reacted similarly: 'Especially the beginning, it's not how I would have seen the Middle Ages. I would have thought that was way before, but – well not way before, but, you know, a hundred years before maybe.' Stephen followed,

I never realised that the Anglo-Saxons and the Vikings were actually part of the Middle Ages; I thought it [the Middle Ages] kind of came after. But I suppose that doesn't really make sense. I suppose in school you think, [. . .] that in the neat segmented view of history that you have the Anglo-Saxons and the Vikings, and then the Middle Ages and then the Tudors.

This is further evidence that their school experience shaped their historical consciousness on a basic, structural level. Having been taught 'Romans, Anglo-Saxons, and Vikings' in primary school in a module separate from 'the Middle Ages', it is unsurprising they did not associate Vikings with the period.

Participants offered a range of reasons for labelling *Beowulf* pre-medieval; they cited most frequently either the material culture or the social culture depicted in the film. That said, they *never* mentioned the date (AD 507) in the opening subtitle. The most frequently cited indicators of period, which, for the participants, placed *Beowulf* either in or before the Middle Ages, were centred on architectural development and the emergence of the monarch. The world of the film, between its second and third acts (between the slaying of Grendel's mother and the beginning of the episode with the dragon) changes immensely. In many ways, during this fifty-year gap, the world evolves from the Early Middle Ages to the High Middle Ages or, as Gwendolyn Morgan argues, from a world of Anglo-Saxon epic to one of medieval romance.[9] This is apparent in three major ways: first, the evolution of the setting from a small village of wooden structures centred on a mead hall to a sprawling city centred on a castle. Second, the evolution from pervasive Norse polytheism to the emergence of Christianity as a major religious and cultural power. And third, from a power structure where Hrothgar stands as a local leader, to one where Beowulf stands as king of a wider region.

Justin initially found that the world of *Beowulf* differed from his expectations of the medieval past because he:

expected it to be a bit more developed and a bit bigger than that really, a bit more advanced [. . .] the settlements would be bigger [. . .] and there'd be a bunch of agricultural things that you could see, like ploughed fields [. . .] I expected it to be much grander really.

This gives some insights into Justin's concept of the medieval landscape for which *Beowulf* lacks the necessary markers: agriculture and cities. Stephen found other markers missing: 'knights and castles and things like that; there's none of that, but presumably that came hundreds of years later'. Justin then added, 'There's kind of a bit towards the end, though, where it looked as if it had developed a bit more.' Jess also noted the change. At first, she reacted positively to the depiction of the mead hall Heorot as exemplary of the Middle Ages 'I like the hall in the first part, it seemed quite hall-y to me, middle-agey.' When pressed for clarification, she expressed discomfort:

> [at first] it was quite [a], primitive, hunting, feasting area, mead hall lot. And then [. . .] I don't believe they'd have gone from that shanty sort of town to that castle [. . .] the second castle as well, just seemed really... why would you build two towers with a bridge next to it? [. . .] a really impractical design. I don't think that was very realistic.

So, whereas Justin and Stephen felt the architectural changes brought the film more in line with their perceptions of the Middle Ages, Jess felt the changes drove it further away from hers. She was uncomfortable with the idea of fast cultural change, not just as a result of the castle's implausible fantastical design, but also due to the castle's very existence. Perhaps she simply found it implausible for economic or logistical reasons (how fast the village would grow into a city, or how fast one might build a castle). However, contributing to this may be a lack of understanding about the often rapid nature of cultural change. While every school child in Britain learns the date 1066 and the events surrounding it, Jess may not have fully understood the architectural revolution brought by the Normans. As Hugh Thomas writes,

> William the Conqueror and some of his followers also had the first stone keeps in England [. . .] many royal castles were built to dominate fortified towns, which helped the Normans consolidate their conquest and give later rulers a way to keep firm control of urban areas.[10]

Moreover, there was a concurrent revolution in church architecture:

> Norman churchmen also brought massive change to ecclesiastical architecture. Within fifty years of the conquest, and in most cases

within thirty years, the Normans began rebuilding every major church in England except Westminster Abbey.[11]

In short, England went from wooden halls to stone castles within a generation. While there are a number of benefits to modularisation in history education, a serious problem is a lack of understanding of the transitions between periods – periods of profound change which, arguably, are the most fascinating parts of the past. But even more, working from Morgan's thesis of *Beowulf* depicting the bridge between literary styles, the castle is not intended to be a real castle at all, but the castle of medieval romance.[12] Its fantastical architecture means to set it out as a symbol rather than as an actual castle. If this was indeed the filmmakers' intent, it was lost on this particular audience.

A few, rather than discussing *Beowulf* within any historical context, thought of the narrative ahistorically. They viewed it as a universal story that was only medieval because it had been placed there by the filmmakers – despite its early-medieval origins. Erica held this view: 'you could have put him in any kind of costume and he would have gone in any time. [. . .] all that's different about him is just the armour'. John also felt the narrative was independent of its period:

> The story's been set on purpose in that age, middle age or medieval times, to make it seem more of a complete story. I mean, the story's the story on its own. If you took away all the little descriptions on it, it's about someone who's in power who had a shameful past, and you could change it to fit into modern day times [. . .] If it's set in medieval times, no one alive today – well some people might have an idea what it's like – but I think [for] most viewers it just makes it much more believable to them [. . .] they can imagine dragons existing in medieval times because they weren't alive.

John accepts the 'shameful past' narrative (which was invented by the filmmakers) as authentic to the original. But more importantly, he here makes an interesting observation about the Middle Ages' role as a common cultural fantasy playground. Since, to him, most viewers don't know the Middle Ages well (being out of living memory), placing a story within the period makes it more easily believable. However John is only partially correct. Ignoring for a moment the medieval origins of the poem, there is no reason a *Beowulf* adaptation need be set in Early Medieval Scandinavia – Neil Gaiman's novella 'The Monarch of the Glen' sets the *Beowulf* story in the modern day, and both the 1999 film *Beowulf* and an episode of *Star Trek: Voyager* set the tale in space.[13] But because the Middle Ages is known in the popular historical consciousness primarily through its icons and tropes – and also has become an acceptable, even default, place-time for the fantasy genre. Placing a fantasy in the Middle Ages has the potential to make it more readily accepted. The film was not set in a place and time truly unknown to its audience (e.g. fourth-century Siberia), but in a place-time already loaded with mental hooks upon which the filmmakers can hang their tale.

In sum, the multiple ideas and images of the Middle Ages they held made it difficult for the participants reliably to place *Beowulf* historically. On the one hand, most accepted the film as very 'medieval' because it portrayed what they perceived as a more 'barbaric' age rife with the extremes of human indulgence – lust, gluttony, drunkenness, and violence. However, the change from Early Middle Ages to High Middle Ages was noticed and celebrated by most – though not all – participants. They enjoyed the depiction of the cultural change towards a world more in line with the Middle Ages they understood. Some had little difficulty viewing *Beowulf* as both medieval and fantastical. They engaged historically with those aspects they deemed historical, and did not with aspects they deemed fantastical. However, some had a more rigid interpretation; for them this hybridity did not sit well. Those people were disinclined to believe that anything on the screen was historical once fantastical elements were introduced.

Filmic Aspects of Beowulf

Criticism of *Beowulf* as a film by the participants centred on two things: the CGI and the language. Their dislike of the CGI or language might not, at first, seem to be related to their knowledge of the Middle Ages (and thus not relevant to this book). However, when criticising these elements, the participants often discussed them in historical terms. Their perception of the film's historicity seemed intimately intertwined with many aspects of the film that have little to do, ostensibly, with its relationship with the past.

For example, almost all participants reacted negatively to the motion-capture CGI used extensively in the film. *Beowulf*, like Robert Zemeckis' other films *The Polar Express* (2004) and *A Christmas Carol* (2009) was created almost entirely by computer. It was filmed using a mixture of traditional filming and computer animation; the actors were dressed in lycra suits pocked with motion sensors, and played out their scenes on a specially designed sound stage (called 'The Volume' by Zemeckis).[14] After this is done, computer artists completed the scene by placing a virtual eye within a virtual three-dimensional space to provide a camera-like perspective, and then overlaying textures, lighting, and backgrounds on the wireframes. By creating the film in this way, the filmmakers had complete control over the final product by manipulating the data within the computer. The shots and camera angles in the film are not the result of the positioning of a mechanical device, but the product of a virtual camera perspective. The movements of the actors provided only a base framework upon which the computer animators then layered flesh, skin, cloth, and light. Every inch of landscape and every stitch of costume was rendered in a computer. Even Beowulf's body was created by stitching together Ray Winstone's face with two other people's bodies – actor Alan Ritchson and fitness model Aaron Stephens – to create a sculpted digital Frankenstein's monster.[15]

Sean said the CGI hampered his ability to engage with the film: 'I do have a bit of a problem getting into the story if it's animated.' Participants also noted that the animation made the film seem to be intended 'for kids'. John was one of only two who enjoyed the CGI, but even he damned it with faint praise: 'I thought the CGI would be much worse'. Robert said 'I felt that [the CGI] took away from it. That was another thing that I thought was, [that] there was a mixture between pandering to the mainstream and [. . .] trying to be historically accurate'. To Robert, 'pandering to the mainstream' is antithetical to making a historically accurate film. The CGI was one part of that division. Chloe was more explicit; when asked what could have been done to make the film more medieval, she replied:

Chloe:	Taken away the computer graphics, and doing it, as he said earlier, with actors and actresses, and using the old animation for dragons, or . . .
Moderator:	So the CGI in and of itself doesn't seem medieval to you then?
Chloe:	Mmm [yes]. I would agree with that.

Moderator: Why? Why do you think that?

Chloe: Because, you know it's computer [generated], not people. And immediately that takes away, I think, [it] puts a big thing in front of me that makes me not able to put it into perspective in real life.

To Chloe, a CGI film cannot be medieval; a historical film's job is to interpret *real* events. The CGI is seen as an interfering layer between her and the history on the screen. Realism, especially historical realism, depends upon a relationship between the audience, the camera and the thing being filmed. Breaking down that barrier – as *Beowulf*'s filmmakers do by creating the entire world with a computer – removes it from reality, and thus history. Erica and Robert also felt the use of technology violated what they expected of a medieval film. Erica reported,

Whenever I think of medieval, I always think of, Robin Hood, [and] crappy, really crappy effects. And, I don't know, that kind of vibe about it makes it seem more medieval. Whereas if it's computer generated and all sparkly and polished, it's too new.

Robert added, 'It's not a very sparkly and polished time, is it?'. Interestingly, co-writer for the film, Roger Avary, echoed their discomfort, saying: 'It was a strange way to be making a film that should be dirty and muddy.'[16] To them, in spite of the grittiness and blood in *Beowulf*, the CGI gives the film a sense of novelty. The filmmaking techniques were new and slick, therefore they could not make a film of something with the patina of age. To all, the technology called attention to the film as a product of the current age rather than the medieval one.

They balked at the CGI in *Beowulf* for aesthetic and historical reasons – implying an unconscious link between them. But despite their criticisms, a film camera is, of course, no more medieval than a motion-capture computer. Yet none of the participants took issue with the Middle Ages being depicted in films at all. Future generations may become accustomed to CGI as a valid way of presenting history, but many in the current generation are not.

The second major criticism levelled against *Beowulf* as a film was that the language used in the film was inappropriate for a medieval film.

Language and accent can play an important role in any film; they can quickly establish cultural aspects of a character and announce the social spaces they inhabit. However in a historical film, these also play a role in establishing the period and can even work to assert – or run counter to – the perception of the film's historical accuracy.

Most participants felt that *Beowulf* did not do this well. All bar one of the participants criticised the accents, particularly the 'cockney' accent used by Ray Winstone (Beowulf), and the 'American' accent of John Malkovich (Unferth). For example Jake felt: 'in *Beowulf* they did have some accents which were American, which obviously don't fit a middle-age film'. However, participants who reacted negatively to the accents in *Beowulf* had difficulty in proposing a better alternative. They were asked, 'what sort of accent would you expect him to have?' Robert replied 'if they're going for historical accuracy, go for a Danish actor, or get Ray Winstone to have a bash [laugh] at a Danish accent'. Justin said the expected accent would be 'Swedish'. Neither of these suggestions would be historically accurate; neither modern Danes nor Swedes speak in the Old English of the *Beowulf* poet or the Old Norse of Early Medieval Danes, though Robert and Justin may not have realised this.

But immediately after requesting a Swedish accent, Justin backpedalled: 'Just like the music in the film, we wouldn't have known as to what the music would have been like or anything like that. But, the accents – I mean, the Cockney accents sounded wrong. John Malkovich's slightly American accent sounded wrong.' Justin seemed aware that his intuition that the accents and music 'sounded wrong' may have had little to do with his knowledge of history. Even assuming participants may have misunderstood that Old English or Old Norse is not the same as modern Danish or Swedish, none suggested that the film should be a subtitled foreign-language film, but rather that it should use the Hollywood convention of accenting English to indicate foreignness.

This is relevant in light of the fact that the film occasionally *is* a foreign-language film. *Beowulf* occasionally switches between modern English and un-subtitled Old English spoken by Grendel and Grendel's mother. In a scene in Heorot, the scops (bards) also perform segments of the original poem in Old English. Stephen noted the use of Old English,

Now, was the monster speaking old Anglo-Saxon? He sounded like, it wasn't English that he was saying, was it? Because I know this is an Anglo-Saxon poem, an epic poem, so I wonder if it's original bits from the poem that the Grendel was saying.

Robert also sensed that the foreign-language aspects of the film were historical. When asked 'what parts of it do you think were aiming at historical accuracy then?' his first reply was 'Well then, the bits that were semi-German.'

Beowulf is the only film in this study in which language is used to establish the film's historicity (a 'history effect', explored more below). To these participants, making a film in a language other than English inherently makes it seem more historical, more 'other'. However, any regional English accent that they could specifically place, especially from places they perceived not to be medieval (in this case the urban Cockney or the colonial American) 'felt' anachronistic. Their lack of negative reaction to received pronunciation (hereafter: RP) accents may be because RP is the default for historical films as much as it is the 'Standard British English'. John H. Fisher calls RP 'the pronunciation that distinguished the British ruling class until the end of the Second World War and is still taught around the world as "Standard British English".'[17] This supports M.J. Toswell's claim that:

the non-English-speaking medieval character is generally the villain, and the character without the Hollywood-approved accent has to demonstrate virtue, rather than be taken at face value.[18]

Though in the case of *Beowulf*, the characters have to demonstrate their medievalness, rather than their virtue, to the viewers against the perceptual headwind that their accent presents.

In spite of these criticisms, *Beowulf* was generally judged to be medieval. Acceptance of what they saw depended upon the expectations latent in their historical consciousness: how it related to their experience with the written *Beowulf*, and how it adhered to their expectations of the Middle Ages. The CGI and accents detracted from their sense of its historicity, but this was set in contrast with a film that almost self-consciously adhered to their expectations of what it means to be from the Early Middle Ages: drunk, dirty, and violent.

Kingdom of Heaven

Kingdom of Heaven is a different kind of historical film than *Beowulf*. It is the only 'true history' film in this study – that is, it is the only one which purports to depict real people participating in real historical events. Obviously films of this type – despite their protestations – do not present history as it was. But, their marketing, genre, and tropes make claims towards historical truth that other films do not. These truth claims are called 'reality effects'.

Reality Effects and History Effects

Roland Barthes first coined the term 'reality effects' in his book *The Rustle of Language* when discussing the literature of Flaubert.[19] Previous theorists, when writing about Flaubert's work, dismissed as 'superfluous' or 'filler' those segments which sought to establish to the reader that the work was realistic.[20] Barthes, instead, saw them as critically important. Barthes also applied the concept of the reality effect to history books and historical films, where detail, and in particular certain iconic details, indicate to the audience the work's historical truthfulness. For example, Barthes analyses the 'Roman fringe' hairstyle seen in Mankiewicz's 1953 version of *Julius Caesar* as a reality effect. The short-fringed haircut in that film is a common signifier of 'Roman-ness' (to the degree that all male Roman characters in that film sport one). And it has gained a life of its own, adorning the brows of the Romans of *The Fall of the Roman Empire* (1964), *Gladiator* (2000), *The Eagle* (2011), and *Monty Python's Life of Brian* (1979) among many others. But its ubiquity has far more to do with the precedent set by films than by history.[21]

Film theorist Vivian Sobchak took this idea a step further in her examination of the phenomenology of historical epic films, saying:

> I want to begin this phenomenological exploration of the Hollywood historical epic not by establishing or debating definitions of the 'epic' and the 'historical', nor by testing the genre's 'truth claims'. Rather, my project here is to describe, thematize, and interpret an *experiential field* in which human beings pretheoretically construct and play out a particular – and

culturally encoded – form of *temporal existence*. Since my aim is to 'isolate the history effects' of the Hollywood historical epic, but to do so 'as they pertain to an *audience*' and 'the manufacturing of public life', my object of study is not so much the films 'in themselves' as it is the rhetorical and semiological *praxis* surrounding the public experience of them – expressed in the prereflexive or 'ordinary' language used in our particular culture to delimit and describe what is commonly perceived as an 'extraordinary' mode of filmic representation.[22]

In other words, Sobchack applies the concept of a 'reality effect' specifically to historical films as an 'history effect', which, for her, is a moment, mode of representation, or generic trope that causes an audience member to experience, even unconsciously, that they are viewing something from another time. They are, in my estimation, a subcategory of reality effect since their purpose is to simultaneously create the sense in the audience that what they are viewing are both real and historical (though neither are, in fact, true).

Some common history effects are easy to identify. Title cards sport heavily serifed (or even mock-blackletter) typefaces to imply authority by association with the printed word. Marketing materials similarly emphasise the truth of what is to be seen, often sporting a variant of 'Based on a True Story': for example Ridley Scott's *Robin Hood* whose trailer and posters (Figure 5.2) purported to tell 'The Untold Story of the Man Behind the Legend' – a truth claim which, when read closely, makes little sense.

And within the films themselves, it could be argued that any element that tacks closely to the popular perception of the past, and which does not serve to advance the plot, could be called a reality effect. *Beowulf*, despite being a fantastical film, had several – the opening title card establishing the date, the opening scene of the drunken feast, and the use of Old English all sought to establish a sort of historical credibility with its audience. *Kingdom of Heaven*, presented as a 'true history' film would have even more potent reality effects. It should be reasonable to expect that the study participants would accept the film as a more valid historical source than the other films. But in spite of this, they did not believe everything presented to them as true, believable, or realistic.

Figure 5.2   Advertising poster for Ridley Scott's *Robin Hood* that makes a bold, if confusing, claim to historical truth (Universal Pictures, 2010).

Kingdom of Heaven, *History, and Reality*

All of the participants accepted *Kingdom of Heaven* as a film that broadly conformed to their image of the Middle Ages, and thus, an accurate portrayal of the age. However, there was some disagreement over whether it was depicting the 'medieval' world or the 'Middle Ages'. Robert labelled this film 'very Middle Ages' – but 'not medieval' – because: 'medieval is less realistic in my head and this was quite real, earthy, rather than more mythological'. Particularly interesting is his use of the term 'earthy' as a quality of 'Middle Ages' cinematic realism, which simultaneously evokes Victorian ideas of the Middle Ages as being closer to nature, and modern perceptions of the period being covered in grime and filth. Despite admitting they know little about the history presented, Stephen believed *Kingdom of Heaven* was realistic because of its genre: '*Beowulf* was going for, I think, just a general actiony-adventurey type audience thing, whereas this one was trying to be a bit more – I'm going to say "real", though I don't know how much of that was truth.' Jake also felt that way: 'you don't know if these characters existed in real life [. . .] because there has got to be bad guys [and] good guys [. . .] At the same time, I thought the story was quite – it's very believable.' Even though Stephen and Jake were self-consciously aware that they may not know how much of what they saw 'was truth', they perceived it as more realistic due to its generic tropes, which caused them intuitively to believe that it was.

Participants did not base their judgement of the accuracy of the film on an overall impression, but on the sum of a series of granular judgements. They analysed specific elements, weighed the realism of aspects individually and then aggregated those results to form a more holistic judgement. Much as in their response to *Beowulf*, they attributed problems with the story to a corrupting influence from 'Hollywood'. Justin felt that the tropes of *Kingdom of Heaven* were more realistic and less manipulative than those in *Beowulf*:

Well, you'd have set pieces that would be destroyed. I mean, you had that in this film, but [in *Beowulf* it was] done in a way that grabbed your attention deliberately and quite obviously, like having someone run across a bridge and have the bridge fall down. [. . .] with this one [*Kingdom of Heaven*] it showed a tactical side on both sides, I thought, in terms of having a battle.

Beowulf's conventions were considered unrealistic because of their transparent attempts to grab 'your attention deliberately and quite obviously'. On the other hand, *Kingdom of Heaven*'s two-sided portrayal of the battle was considered more authentic. Justin was a sophisticated movie-viewer, familiar enough with film conventions that he understood they are intended to manipulate his emotions – a familiarity that caused him to recoil from that manipulation.

But some Hollywood manipulations went unnoticed. Unlike with *Beowulf*, none of the participants commented upon the characters in *Kingdom of Heaven*'s accents (nor the use of Tolkien's invented languages in *Return of the King*). All of the Christian characters in *Kingdom of Heaven* (except the token 'big Germanic barbarian' stereotyped character seen in Balian's father's entourage) speak English with a RP accent. Despite their use of this accent, all Christian characters in that film are French.[23] Participants did not recoil from the RP accents used for French characters, because RP has become the conventional way for Hollywood films to denote European historical people, particularly pre-modern ones. This may also contribute to the overarching expectation that films about the Middle Ages are about *English* people, and that the Middle Ages are definitively about England. Jess even expressed surprise that *Kingdom of Heaven* was about French people at all.

Many focused on the material culture of the film as particularly – and laudably – accurate. The plot did not fare so well. Robert said, 'it evoked the period quite well, like the costumes, and it did give you a feel for it. The story, seemed a little clichéd and stereotyped [...] the story itself didn't make it seem very real.' Other participants, like Robert, clearly distinguished between the visual and narrative aspects of the film.

In terms of the film's visuals, participants' judgement of a film's accuracy seemed based on an impression of detail – which seems to stand as an important reality/history effect. For example, despite claiming that he did not know much about how the period looked, when asked if he felt the film seemed realistic, he replied:

I suppose, in a way, it did. I mean, not knowing anything beforehand, if somebody came up to me and said 'that's what it looked like', then I would believe them. But, obviously I'm judging this from a movie. So, I would judge it as being realistic. But, as to whether it was real: it wouldn't shock me if it wasn't.

Interestingly, he differentiated between the film being 'real' – meaning actually historically accurate – and 'realistic' – meaning that it *seemed* real. This impression of detail was an important influence upon others' perceptions as well. For example Robert said:

> personally, I felt like they spent a lot of time working on the details of it, so I couldn't fault it on that. In my personal thought [...] it seemed like quite an important thing for the director to really get all the details right.

The participants had a sense that the material culture of *Kingdom of Heaven*'s historical period was well represented by the filmmakers, who had thus made the film into a trustworthy visual-historical source. It is difficult to know what specifically caused this impression, but it is an understandable logical leap. If the world of the film seems as detailed as the one which surrounds us on a daily basis – with a similar variety in costume, or a scene filled with well-detailed objects of everyday life – it will intuitively feel more realistic. This feeling will persist even if it remains unknown whether it is depicting something 'real'. In many cases, the accuracy of the details are less important than the impression given by them: that they exist within a fully realised world. This gives credence to Barthes' theory of reality effects – the 'unnecessary' details are, in fact, necessary to convey a sense of reality as much in Scott's film as they were in the novels of Flaubert.

Many focused specifically on the violence in the film, feeling that it matched their expectations and made the film seem more realistic. At first, the film conflicted with Mark's understanding of the Middle Ages as a pre-technological age: 'I didn't know they had siege towers that early, I would have thought [...] that would be a later technological development.' The way Mark phrases this is important; by starting with 'I didn't know', and by using the subjunctive 'I would have thought' (rather than the more assertive 'I don't think' and 'I think that'), it is clear that he has judged the film to be a reliable source of knowledge – perhaps even more so than his historical consciousness. In short, this was a learning moment. Dan, Mark, and Jake also felt the violence in the film was believable:

> Dan: I felt the general storyline was very believable. It's
>   something that always irks me in films is when swords,

when they cut people to death with swords – which just
doesn't happen. It sort of glamorises battle a bit, where you
can die quickly from just cutting off the head.
Whereas, actually, the swords weren't actually sharp
enough, and they would have to beat each other to death
with them.

Jake: Same with arrows as well. It's like, in that first sort of
battle scene when they're in France, it's not like [a] one-
shot-kill sort of arrows, sort of situation =

Mark: = well, one-shot-not-kill especially =

Jake: = you've got a sharp pointy thing in you, somebody will
still fight on. I thought that was quite good. More
believable.

This group applied a combination of knowledge and intuition to these
film tropes – a previous understanding that medieval swords were less
sharp than typically depicted in films,[24] and that a person would not
necessarily die instantly from an arrow wound. The violation of typical
Hollywood tropes in *Kingdom of Heaven* is celebrated. Film tropes can
thus be self-defeating; sophisticated film viewers see them for what they
are and, instead, celebrate deviations from them if they seem more
plausible.

It was not only the weapons themselves which contributed to the
film's realism, but also the way in which the battles were shot. Stephen
and Justin felt the cinematographic style of the battle scenes made the
film more realistic.

Stephen: I do think you get a sense of the melee though, which
was the =

Justin: = the chaos of melee =

Stephen: = you're not seeing it all, you just see chaos around
you. You see some people [and] you don't know who's
hand has just been hacked off, whether it's a Muslim or
a Christian. And [the] fray of the battle, you can't really
see what's going on. [. . .] I suppose that's where the
realism came from. The fact that it's right down on the
actual ground level of the troops, close-up
in the battle.

Justin: But you're not hiding the fact that this was quite a
            horrible thing for individuals to have to go through.

Several of the battle scenes in *Kingdom of Heaven* (most particularly the
large melees after the cavalry charge at Castle Kerak and the battle in the
breach at the conclusion of the siege of Jerusalem) employ a recently-
adopted technique of shooting battle scenes. This technique employs
extreme close-ups, hand-held camera work, first-person perspective
shots, and an alternation between quick cuts, fast-forward, and slow
motion in order to portray the disorientation and chaos of the melee.
This technique for filming fight scenes has become common in recent
years, employed by a variety of film and TV across genres, including
Saving Private Ryan (1998), *The Bourne Identity* (2002), the Christopher
Nolan *Batman* series, the rebooted James Bond franchise, and *Game of
Thrones*.[25] The technique differs markedly from the older cinematographic mode of depicting battle (as seen, for example, in *Beowulf*,
The Return of the King and the other battles in *Kingdom of Heaven*), where
the audience is shown the faces and bodies of the combatants, typically
from medium-shot. In this new approach, the audience is disoriented, and
the fighting prowess of the hero is implied rather than made explicit.
Body parts and weapons become disassociated from their owners, and
friend is difficult to discern from foe. The results of combat – who is dead
and who is alive – only become clear when the fog of the melee lifts.
The pleasure of viewing the hero's fighting prowess is de-emphasised.
In *Kingdom of Heaven* – as in many of the other films that have adopted this
technique – this method of shooting battle is meant to convey the idea
that war is chaotic, random, and awful. This contributes to the overall
message of the film: war itself is the antagonist.

The participants responded positively to what they felt were breaks
with Hollywood generic tropes (in which death by sword or arrow is
often quick and bloodless in an attempt to minimise the violence and
thus avoid censorship) in favour of a more violent, chaotic, less
'Hollywood', and, to them, more realistic vision of medieval war.
Limited deviations such as these from Hollywood generic tropes can be a
history effect. All of these things contributed to a sense among the
participants that *Kingdom of Heaven*, especially in its depiction of
medieval warfare, was a very trustworthy source for historical knowledge
(especially about the material culture of the Crusades) and an appropriate

source from which to learn. Of course, as with the shooting style in *Kingdom of Heaven*, these deviations can quickly lose their potency when they are adopted by the mainstream and become a new 'normal'.

Based on a True Story?

The plot was not generally regarded as highly as the material culture. Many characters in *Kingdom of Heaven* are based upon real people. Balian of Ibelin, Guy de Lusignan, Reynald de Chatillon, Count Raymond III of Tripoli, Count Raymond of Tiberias, Princess (and later Queen) Sibylla of Jerusalem, King Baldwin IV of Jerusalem, Saladin, Imad-Ad-Din, and Richard I of England were all real. However, participants in this research were likely not aware of this (barring Richard I and Saladin). There is often no way for the casual viewer of an historical film to know, while watching the film, which of the characters are real, and which are inventions or amalgamations. It also remains important to remember that all film characters – no matter their historical provenance – are the inventions of filmmakers. As Roger Ebert noted in his review of *The Hurricane*:

> Several people have told me dubiously that they heard the movie was 'fictionalized'. Well, of course it was. Those who seek the truth about a man from the film of his life might as well seek it from his loving grandmother. Most biopics, like most grandmothers, see the good in a man and demonize his enemies. They pass silently over his imprudent romances. In dramatizing his victories, they simplify them. And they provide the best roles to the most interesting characters. If they didn't, we wouldn't pay to see them.[26]

Despite this, depicting a person who actually existed in an historical film says to the viewer that this story could, or even should, be believed to have *literally* happened. Purporting to be based on a true story pushes the expectation of historical authenticity and realism for *Kingdom of Heaven* far higher than it was for *Beowulf*. While *Beowulf* had only to seem realistic (in an archetypal or iconic way), *Kingdom of Heaven* had to seem *real*.

Believing that the characters on screen were not just realistic, but *real*, was central to some participants' beliefs that the story was true, and their subsequent enjoyment of the film. For example, Katy felt that she was better able to believe the story and empathise with the characters in this film because she felt *Kingdom of Heaven*, unlike *Beowulf*, portrayed real people. 'I think the majority of it was realistic. And I thought [it was] a bit easier, because there was no mystical, mythical characters in it; it was all very human. [...] You could kind of, not sympathise, but see the reality of it.' That said, many questioned whether the protagonist – Balian of Ibelin – and his story were real. As mentioned above, Balian was a real person (and Ibelin a real place). However, the historical Balian of Ibelin was, perhaps unsurprisingly, very different from his portrayal in the film. In order to elicit empathy from the audience and add drama to his journey, Balian is presented in *Kingdom of Heaven* as a blacksmith who attains power and prestige after taking the crusade. This fits a typical 'rags to riches' narrative, and, like many films featuring this narrative type (see, for example, *A Knight's Tale*), Balian's lower-class morality is juxtaposed against the venality of his aristocratic rivals. The supposed superior morality of the working class is a common meta-narrative in popular culture and political discourse in both the UK and the USA. The real Balian was born a nobleman in the Holy Land and inherited the lordship of Ibelin from his brother.

There are also a number of other deviations from the historical record with regards to Balian's character in the film. The filmmakers cast the youthful Orlando Bloom in the role, and engineered a romantic tryst between him and Princess Sybilla of Jerusalem. However, during this period, the real Balian was in his fifties and married with four children. Unlike the film, Balian's family were not unwavering supporters of the King of Jerusalem. During the siege of Jerusalem, Balian is reported to have worked closely with the patriarch of Jerusalem, contrary to the adversarial relationship depicted in the film. The historical Balian fought in the disastrous Battle of Hattin, but escaped with his life and fled back to Jerusalem. The cinematic Balian abstains from the battle as a conscientious objector.

With that having been said, the real Balian of Ibelin did perform some of the heroic deeds depicted in *Kingdom of Heaven*: he led the garrison of Jerusalem to a stalemate with Saladin's vastly superior force, knighted sixty of the burgesses of the city in one day, and successfully negotiated the surrender of Jerusalem (in which most of the citizens were allowed to buy their freedom in order to avoid being taken as slaves by the Saracens).[27] But beyond this, it is difficult for the historian to discern an unvarnished view of the character traits of Balian of Ibelin, because there exist several accounts of his life from different chronicles. Those chronicles differ vastly due to the political allegiances of their authors – some of whom were aligned with Balian and others with King Guy (Abroise's *Estoire de la Guerre Sante*, for example, calls Balian 'more false than a goblin').[28] As a result, the medieval accounts (not unlike historical films) paint an unrealistically heroic or villainous portrait of the man.[29]

But were these differences between the historical record and the film perceived? The participants often questioned whether Balian was a real person, for two reasons. First, there was a perception that the hero's journey – both his moral, social and geographical journey – was unrealistic. His geographical journey takes him from France to the Holy Land and back; his social journey is from an unknown blacksmith to the Baron of Ibelin, commander of the garrison of the city of Jerusalem and lover of the Queen of the Kingdom of Jerusalem;[30] his psychological journey is from the perspective of a jaded Christian seeking absolution to a victorious hero who has embraced secular humanism. The Crusades are only the backdrop and facilitator of these personal quests. Many participants felt these character arcs were unrealistic. Mark said, 'I'm a little sceptical about the, I'm not quite sure what the timescale of the movie was but, blacksmith to, at one point, ruler over Jerusalem. I'm a little sceptical.' Erica echoed this. 'Orlando Bloom, he was, not a wuss, but was [a] happy little blacksmith doing his own thing, and then all of a sudden he was this massive, big knight, and he knew everything – this seemed a bit unbelievable.' Justin, Sean and Stephen cited this as a reason not to believe Balian was real:

Justin: I think Orlando Bloom's character might not have been real.

Sean: [Yeah I thought he was just a smith, and then [he] became this amazing warrior.

Justin: Yeah he was just used as a}

Stephen: It was a stylised, I suppose, like Shakespeare did with Henry the Fifth – that kind of big, heroic leader that's going to lead Jerusalem to ... surrender. [laugh] But no.

Justin: It was almost, *almost* a rags-to-riches thing.

This specific aspect of the hero's character arc may have provoked such a negative reaction because of the participants' understanding that the Middle Ages were a time of little social mobility, and with vast differences between the rich and poor. To them, heroism has a class component; any peasant rising to the level of the heroic nobility requires explanation. The filmmakers explain this rise in ranks as a feature of the Holy Land, which Finke and Shichtman compellingly link to a narrative of American exceptionalism.[31] In the film, Godfrey presents it as a unique land of opportunity with words clearly chosen to resonate with an American audience's imagined history of their own country:

> Do you know . . . what lies in the Holy Land? A new world. A man who in France had not a house is, in the Holy Land, the master of a city. He who was the master of a city, begs in the gutter. There, at the end of the world you are not what you are born, but what you have it in yourself to be.

Part of the opening title card presents Jerusalem similarly: 'Europe suffers in the grip of repression and poverty. / Peasant and lord alike flee to the Holy Land in search of fortune or salvation'. However, these statements – even though deployed with a reality-effect title card – did not seem sufficient to overcome the participants' perception that this was improbable. This narrative might have been effective with an American audience, but it was not so with this English one.

Rags-to-riches narratives are common in films and form a common metanarrative for American self-definition under the iconic phrase 'the American dream'. The film also contains the cultural meme of the working class, virtuous outsider's rise to political power and prestige (most famously articulated in *Mr Smith Goes to Washington* (1939) – which is surprisingly similar to *Kingdom of Heaven* if one imagines Jimmy Stewart in a mail coif and the filibuster enacted through siege warfare).[32] The inclusion of these seemingly modern ideas in a film depicting the Middle Ages provoked the negative reactions witnessed – and the film's story was roundly rejected by the participants as unrealistic.

The Star System and Medieval Masculinities

Orlando Bloom's very presence in the film also made some participants less inclined to believe that his character was real. Interestingly, this was largely because Bloom himself did not fit their expectations of a medieval leader. In fact, they seemed more aware of the actor than the character he was playing. During discussions, participants used the name of his character (Balian) very infrequently, instead referring to him as 'Orlando Bloom's character'. Occasionally they substituted the actor for the character entirely, such as Erica's: '[. . .] right at the beginning where Orlando Bloom's wife got her head chopped off'. By contrast, the characters of *Beowulf* and *The Return of the King* were described by the character's name rather than the actor – even Orlando Bloom's Legolas in *The Return of the King*. This indicates that something in *Kingdom of Heaven* prevented them from seeing the character, rather than the actor. This may have been the star system that made Orlando Bloom a household name at the time, the portrayal of the character, or the fact that 'Balian' is an uncommon name (though no less than 'Frodo', 'Aragorn', or 'Beowulf').

Participants disliked the fact that they recognised the actor playing the leading role. For example, Katy felt the casting of Orlando Bloom was a marketing ploy, and that he was only present as a sexual object: 'Orlando Bloom, a character like that, using an actor like that, [it] is probably kind of a ploy to get people to watch it [. . .] it forced them to watch it because, particularly, females liked it.' Stephen concurred. 'I think that's why we didn't necessarily believe it or respond well, because we're aware that he's in there as the star [. . .] and he's there to draw people in to watch the film.' Participants seemed hyper-aware that they were watching a star in the lead role, and bristled at what they perceived to be another attempted manipulation by Hollywood.

Dislike of Orlando Bloom, however, was not only because he was a well-known star. Stephen cited Bloom's androgynous physical features as a reason for disliking him in the role: 'Orlando Bloom is known as a celebrity and a bit of a dish [. . .] [he is] a little bit too glossy [. . .] you see Orlando Bloom and you make a snap decision that he's a pretty boy.' The last two words, 'pretty' and 'boy' are of equal importance; his perceived appeal to a heterosexual female or homosexual male audience, and also his youthfulness, both detract from his perceived appropriateness as the lead in a medieval epic.[33] When asked which actor might be more appropriate, Justin said 'Liam Neeson [who plays Balian's father] was a bit more of the look I thought – of that kind of character.' When compared with Neeson, some saw Bloom as too young or immature.

Stephen said 'I think a big part of it is age', and that an appropriate hero should have 'silver hair'.

This treatment of Orlando Bloom in this film is quite similar in to the reaction of heterosexual men to 1920s film star Rudolph Valentino, famous for his portrayal of a number of highly sexualised 'Latin lovers'. As Harry Benshoff and Sean Griffin recount,

> While multitudes of female fans actively worshipped him, some male moviegoers grew antagonistic towards him, partly because he was competition for their women's attention, but also because Valentino's objectified star image was uncomfortably close to the objectified star images of female bodies. He was deemed too pretty. Men weren't supposed to pose like that! Male newspaper columnists began to smear Valentino's masculinity by suggesting he was effeminate.[34]

There may also be a biological component to the perception that Orlando Bloom's youth and androgynous features make him less appropriate to play a medieval hero. Recent research at the Schools of Psychology at Aberdeen and Stirling Universities has found a significant correlation between masculinity (and masculine facial features) and desirability in societies with low overall health. By contrast, in healthier societies, feminine features were more desirable in men's faces. They report,

> Across 30 countries, masculinity preference increased as health decreased. This relationship was independent of cross-cultural differences in wealth or women's mating strategies. These findings show non-arbitrary cross-cultural differences in facial attractiveness judgements.[35]

This phenomenon may play a part in the formulation of the expectation that appropriately attractive medieval men have very masculine features, since the Middle Ages are commonly understood to be a time featuring poor health and intense poverty. This may be emphasised in films like *Kingdom of Heaven*, which are part of the darker vision of the Middle Ages. Perhaps jolly, light adventure films can star Douglas Fairbanks or Errol Flynn, but our current crop of muddy and bloody medieval films require someone more butch. Our vision of the ideal man of the Middle

Ages is surely different from his counterpart in the eighteenth century (think *Dangerous Liaisons* or *Amistad*), and even further removed from the Victorian (think *Sherlock Holmes* or *The Prestige* – Dr Jekyll's alter ego Mr Hyde seems practically medieval).

Alternately, this could be purely a product of the ways in which the Middle Ages have been represented in previous films. As Finke and Shichtman argue (in a discussion of the work of Susan Jeffords), films in the 1980s featured 'hard-bodied', hypermasculine male heroes who 'were not restricted by diplomacy, military protocol, or police procedure', and who were 'competitive, athletic, decisive, unemotional, strong, aggressive, powerful, and, above all, never feminine'.[36] And while the action heroes of the twenty-first century have moved on from 1980s-style machismo, the medieval hero has been slower to reform. Finke and Shichtman cite *Braveheart*'s William Wallace as its continuation into the 1990s, and Susan Aronstein analyses the rise and fall of the hard-body Arthurian knight in her *Hollywood Knights: Arthurian Cinema and the Politics of Nostalgia*.[37] The same can be said of *Beowulf* where, as discussed above, a hard body was constructed for Ray Winstone from first computerised principles.

Or perhaps leadership in war is the crucial difference. Bloom was particularly criticised by the participants because he did not fit the image of what the protagonist of a medieval *war* film should be. Many saw leadership in war as the highest quality of the medieval hero. For example, Carin said,

> I don't believe when all the men are following him. I just, I wouldn't follow him [. . .] I don't think he's a very good actor, and he's just . . . I don't think he's your typical kind of . . . I don't know, just seemed a bit . . . wimpy.

She did not specify what was 'wimpy' about Bloom, though others did. With apologies to Mr Bloom, some said he was inadequate because his voice or demeanour lacked 'gravitas' or 'power'. Stephen said the main problem was:

> Because of the context of having a great leader, leading people into battle is quite a medieval thing. Well, historical, maybe, not exclusive[ly] medieval. But it's not, you don't need gravitas in *Pretty Woman* [. . .] I just wasn't really buying Orlando Bloom

when he was doing the speeches and things [. . .] [he] doesn't have
the voice for it, he doesn't have the gravitas for it.[38]

Justin pointed this out as well, 'I think the reason he couldn't pull it off
is that he didn't have the look, really. He seemed a bit too . . . [he] didn't
seem to have the power behind him to suggest that he could lead people'.
It is unknown whether the participants were being coy or exploring
nuances – whether it was his voice, his manner, or his muscles that were
lacking. Whatever it was, the filmmakers themselves also seem to have
shared these concerns; the companion book to the film states:

> Bloom's preparation required a great deal of physical training [. . .]
> Vocal training was also part of the package: Scott wanted him to
> use a deeper, more mature voice for Balian.[39]

Unfortunately, Bloom's training seems to have been insufficient to
satisfy the participants.

An image of the ideal medieval man is being revealed from the
participants' historical consciousness: he needs a deep voice as a marker
of age and maturity, and is associated with aggressive, heterosexual,
hard-bodied masculinity. His value is as a warrior, particularly as a war-
leader. Queerness or androgyny have no place in this image of the
medieval man. This is not an age when tenors were heroes.

To these participants, there was a certain 'type' which is visual
shorthand for a war-leader, either in a broad historical sense, or a
specifically medieval sense. Most felt that Orlando Bloom did not fit this
image. Bloom was too well known, too 'dishy'. He did not have the
'gravitas' that age or maturity would lend, or the masculinity that would
make him a more appropriate medieval war hero. In sum, medievalism's
heroes are not 'pretty boys'.

Political Allegory and Believability

Another unique feature of *Kingdom of Heaven* is the allegory central to the
film. The narrative of the film ties the Crusades to the current conflicts in
the Middle East. It can therefore be interpreted as a parable in which the
Crusades, and by extension all religiously motivated war, are revealed to
be morally bankrupt. The real heroes are those secularists, like Balian,
who strive to make and keep peace. Or as Finke and Shichtman put it,

[Ridley] Scott seems to understand that he needs to detach at least his heroes both from the religious zealotry and materialistic motives that drive his crusaders. His heroes, Balian and his father Geoffrey, must be seen as secular crusaders struggling for freedom and religious tolerance against the forces of fundamentalism on both sides.[40]

Many participants saw this message in the film – though they did not necessarily see the film as trying to teach a lesson. And even those who did not explicitly identify the film as an allegory for modern conflicts viewed the film through the prism of their experiences with war.

When asked if he had learned anything from the film, Stephen pointed to the pacifist parable in the film: 'I think the goodie/baddie divide in the film came from those who wanted peace and coexistence, [like the] Leper King [and] Orlando Bloom, and those who wanted war such as Guy and Saladin.'[41] Jess responded positively to this division, indicating this made the film more realistic, 'I thought it was good the way there were lots of goodies and baddies on both sides, it wasn't [a] one-sided film [. . .] I thought it made it realer.' Sean agreed, 'I think it did quite a good job of not splitting up Christians versus Saracens, and it wasn't like Christians are goodies Saracens are baddies, as is often done. I thought it was quite good.' Jake also enjoyed the moral divide not being defined by religion: 'I liked the way he [Saladin] wasn't like, [the filmmakers] didn't do the obvious thing of making him the bad guy and the army of Jerusalem and everybody are the good team [. . .] [I] kinda questioned people's morals.' Jake and Sean both felt that the default position would be one in which the Christians are the protagonists and the Muslims the antagonists. However, at least among Crusade films, this is hardly the case – Saladin has long been a heroic figure in Western conceptions of the Crusades (discussed more below). Though in DeMille's 1935 film *The Crusades*, the rank-and-file Saracens are certainly portrayed as villains, it is doubtful that the participants saw that particular film. The only other 'crusade' film mentioned by participants was *Robin Hood: Prince of Thieves* – which notably includes a positive (if problematic) Muslim character in Morgan Freeman's Azeem.[42] Instead, their opinion is likely a product of what Jack Shaheen identified as a 'pervasive stereotype' – particularly since the 1970s – where Arabs have been painted as villains in films of all genres and topics (whether set in the Middle East or not).[43] This cinematic stereotyping, in place since before these participants were born, has led them to see 'Middle Eastern' as a marker of villainy, no matter the place or time period.

When asked whether the division of good and bad in the film along the lines of pacifism and warmongering – rather than along European/ Middle Eastern – was believable, Justin felt:

> I think it probably is. I think that makes it more believable, [...] because you know that in a situation like that, not everyone is going to have that sort of full belief [where] you're going to go along with the zeitgeist. [...] I think that if you're putting across the idea that everyone was happy with this and everyone wants to go fight the opposition, the opposition wants to go fight you, and everybody wants to, then it's just becoming kind of a sullied them-versus-them, good-versus-evil type thing, rather than if you show them within a society that they've got people wanting different aspirations. Then, you're putting across a bit more of a human thing.

Justin here took a postmodern approach; to him a perceived a traditional 'good-versus-evil' approach to the Crusades would be 'sullied' and less 'human'. He preferred a vision of the Crusades in which the movement is shown to be made up of individuals with differing motivations and levels of commitment to the cause. This is likely a reflection of the deeply conflicted, complex attitudes towards war held by a significant portion of the British public since Britain's involvement in the war in Iraq. To him, it would simply be unrealistic to depict a war with widespread popular support, since he had not experienced one.

Stephen was one of the few to disagree with the idea that this was realistic. He felt that the pacifist message of the film did not fit his knowledge of the Crusades. However, he felt the film was presented realistically enough for this narrative to be accommodated as a new nuance in his understanding:

> It did seem more, in my opinion, of the Crusades as being about people really fighting for their religion. But, it did show that there is an element of people who just want power and [...] just want war essentially.

That said, he balked at the degree to which the Crusades were depicted to have been motivated by secular concerns:

> I expected that in any war it's going to be people manipulating people's feelings and manipulating people's religions for the sake of power. But, to the extent that it was shown in the film, it didn't seem as though anyone was really fighting for their religion. It was either the people who had the lust for power, or in the case of the people who wanted peace, they were fighting for humanity, they were being humanists. They wanted both sides to be able to coexist; there didn't seem to be a strong ideological thrust from either side that we've got to keep this city for our religion.

Perhaps without knowing it, Stephen is echoing the scholarly debates which have raged over the question of the motivation of the Crusaders – whether they went on Crusade to seek financial gain, as an expression of their religious beliefs, or for other reasons. Stephen is reflecting the ideas of Jonathan Riley-Smith, who in the 1970s shifted Crusade historiography away from the view that the Crusades were a form of early colonialism wherein second sons went abroad to seek their fortune.[44] Instead, Riley-Smith argued that many of the crusaders were motivated by deep religious sentiment, even going so far as to famously call Crusading 'an act of love'.[45]

But Stephen's knowledge that the Crusades were fought by individuals motivated by religion was malleable. This idea was ultimately trumped by what he regarded as a more realistic assessment presented by *Kingdom of Heaven*. When asked if the depiction as he described it above was realistic, he said, 'I imagine so [...] religion is used as a camouflage for people's desire to make war.' Stephen's interpretive process is on display; he recoiled from the idea that no one during the Crusades was motivated by piety, but also agreed with the overall principle that religion is sometimes used to justify war. His ultimate position was one synthesising the old knowledge and new ideas. The film's resonances with contemporary conflicts may have been the source of participants' resistance to a clear 'good-versus-evil' narrative; these connections to contemporary conflict necessitate a different kind of identification scheme, lest the film seem 'sullied' or its characters 'not human'. According to Evelyn Alsultany, this has been, arguably paradoxically, a trend in post-9/11 media. Though after 9/11, several American TV shows presented the tried-and-tested stereotype of the 'bad Arab' explored by Shaheen above, a new countertrend also emerged. As she writes:

> The shift around 9/11 is not one in which Arabs are represented solely as terrorists to one in which Arabs are represented sympathetically. It is from a few exceptional, sympathetic representations of Arabs and Muslim identities to a new representational strategy whereby sympathetic representations are standardized as a stock feature of media narratives. [. . .] After 9/11 these strategies, especially that of including a 'good' Arab American to counteract the 'bad' or terrorist Arab, came to define the new standard when representing Arabs.[46]

Kingdom of Heaven deploys this post-9/11 strategy in its depiction of both 'good' and 'bad' Muslim characters (as well as good and bad Christian ones). The participants noticed, and responded positively, to its use.

Direct Comparisons to Current Conflicts

As explored previously, the interview questions in this study were open-ended, in order to allow the participants to decide – and vocalise – for themselves what was important about each film. As such, they were not asked about any relationship the film had to contemporary politics or conflicts, since to have done so would imply that such an interpretation was either correct, or that such a relationship existed. Only one of the groups (the June group) spontaneously raised this issue after viewing *Kingdom of Heaven.* This group was already attuned to comparisons between the past and present, since their pre-film discussion also focused on the relationships between the Crusades and current conflicts in the Middle East. This group did not view the film's political message as a hindrance to the film as a representation of the past; often the message of the film seemed to coincide with their political ideology and expectations. The members of the group projected their understanding of the contemporary world onto the Crusades, and used the film as a support for the links they were already inclined to draw.

For example, Stephen viewed current conflicts in terms of realpolitik: 'at the end of the day, [it] is probably still motivated by people, on both sides, who are hungry for power'. Katy agreed, saying 'I agree that it's about power. A lot of it is about power [. . .] they think they're trying to show power by imposing their religious views on the world.' When asked to clarify whether she was speaking about the film, the Crusades or the conflicts today, Katy said 'Both. [The] Crusades battles, and [the] movie, and what's going on now as well. I think [they] all [are] about imposing a set of beliefs that you believe to be true and unquestionable on the rest of the world to save the world.' Their fundamental interpretation of conflict as a result of the desire for power is a link that can be drawn between past and present, and between history and *Kingdom of Heaven*. Justin did not believe that all of the aspects of the Crusades depicted in the film corresponded with his understanding of present-day conflicts. He defined the difference based upon which side was the aggressor:

But it's very much from a – it's kind of an exchange now though isn't it? [. . .] In the past it was the Christians putting their beliefs across on [. . .] the Muslims, but now you've got [a] very few, but they do exist, fundamentalists that are generally going up against Christianity.

Justin saw the Crusades as an aggressive act by Christians whereas the current conflicts are due to the aggression of Muslim fundamentalists. Stephen also felt that the Crusades, as presented in the film, were solely about control of Jerusalem, whereas current conflicts in the Middle East have a different focus, 'it's not about control of a particular city, it's about what they think that the world should be'.

It is difficult to discuss with confidence the reasons why the participants in the other groups did not discuss the political implications of the film; a lack of evidence can say only so much. That said, very few participants viewed the film allegorically at all. This is in spite of the fact that the film presents itself as a political allegory quite explicitly. Even after having just seen the final title card (Figure 5.3): 'Nearly a thousand years later, peace in the Kingdom of Heaven remains elusive', most participants seemed uninterested in relating the film to modern politics. Perhaps this was in an effort to keep the

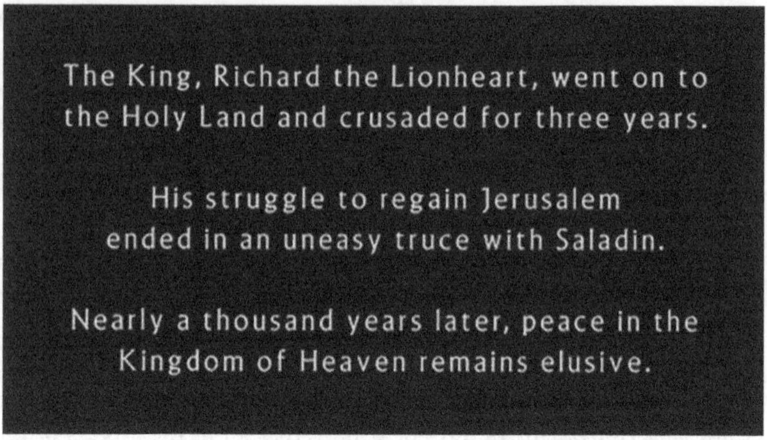

> The King, Richard the Lionheart, went on to
> the Holy Land and crusaded for three years.
>
> His struggle to regain Jerusalem
> ended in an uneasy truce with Saladin.
>
> Nearly a thousand years later, peace in the
> Kingdom of Heaven remains elusive.

Figure 5.3   Driving the point home; the final title card of *Kingdom of Heaven*. Source: Ridley Scott, *Kingdom of Heaven – Definitive Edition* DVD (20th Century Fox, 2005).

conversation polite – the one group who did discuss the political implications was the group of friends. That said, the other groups had few qualms assertively opining on many other controversial topics (i.e. religion and sexuality). Therefore, it is unclear why they might not have discussed the politics *Kingdom of Heaven* wears on its sleeve.

Anti-Muslim Prejudice

While most did not overtly compare the film to modern conflicts, many of their comments were revelatory about their ideas about Middle Eastern people and cultures, both medieval and contemporary. As already mentioned, many regarded the film as a positive challenge to a tradition which dictates that Christians should be depicted heroically and Muslims as the enemy. For example, Mark forcefully praised the depiction of Saladin, the Muslim ruler: 'I'm glad they didn't display the Salah-ad-Din[47] as a bloodthirsty murderer, because that would have just been completely untrue.' Saladin is an interesting figure in the discussion of the stereotypical depiction of middle easterners in Western culture. Contrary to Mark's expectation, Saladin has more usually been depicted as a hero in Western popular culture, particularly since Sir Walter Scott's 1825 novel *The Talisman*, which solidified his position as 'the only noble enemy' of the crusaders.[48] It was from this orientalist, Westernised image of Saladin as a noble opponent that Saladin has been taken by some in the Middle East to be their *non plus ultra* anti-Western-imperialist hero.[49] Mark was likely not aware of this, as he seemed to take pride in his belief that he held special knowledge that Saladin was not 'a bloodthirsty murderer'.

Erica saw the controversial scene where Balian assists his serfs in the building of a well as a timeless one:

> I thought the bit where Orlando Bloom went to visit his new plot of land and they built the well, that could have been done at any time. I didn't really see the middle-agey, medievalness in that couple of scenes. That could have been shot in any time, any place [...] That just seemed like it could have [been] done yesterday because the clothes and everything, I didn't really think as being medieval.

In this scene, Balian surveys his newly inherited lands, and, finding them well-populated but parched, orders his men to build a well. Balian himself leads the team of well diggers, even jumping into the muddy hole. Water is struck and, in the following scenes, his lands are transformed into an oasis paradise. This scene is controversial because it calls back to an imperialist, Orientalist, and colonialist narrative wherein Europeans were needed to 'make the desert bloom' – bringing civilisation to the Arab world.[50] In short, the people living on Balian's lands did not need a French blacksmith to teach them how to dig a well. More than anything, the scene is about leadership – Balian's father did not care about his lands, so it wilted. Balian did, and thus it bloomed. This sets up a problematic paradigm where without dictates from a strong (European) leader, the people are so listless that they will not even work together to provide for their most basic needs. Erica's perception of the universality of the scene is based on an incorrect belief that Arabic material culture, landscape, and clothing has not changed significantly since the Crusades. Her assertion that 'it could have [been] done yesterday' also implies that she sees the medieval Middle East – and probably its contemporary analogue – as an impoverished failed state in need of water aid. This aspect of her Middle Ages seems drawn from commercials for international aid charities.

Participants also thought that the Crusades were fought similarly to modern conflicts. For example, Justin said that *Kingdom of Heaven* differed from his knowledge of the Crusades:

> I didn't expect the opposition side [the Saracens] to have such a strong force for them. I didn't expect them to be like that; I thought it would be much more, as I said, more of a guerrilla-type warfare, just a population resistance rather than an army resistance. [...] I suppose this is, maybe, looking at it in the same way as I'm seeing the war in Iraq at the moment. [...] I suppose it's because America has just gone in there and just invaded them. But that's the way I saw that the Crusades would be; I didn't expect them to be two big armies against each other.

Justin instinctually related the war in Iraq and the Crusades (though he seemed uncomfortable with this instinct); he saw the American military as similar to crusaders – at least in terms of their military superiority. As a result, he expected the Saracens to be analogous to the Iraqi insurgency. Katy also expected asymmetry between the forces of the crusaders and the Muslims, 'whenever crusade comes up, I just always think of that, and weak and strong kind of armies'. Justin and Stephen went even further, in a discussion that tied together their ideas of Britain, the Middle East, the past of the crusades and contemporary conflicts. Justin quickly became uncomfortable as he spoke:[51]

Justin:	In a way, I didn't expect that. Which is why I wasn't really sure about there being two big armies, because I assumed that, I wasn't, I mean, not knowing anything about Jerusalem back then I didn't realise that, as a culture, you know, because Britain's always been very much, especially in the past has always been very much, you know, as an, advanced. I mean, I don't want to say advanced, do you know what I mean? It's been on the, on [the developed side of things
Stephen:	E-e-even though,] even though I know in my head that around that period the Islamic world was the centre of learning, pretty much, but you know a lot of

mathematics and stuff comes from that period, for some reason maybe it's, you know, some, some gut feeling some gut, thing that's been instilled in me from somewhere, from some book from some film from some TV programme or whatever, I, I agree with you that you don't think of them as civilised.

Justin: I don't, I don't think it's un-, I don't think that they're uncivilised they're just, I don't think of them as being

Stephen: = sop – sophisticated [is the word

Justin: Yeah,] sorry [sophisticated.

Hearing these views was chilling, but revelatory. There is much to unpack here.

It might be simple to dismiss their views, but it is important not to. These people were not stupid – they were intelligent upper-level students at a good university. Moreover, that university was in Yorkshire, a region of England with a significant Pakistani Muslim community – meaning that they most likely encountered Muslims in their daily lives. Their politics were not right-wing, nor did they outwardly espouse racist, xenophobic, or Islamophobic views aside from here. In fact, at other points in the conversation they took pride in their liberal worldviews and revelled in deriding right-wing figures and media sources. And yet, they clearly have some deep-seated prejudices about Muslims about which they are only partially aware, and which make them very uncomfortable.

This represents a remarkably introspective struggle they had between two pieces of knowledge, one of which they felt to be morally abhorrent. Their increasingly halting speech pattern shows that they had difficulty admitting they felt it, and even when they did, they sought some external source for it onto which to shift blame. Still, they had difficulty ignoring their prejudices. Though they remembered learning about the culturally and technologically advanced Islamic world, they simultaneously held the contradictory perception that the medieval Islamic world – or perhaps the Islamic world by definition – was not, and seemingly could not be, 'sophisticated'. This is a clear conflict between learned historical knowledge and knowledge inductively projected from the present onto the past. This clearly shows the benefits, and limitations, of history education. On the one hand, their education – whether from classroom or informal sources – provided a counterpoint to this prejudice. However, their historical knowledge was clearly less evident in their minds, as a confounding fact in the face of a much deeper belief.

Their perception that the contemporary Middle East is 'uncivilised' may have a basis in the way that the region has been portrayed in the media, especially (but certainly not exclusively) since 9/11.[52] Between the reports of civil war, suicide bombings, honour killings, the oppression of women, abrogation of civil rights, and the bloody repression of democracy by autocratic regimes, it has become too easy, without any correctives, for them to see Middle-Eastern cultures as fundamentally 'other'. They coupled this perception with the seemingly intuitive sense that cultures do not change – or at least that Britain has 'always been [...] advanced' or on the 'developed side of things'. This is very arguably not the case.[53] However, considering that their history education focused on the history of Britain nearly to the exclusion of all others (as discussed), and that the preponderance of their encounters with history in popular culture focused on Britain, it is understandable that they would think Britain more 'advanced'. It reflects a confirmation bias: their knowledge that Britain was relatively advanced is based upon the fact that their knowledge *of* Britain is relatively advanced (at least by contrast with their knowledge about other places).

They had difficulty negotiating a compromise between these two conflicting ideas – of a technological medieval Islamic world and an uncivilised Islamic world – and did not come to a satisfactory reconciliation during the course of the focus group. At the next meeting, they admitted that this debate continued on the bus ride home. In one regard, these statements are a reason to praise the film. Despite its flaws, *Kingdom of Heaven* has shown these two participants a compelling image of a powerful, 'civilised' and sophisticated Islamic world that contrasted with their incorrect perceptions of the past. It forced them to confront a prejudice they might not have realised they held. This interchange shows the potential of historical film to cause individuals to challenge their own ideas – essentially, for better or worse, to act as an history educator.

However, it is appropriate to be cautious. Firstly, these participants never came to a clear conclusion on which idea to believe. Secondly, the political allegory in *Kingdom of Heaven* was only noted here because it presented a similarity between modern and medieval that was *less* obvious than they thought. None of the participants directly cited the film in helping them to draw the link between medieval crusades and the war in Iraq, because the participants felt that the Crusades were *more* like the war in Iraq than the film depicted, rather than less. As a result, the allegory in the film seemed natural to them, even not going far enough. Thus, this film possibly reinforced their ideas that the Crusades and current conflicts in the Middle East are related or similar, even while showing them a more nuanced view of the past than they held. Finally, *Kingdom of Heaven*'s view of a powerful and sophisticated Islamic world was hardly universal: on the one hand is Saladin and his armies, on the other are the deprived peasants of Ibelin who need a white man to teach them basic irrigation. Both images resonated, even though both images are problematic.

In sum, the participants came to a number of complex conclusions about *Kingdom of Heaven*. Certainly, most participants saw it as very medieval and very realistic. But, the protagonist was considered too formulaic to have been real – the strict social order in their idea of the Middle Ages would not allow for Balian of Ibelin's sudden rise to power. Orlando Bloom was universally panned as 'not medieval', not for his acting, but for his very voice, body, and sex appeal. Defining what a 'medieval man' really entails was less apparent, though this 'pretty boy' was its very antithesis.

Despite what seemed to be an obvious link made between the past and present by the film, many participants did not find that aspect of the film noteworthy. For those who did, they were torn between the depiction of a powerful Muslim world and their prejudices about current-day Muslim-majority countries – between a Muslim world of technology and culture, and one rife with civil wars, foreign occupations, and famine. Ultimately it is difficult to know which image they found more compelling – whether they 'learned' from the film that the Muslim world at the time was, in fact, made up of powerful sophisticated societies, or whether they ultimately backslid to their perception that the Muslim world is currently as it always has been in the past. *Kingdom of Heaven* is just one point of data in their lives, and when placed alongside the constant depictions of the Muslim world across all media that paint it as a fundamentally broken place, it is easy to see how that one contrary image might be discarded.

Like all films, *Kingdom of Heaven* presented a number of messages, some of them conflicting with themselves, and many of them conflicting with what the participants thought they knew. The viewers recalled and engaged with those they found relevant, and which coincided with beliefs they already held. It is not simply that the viewers decoded these messages differently, but they only recalled the messages which were most interesting to them. With few exceptions, they ignored the rest.

The Lord of the Rings: The Return of the King

The Return of the King was the final film viewed, and the one least directly related to the Middle Ages. It is neither based on the product of a medieval imagination (like *Beowulf*) nor is it 'based on a true story' (like *Kingdom of Heaven*). Rather, *The Lord of the Rings* films are a prime example of medievalist fantasy.[54]

Unlike *Beowulf* (or most fantasies written during the medieval period), *The Lord of the Rings* is not set in our world. While Middle-Earth bears many comparisons with our world, it is not ours.[55] And even though it is not our history, it is designed to seem as though it might be. *The Lord of the Rings* series (both book and films) is recognisably medieval in flavour, in their material and social cultures, in their similarities to medieval literature, and in the languages used by the characters.[56] However, to what degree did participants see this connection between medievalist fantasy and medieval history? Was *The Return of the King* considered recognisably medieval? If so, did they rely upon their historical knowledge when interpreting the film – could they possibly have learned about the Middle Ages from a fantasy?

Novels and Fandoms

One factor that clearly affected the participants' interpretation of the films was their previous experience with the novels. Many expressed familiarity with *The Lord of the Rings* books. Among the participants, all of those who indicated they had read the books had also seen the films, and some who had not read the books had seen some or all of the films. While there were no clear indications that having already seen the film influenced their interpretation in the focus group, previous experience with the novels clearly did. Some participants were self-described 'fans' of the series. For example, in the May group, Carin said she was 'a big

Lord of the Rings fan', both 'the books and the films'. In the June group, Sean and Justin both said they had read the books, and Sean often referred to his knowledge of the books during the discussion. Those participants sometimes used their fandom to assert a social authority over how *The Return of the King* should be interpreted. The June focus group's familiarity with the historical provenance of *The Lord of the Rings* (as an early-twentieth-century book) made participants reluctant to label *The Return of the King* as 'medieval fantasy'. Stephen postulated:

> I wonder if some of the fact that we don't see it as a medieval fantasy comes from the fact that it was written, it wasn't written then [in the Middle Ages], or it doesn't directly originate from then, that it's quite modern. [I] suppose it's a modern view, well, [a] relatively modern view of what a medieval fantasy is. We don't accept it as authentic because of that – because it's written hundreds of years after the medieval period.

Unlike *Beowulf*, the participants who had read *The Lord of the Rings* novels did not criticise the film in terms of its fidelity to the book. This may have been a result of the fact that, as a piece of popular fiction, *The Lord of the Rings* would not have been taught in school. As such teachers would not provide interpretive frameworks – such as that which Erica's teacher provided for *Beowulf* (above) – that contradicted the film. Alternatively, it is possible the participants simply felt the film was relatively faithful to the novels. Prior to its release, the films were explicitly marketed to Tolkien fans as a faithful rendition, and the participants may have agreed.[57] Since those who had read the novels regarded their having done so as conferring a social authority over its interpretation, the novel, as the source for the film, was regarded as the 'true story', against which the film must be measured (not entirely unlike how *Beowulf* was interpreted). Ironically, since they were not familiar with the history behind *Kingdom of Heaven*, it was the only film not subjected to scrutiny based upon fidelity.

Medieval Lord of the Rings

But was the film 'medieval'? As would be expected, none of the participants believed *The Return of the King* depicted real events. However, most reported that they felt the film was recognisably medieval, or contained elements that coincided with their expectations of the Middle Ages. Justin felt the film: 'fit in with what I imagine a medieval world to look like, in a way'. When asked how this film compared to the others, Erica responded: 'I thought it [was] kind of a mixture of the two that we'd seen before. Like, it had the fantasy elements, loads of it. It's obviously set in a middle-agey, medieval times.' When Erica was asked what made it seem that way, she responded: 'the battles, the knights, there was the kings, there was, not so much the feasting apart from the king [Denethor] [...] And it had the mythology part of it as well.' When asked to clarify what she meant by 'mythology', she, Carin, and Claire named 'the dragonish things', 'the wizards' and 'the ring'. Similarly, when asked what in the films seemed medieval to them, the June group listed, 'I think chiefly [...] the clothes and the weapons' and 'The clothes, the weapons, Rohan I would say as well.' Dan went so far as to claim *The Return of the King*, 'probably depicted medieval England better than *Beowulf* did [...] I think that reflected culturally [the culture] better. Obviously I don't know if it did, but in my mind it seemed to gel.' Once again, the reflex to see the medieval exclusively in England is apparent, despite neither *Beowulf* nor (clearly) *The Lord of the Rings* being set there. But, to Dan, the culture was similar enough to his idea of medieval England to be identifiably medieval; there was an unidentifiable quality to the film that made it *seem* like a good depiction of medieval England in spite of his admission that he would not know precisely how medieval England looked.

When asked whether they learned anything from *The Return of the King* about the Middle Ages, many said no. For example, Erica said 'I think it's just fantasy. But they based the time period on medieval. [...] It's too much of a fantasy to learn anything historical about medieval times from it.'

However, some identified instances where what they viewed corresponded with their knowledge of the medieval world. Furthermore there was evidence that showed that their knowledge of the medieval world *had been formed by the two previous films they had been shown*. In fact, comparisons with the previously shown films were frequent. Erica found similarities in 'the battles like the big [siege] towers they use and the throwy things [trebuchets] they used in *The Lord of the Rings*; they used the same ones in *Kingdom of Heaven* [...] it seemed to be a lot based on medieval times'. Sean also focused on the battles:

the battle scene is [...] very similar to the one in *Kingdom of Heaven*. It's the same. The same kind of weaponry being used. It's the same kind of tactics being used by both sides. They look like medieval battles, discounting the fact that one side were [non-human] monsters. But they looked medieval.

It is important to note that these battles do not look like medieval battles, *per se*, but look like medieval battles as they have been portrayed in cinema and popular culture; these are not *medieval* battles, but rather *medievalism* battles. For both Sean and Erica, siege warfare and technology is a defining feature of medieval battle and its presence in both films opens them for comparison. Although Laura was insecure about her knowledge of the Middle Ages, she also cited similarities between the depiction of the siege of Minas Tirith in *The Return of the King* and the siege of Jerusalem in *Kingdom of Heaven*:

I don't really know anything about medieval battle and stuff like that. But there seemed to be a lot of similarities to me. Obviously there was the fantasy element, so there weren't giant elephants in the last one [*Kingdom of Heaven*] or anything. But, there were, I don't know what they're called, but the towery things [siege towers] [...] and there are also ... called trebuchets or something? Or catapulty things, there was stuff like that.

Kingdom of Heaven's detailed depiction of medieval warfare rendered it an authoritative source of information. Thus, *The Return of the King*'s similar depiction – despite the fantastical additions – rendered it recognisably medieval. If a particular film becomes an authoritative source for historical knowledge, it seems that positive comparisons with other films can confer that authority and allow the public to see history where it might not otherwise be seen.

Some also judged the narrative aspects of *The Return of the King* to be medieval because of its similarity to *Kingdom of Heaven*. For example for Erica, 'it also had the whole sort of crusade, in going to burn the ring'. For Justin:

coming back to what they [the others in his focus group] said about the crusade last week about it being sort of a journey, I think that came out in this movie [*The Return of the King*] more than in the other one [*Kingdom of Heaven*] because you've got Aragorn's road to being king, and you've got Frodo's quest to destroy the ring.

This equates the idea of 'crusade' with the idea of 'quest' – or perhaps subsumes crusade *into* the idea of a quest (perhaps as a subschema), removing its violent implications in the process. The fantasy quests of *The Return of the King* are thus rendered medieval for the participants, by association with the Crusades. These two films were not simply being compared, but were used to reinforce each other. This process indicates that people who consume several medieval films may enter into a self-reinforcing cycle of intertextual references. They see a narrative feature in film A. Film B also contains this feature – which both validates film A and makes film B more believable. The knowledge becomes further fixed with each reiteration, despite there being no external validation of this knowledge. The more films they see, the more their knowledge is reinforced.

Several types of knowledge became fixed in *The Return of the King* through this process. As mentioned, the participants most frequently referred to material culture when describing *The Return of the King* as 'medieval'. Dan thought one very medieval aspect of the film was 'The idea of horsemen, and the way they were armoured, and the way they made camp, I thought was quite good. And also, the dress of it seemed quite what I imagined the lords to be like.' Carin agreed: 'The costumes were quite medieval. And the armour.' When asked to clarify, she said: 'It's just that kind of dress, the dresses the women were wearing and obviously the armour.' Her seemingly instinctual first response is to comment upon the costume. When asked how medieval the world of *The Return of the King* was, Justin, Sean, and Stephen responded with this exchange:

Justin: In a way it was pretty medieval. In terms of what they wore =

Stephen: = yeah, the way it looked.

Justin: Maybe in the way that they presented the speech and things almost in a way. Just the way they talked.

Stephen: Quite archaic.

Mod: What do you mean?
Justin: I can't really think of instances, but, you know, there
            was a certain way of speaking sometimes that was
            similar to, maybe what you saw in *Kingdom of Heaven*,
            in that it was very [...] I'm trying to think of the
            word but I can't.
Mod: Can anyone help him out?
Sean: I know what he means, but I can't really explain it.
Justin: It almost, it almost seemed a bit grandiose really. And
            especially when someone like Aragorn [was] talking
            [...] he was kind of similar to Balian from yesterday
            in the way that he spoke. [...] I think in medieval in
            the, in the sense of [...] what I would imagine it to be
            medieval [...] if it was put on a screen and somebody
            told me it was medieval then I would succumb to it
            knowing that maybe it isn't truly medieval like that,
            but because it's on a film like that I can believe it
            because in other films that's how it's presented.

Justin initially (and seemingly instinctually) referred to the costume as
being a very medieval element, then referred to the visual aspect of the
world generally. However, the conversation then turned to language.
To these participants, the language had a certain 'grandiose', archaic
cadence which fit with their ideas of the Middle Ages. Despite a
difficulty in expressing himself, Justin astutely identified a commonly
accepted trope that may have little to do with historical reality. But, it is
a history effect specific to the Middle Ages – grandiloquent speech
signals the Middle Ages, particularly in the mouths of the nobility.
It stands as a history effect for pre-modern speech, likely derived from
the archaic-sounding (but still recognisable) linguistic patterns of the
Early-Modern English of Shakespeare and the King James Bible.
    On the other hand, similar to their critiques of *Beowulf*, John
disliked some of the accents used in this film: 'A lot of the orcs had this
weird sort of Cockney accent, which is not in the right time period
obviously because it wouldn't have been around in medieval times.
And when I watch it, that actually does bring it down a bit, bring
down the realism a bit.' To him, the urban environment of east
London that gave rise to the Cockney accent is definitely not

medieval, and therefore the orcs' use of it (recalling also the protagonist's use of it in *Beowulf*) 'brings down the realism'. This is possibly also a product of the broader (incorrect) perceptions of the Middle Ages as a time without urban spaces, where the participants only saw castles, villages, and fields as appropriately medieval (explored further in Chapter 6).

That said, it is noteworthy that while John was disturbed by an inappropriate accent, he seemed willing to accept the breach of reality represented by *the very presence of orcs*. This shows that the participants have a multi-layered understanding of historical realism. They seem willing to accept large violations of realism as part of the fantastical world of the film (so long as they fit the general outlines of 'medievalist fantasy', i.e. dragons and elves, but not robots or aliens). But even when doing this, they do not surrender their critical perception of historicity. Orcs are fine – so long as they look, act and sound appropriately medieval. The savagery that the orcs represent is, in many ways, a hypermedievalisation of the barbarity, darkness, and monstrosity that have become emblems of the period. As a result, many of the participants understood the film to be medieval and not medieval, historical and not historical, at the same time.

To an historian this may seem odd. *The Return of the King* is not medieval. Similarly, some participants felt that some aspects of the film were less medieval than others, while some rigidly stated that since the film does not depict our own world, it cannot be considered medieval at all. John labelled anything fantastical or magical not medieval:

Anything which isn't real ... anything like the magic stuff, for me, that makes it un-medieval. Because I only see medieval as what actually happened. But I know [...] that can't be a common point of view [...] I know a lot of people feel like those sort of things fit with the medieval [...] magic, or kinds of weird creatures, stuff like that.

Carin reported that her initial reaction to the film when she saw it before participating in this study was not to identify the film as medieval. She felt the environment of the focus group itself may have led her to relate it to the Middle Ages where:

I did notice watching it this time that, after watching the previous two films, it is kind of, yeah, with the battles and stuff, it is kind of like that era. But when I'd watched them normally, I just think, *Lord of the Rings*, Middle Earth, rather than how it relates to our history.

Erica also reported that the mindset of having watched *Beowulf* and *Kingdom of Heaven* immediately prior led her to compare this film to the previous ones: 'when I was watching it I was pinpointing, trying to compare it to the other two. I didn't really think about it being not [medieval].'

It is probable that the focus group setting, and watching this film last out of the three, influenced ideas about whether or not *The Return of the King* was medieval. This is a limitation of the study, and leaves room for further research into whether fantasy films are consistently identified as medieval. However, this finding also implies that those who are more familiar with the Middle Ages – or with medieval films – may be more inclined to identify fantasy films like *The Return of the King* as medieval. The frequent comparisons made between *The Return of the King*, *Kingdom of Heaven* and *Beowulf* implies that connections can be seen. However, they may be most apparent to frequent consumers of medievalisms.

The Return of the King *and Realism*

Even though many participants regarded the film as medieval, they were less inclined to label the film 'realistic'. This contrasts with the idea, observed with the reactions to the other two films, that a perception of historicity is dependent upon a perception of realism. Their judgement that it was not realistic was primarily due to the fantastical elements and the setting in a separate world. Some tried to draw allegorical parallels between these fantastical elements and reality, but most saw the two as mutually exclusive. When asked how realistic *The Return of the King* was, some expressed difficulty deciding whether to judge the film based upon the rules of our world, or of Tolkien's (and Jackson's) invented one. When asked whether the film was realistic, Erica and Chloe had differing understandings of what that meant:

Erica: Obviously not with the whole middle-earthy elves and that kind of jazz =

Chloe: = you want to believe it though, don't you? [laugh] I was
sitting there going, come on, get up the hill!

Chloe's sense of realism was tied to the emotional, empathetic affect of
the film, whereas Erica's was bound to its correlation to objective reality.
Justin also understood realism to include empathetic emotional affect.
When asked if the film was realistic, he asked, 'In terms of what,
expressing emotions and things like that?' Justin and Stephen argued
that the fantasy elements made *The Return of the King* more emotionally
satisfying than *Kingdom of Heaven*, if less realistic. Stephen felt that the
fantastical world lent it a scope that the other two films did not have:
'that's where the fantasy element comes in that they were fighting for a
big, big thing, with the ring and stuff. Whereas [they were] just
fighting for control of a single city in *Kingdom of Heaven*.' Justin felt that
the fantasy world was more immersive than the real one:

I think the fantasy element helped it a lot though because you felt
you could immerse yourself into it a bit more, knowing it was a
completely different world as well. [. . .] with *Kingdom of Heaven* it
was very rooted in real religious things that have happened and
you can believe have completely happened. Whereas this, you
know it's fantasy and you know that anything is possible in this
world.

This offers some insights into how larger-than-life fantasies can be even
more effective – and emotionally affective – films than strictly
historical ones. The heightened stakes of *The Return of the King* simply
made it more compelling viewing. A fantasy epic such as *Return of the
King* can be satisfying not just in spite of, but because of not being bound
to reality. In that environment where 'anything is possible', Justin was
able to emotionally invest more readily, because the story was crafted to
be satisfying. Realism was defined differently here than for *Kingdom of
Heaven*. For *Kingdom of Heaven*, the sense of realism was grounded in
extensive historical details, particularly in the material cultures, that
acted as a history effect. *The Return of the King* is certainly not short of
detailed material cultures (in some ways arguably providing a template
for *Kingdom of Heaven* and other epics like it). But it was the *The Return of
the King*'s ability to move them emotionally, rather than dazzle them

visually, which was the most-noted effect – although this was a reality effect rather than history effect. Obviously both spectacle and empathy are important in terms of creating a quality piece of cinema. But for these participants, fantasy films and historical films demanded different priorities.

In summary, many aspects of *The Return of the King* were regarded by the participants as being 'medieval', even if the world itself was not. Furthermore, certain elements were still judged based on historical accuracy even though they were entirely fantastical. It is possible this is simply a part of a wish to have the world present itself as a coherent whole. Interestingly, it seems as though history is the glue which binds these fantasy worlds together, and deviations from history are thus considered to be a break within the imaginary space. The participants did not describe the film as 'realistic' in anything other than an emotionally affective way, though many of them saw it as believable. Though they did not mention the lush material cultural details as a driver of their perceptions of realism (as they did with *Kingdom of Heaven*); it is likely that, were they not there, it would have been cause for complaint. Perhaps their efficacy was powerful enough to not bear mention. In discussing what aspects of the film were 'medieval' or not, participants frequently compared this film to the ones shown previously and saw elements of the previous films in this one. This implies that they saw any directly comparable elements of the films as part of a self-perpetuating cycle, where the arguments, messages, and visuals of previous films lend credibility to the current one, and simultaneously, vice versa.

Conclusion

Each film had unique characteristics to which the participants responded. The Middle Ages that they found in each was as dependent upon the unique characteristics of the film as it was their historical consciousness. Their interpretations were vastly different from what a scholar might see in these films. For example, though they interpreted *Beowulf* as an adaptation of the medieval poem, they did so through the fuzzy half-memories of their encounters with it in their early years in school, which also played a major role in their perception of the time and place. They were far more concerned with those elements which they felt grated *both* against their perceptions of the past and their perceptions of good filmmaking, namely the CGI and the accents. To them, the film would have been regarded as a far better history if it were a better film. *Kingdom of Heaven* had similar issues, particularly when the participants focused on the main character and the star. And while their criticisms of Orlando Bloom may seem petty, they cast some light on what, to them, makes an appropriate hero in the medieval world. While many scholars (myself included) have written about the film's allegorical relationship with modern day conflicts, most participants either did not notice this connection or did not feel it was important enough to mention. And those who did were unsure how to interpret what they had seen, since it clashed with some deep-seated prejudices about the Muslim world.

Finally, the participants were divided on whether *The Return of the King* should be regarded as medieval at all. Despite some iconic similarities, it was found that the participants relied on the knowledge they had gained from viewing the previous two films far more than any external sources. Those who did label it medieval saw the Middle Ages in Middle Earth within specific elements of the material culture(s). However, overall many saw that, while the world was not our own, they judged it by historical standards nevertheless. This indicates that while some may not outwardly feel that the film is 'medieval', that it is judged by the standards of the historical film and may thus influence their broader ideas about the medieval world. This influence seems to work through a cyclical pattern where the more medievalisms that are consumed, the more the ideas about the past latent in medievalisms are reinforced. This was seen even in these groups, where discussions on the third day of each focus group, intended to be about *Return of the King*, ultimately focused almost exclusively on comparing that film with the other two. It was from this milieu that a more cohesive (or at least broader-ranging) idea about the medieval world began to emerge.

It is those broader ideas about the medieval world that we will explore next. The question of the degree to which these participants learned about the Middle Ages (meaning that their historical consciousness changed noticeably) remains open. As seen in the discussions of *The Return of the King*, the participants frequently compared and contrasted the images presented to them in these films, and seemed to be learning from them. As the groups progressed from first day to third, these moments of comparison became more and more frequent.

CHAPTER 6

THE MEDIEVAL WORLDS
THEY FOUND

He belonged to a walled city of the fifteenth century, a city of narrow, cobbled streets, and thin spires, where the inhabitants wore pointed shoes and worsted hose. His face was arresting, sensitive, medieval in some strange inexplicable way, and I was reminded of a portrait seen in a gallery I had forgotten where, of a certain Gentleman Unknown. Could one but rob him of his English tweeds, and put him in black, with lace at his throat and wrists, he would stare down at us in our new world from a long distant past – a past where men walked cloaked at night, and stood in the shadow of old doorways, a past of narrow stairways and dim dungeons, a past of whispers in the dark, of shimmering rapier blades, of silent, exquisite courtesy.

Daphne Du Maurier, *Rebecca*[1]

There is much that is immortal in this medieval lady. The dragons have gone, and so have the knights, but still she lingers in our midst.

E.M. Forster, *A Room with a View*[2]

As the participants saw more medieval films over the course of the study, they began to compare them without being prompted to do so. Analysing these comparisons reveals further layers of nuance in participants' historical consciousness and indicates how their knowledge was challenged, supported, or revised by the three medieval cinematic worlds they experienced. The discussions were far-reaching, but often focused on one of five key themes: society, gender, power, landscape, and religion. These themes emerged from the interview data, but not discretely – participants routinely linked them. For example, social classes were often described as both a product and producer of the built landscape. Kings are the apex of both medieval power and medieval masculinity. Knighthood was, to them, simultaneously a class distinction, a quasi-religious moral ideal, and an icon of medieval masculinity. This chapter traces the complex relationships among these issues and describes how they relate to the participants' wider historical consciousness of the Middle Ages.

Medieval Society: Mad, Bad, and Dangerous to Know

Every historical film is reflective both of the society that the film depicts and (usually more so) the society that produced the film; as discussed in the previous chapters, they are culturally positioned. Each of the films the participants watched also imagined medieval social relationships differently, showing varying relationships between people, social structures, intellectual cultures, and social conditions. The participants reacted strongly to the depictions of social conditions in these films. Sometimes they drew links between contemporary British culture and the medieval, and saw the Middle Ages as a distant cultural ancestor. But more often, they revelled in presentist *schadenfreude*, deriding what they perceived to be the alien qualities of medieval culture, asserting their authority over a past they felt was inferior.

Each of the contrasting images of the Middle Ages in their minds implies a comparison between the Middle Ages and the present day. Either the Middle Ages were better than today (i.e. an era of light, chivalry, nobility, beauty, and fantasy), or they were worse (i.e. an era of squalor, barbarism, torture, suffering, and disease). The idealised Middle Ages were only very rarely discussed after viewing the films; far more often, participants saw in them a support for their image of a squalid and barbaric Middle Ages.

Robert felt that the alleged barbarity of the historical Vikings would be impossible to depict accurately in *Beowulf* without the film achieving higher than its 12A rating:[3] 'the Vikings were quite barbaric people, so if you want to really make it accurate, then I don't think you can fully show it to twelve-year-olds'.

By contrast, Dan pushed back against the emphasis on sex in *Beowulf*, feeling that it was ill-placed:

> It seemed to focus on sex a lot. [...] I know that that went on, but I don't think it was the focal [point] of life to the extent that the movie portrayed it. [...] there are plenty of buildings today where there are just drunken orgies going on, but that doesn't mean that you say that that's what life's about. That seems to be, 'look what happened in the Middle Ages'.

Robert and Dan used the same source material to come to radically different conclusions, both about the film and the medieval world. Robert deployed the pervasive idea wherein the Vikings stand as the figurehead of the 'barbaric Middle Ages', as Joseph M. Sullivan puts it, 'standing for a more generalized idea of foreignness, barbarity, and evil'.[4] This perception of Vikings is further entrenched by the litany of films and TV shows that depict Vikings in just such a way, the most recent of which being the History Channel series *Vikings* (2013–). Seemingly aping the formula of *Game of Thrones*, *Vikings* depicts a Viking world rife with sex and extreme violence. But Dan seemed to regard *Beowulf* as a culturally positioned work of art, appreciating that the limited frame imposed upon the world by a film never represents the totality of experience, or even the norm. His relatively sophisticated historical and media literacy caused him to, if even momentarily, reject the 'otherness' of the Middle Ages and see his historical forebears with empathy, regarding them as not so very different from people living today.

Jess echoed Robert's position. For her, in the Middle Ages, violence reigned. Jess felt that *Beowulf* was an accurate depiction of the Middle Ages because it focused on what were, to her, the two biggest forces in medieval society:

> fighting and [...] power. I mean, it's not like they had much else to do, is it? [...] I kind of liked the drunkenness and the sexy stuff; that made sense to me. It being set when it was, because they didn't want to drink water did they, because it was filthy, so they did all just get lashed all the time.

This shows that a little bit of historical knowledge can be a dangerous thing; her conclusion is based on a piece of correct historical information she learned (that beer was sometimes safer to drink than water). But she then expanded that idea to an extreme conclusion: a thousand years of drunkenness. This fits neatly into the common perception that the Middle Ages was an unruly and lawless place, filled with taverns full of happily (or unhappily) drunken townsfolk. This common myth is blind to several complicating factors: a lifetime of tolerance to moderate consumption, the difference in strength between modern and medieval beer, the fact that medieval people were unaware of the disease vector that unpurified water represented, and a conflation of *any* drinking with *binge* drinking. Of course, people got drunk in the Middle Ages. But assuming they did any more so then than they do now without evidence reveals an idea that runs counter to historical empathy – seeing medieval people as 'other', and, in this case, lesser. Perhaps more provocatively, in constructing this myth, do our 'drunken' historical forebears justify modern-day binge drinking (despite advances in water purification) as 'tradition'? Or does this boozy Middle Ages simply make it more attractive a place to fantasise about, or to shun?

Discussions about medieval society in *Kingdom of Heaven* rested on similar lines of lawlessness. Dan declared one scene to be unrealistic because 'they were able to kill all the Bishop's men, then get away to Jerusalem, then come back to the same house and his crime of murder, and then [their] rebellion on a small scale was completely overlooked and he could live a normal life'.[5] In reply to this, Mark used his knowledge of the Middle Ages as a barbaric age to support the film:

> yeah, but bear in mind most of the authorities back then were corrupt and inept [. . .] they didn't exactly have forensics so, a sneaky arrow in the gut or a bit of a poison ivy in the glass and bye-bye.[6]

Mark then explained that lawlessness was pervasive in the Middle Ages 'just because the fastest way to travel was by horseback, it's hard to maintain the same level of control'. To Mark, the Middle Ages were lawless because law (or, in his eyes, 'control') cannot be enforced without forensics and technology (which Mark felt is necessary for civilisation); medieval law keepers were all as corrupt as the Sheriff of Nottingham.[7] Mark seems to see policing like an episode of *Law and Order* or *CSI*;

without professional investigators, crime labs, and car chases, how could medieval society possibly bring criminals to justice? Mark's view – certainly shared by others – is that contemporary society is so reliant upon technology that it is impossible to imagine a world that functions without it. This is an example of one of the primary challenges to the historical imagination: a failure to imagine how people unlike oneself could live.

Class

Class plays a significant role in each film as well. *Beowulf* is primarily about the warrior elites – Beowulf begins the film a warrior, and ends it a king. In *Kingdom of Heaven*, the protagonist journeys across not merely geographical boundaries but those of culture and class as well: he begins the film as a blacksmith, becomes a baron (and nearly a king), and by the end of the film loses (almost) everything. *The Return of the King* has a dual focus: one narrative strand follows the actions of royalty from two kingdoms and their warrior elites as they fight for their continued existence; the other features hobbits who represent an ideal of the rural gentry as they transcend their rustic roots and become heroes. Participants picked out the films' depictions of class structures, but focused primarily on the gulf between the rich and poor. The former category included knights, ladies, kings, and queens; the poor were conflated into a homogenous mass of peasantry. John, Jess, and Dan noticed that all of the films were stories about the upper class:

John: They taught us [in school] a bit of history about it, the peasants and stuff, but you're not going to know about them all. I guess that's why we associate the kings and queens with them [the Middle Ages] so much, because that's mainly the amount of information that comes out about them. They're the important things at the time.

Jess: I mean, you just don't really care about what peasants have to do each day, 'oh we have to farm, and we have to tend the fire'. It's a lot more interesting to read about kings and queens. So yeah, I get that – why they focused on that part. [. . .]

Dan: I think it's best to focus around the monarch because they were doing most stuff.

To these three, the focus on the monarchy rather than the peasantry is natural, even preferable due to their perception of a lack of information about peasants. Even if it were possible to know about their lives, the poor are unimportant, inactive, even boring to them; as a result, it is natural that stories involving them are infrequent. Sean, Stephen, and Justin took the opposite view. *Beowulf* 'focused upon the knights and the lords a bit too much'. Stephen noted that the only poor character in *Beowulf* was 'the peasant servant that was always getting kicked'. He also misremembered that the servant character, Cain, was the one who 'ends up getting his face burned' (it was actually his master, Unferth); he replaced a moment of poetic justice against an abusive master with a false memory of yet another cruelty towards the poor. Stephen also misremembered Cain as a 'servant'; in the film he is explicitly referred to several times as a 'slave'. It is possible that Stephen may have misremembered Cain as a servant because slavery is not an expected part of the Middle Ages whereas servitude is – even though slavery was common.[8] It is also possible that he misremembered Cain in this way because he instinctually associates the word 'slave' with the African slaves of the Colonial period; thus, Cain, being white, may not seem like the typical slave. The very fact that the problematic term 'white slavery' – where 'white' is needed as a modifying prefix – exists is due to this expectation in Western culture.

Stephen saw the lack of class hierarchy as a reason to criticise *Beowulf* as a poor depiction of the period. 'I got, again, the picture of the Middle Ages as a very stratified society and very hierarchical. But the king was there drinking with everyone, and he was pretty much one of them.' This led Justin to conclude 'He seemed almost more like a chief than a king [. . .] someone who was just getting everyone to move, getting everyone to do as he says, rather than standing in this big room at the top of a castle somewhere.' To Justin, the image of the king is not just removed from his subjects in terms of class, but also physically: an isolated figure ruling from the top of a castle, separate from his subjects. No matter what he is called in the film, Hrothgar, therefore, was a chief rather than a king. That confers upon him a diminished status because he fraternised with his subjects in a way inappropriate for a 'true' medieval king.

In summary, the depiction of medieval social class was a notable part of each film. However, there was little agreement on whether the depiction was accurate. Some recoiled from the abuses heaped upon the lower classes, whereas some saw the focus on the nobility as natural, even desirable. Slaves placed in the period were unconsciously edited out. But whatever the depiction of society, there remained in the participants' minds an unchallenged idea that the Middle Ages featured a rigidly stratified society, marked out by drunkenness, lawlessness, and sex – despite being provably untrue.

Gender

For many participants, the Middle Ages were characterised by strict, rigid gender roles and social boundaries between the sexes. Men were kings and knights, always heroic, martial figures. Women, on the other hand, are generally seen as passive: the good queen, the good wife, the princess, or the lover. Each of the films relies upon this strict stereotyping, but as often to subvert as to reinforce them. The participants bristled at depictions of these strict gender boundaries and of misogyny, but usually attributed them to problems with medieval society rather than a flawed depiction of the medieval past.

Women

Women do not play a central role in any of these films. None feature women in a leading role; none pass the Bechdel test.[9] In the poem *Beowulf*, women are relegated to a secondary role. There, aside from Grendel's mother, women rarely appear at all (though some have recently argued that in spite of their limited appearances, their roles are nevertheless important).[10] The film features women somewhat more, but recapitulates the oft-criticised virgin/whore dichotomy of femininity pervasive in popular culture. Queen Wealtheow is good, wise, virtuous, chaste, and passive. Grendel's Mother is powerful, evil, violent, sexual, and active. Participants saw this relegation of women to the sidelines as reflective of medieval social realities rather than sexism within the film. Sean joked about the difference in the depiction of men and women in *Beowulf*, 'the men were all running around doing things and there was the women who were sort of fussing over their clothes – and, with an ember on their skirt they're like "oh dear" [. . .] The guy had *one arm* at that point.' Stephen, Justin, and Katy looked more critically at the passive role of the women in *Beowulf*:

Stephen: I thought it was quite interesting about the role of women [...] the previous king, he left his wife. And then she was very accepting when he started sleeping with that younger woman. So I don't know whether that was =

Justin: They didn't seem to have any kind of free will, did they? They kind of had =

Stephen: = And likewise they didn't have any kind of strong, equal partnership in the marriage or any kind of strong =

Justin: = Or even, in fact he had that mistress on the side =

Stephen: = yeah. And that his wife knew about it and was, to some extent, fine with it. Yeah.

Katy: The queen being passed down as well =

Stephen: = Yeah, yeah, exactly, yeah.

Justin: But in a way it made men look a bit weak, I think, as well at the same time.

To these three, *Beowulf* depicted a time when women did not have autonomy and were passed as property from one man to another – implying that this would not happen today. They also felt that women being powerless to stop their husbands' philandering and obliged to accept infidelity passively was indicative of medieval, not modern, realities. Chloe, by contrast, took a more feminist tack. She felt very strongly that the role of women in *Beowulf* reflected poorly on both the filmmakers *and* the Middle Ages:

It's tried to make it appeal to lots of people, I think, by the way they portray women in it as well, making them objects and the men are the ones who go and fight. [...] So, I think they've tried to bring medieval and Middle Ages a bit closer to how we view it and incorporate modern-day society into how it was then. [...] It's just [that] they're there on the side, you go back to them in the evening, they're just objects, nothing more. [...] And what happened then is probably still happening now.

To her, the mistreatment of women in *Beowulf* is both an objectification scheme intended to draw in audiences and a projection of modern problems onto the Middle Ages. This projection is, for her, an *accurate* link between modern and medieval; in portraying women in this fashion, the filmmakers were rightly linking the mistreatment of women then and now. This seems to imply that Chloe saw *Beowulf* both as a story that recapitulates (and possibly perpetuates) modern patriarchal structures, but at the same time is an authentic depiction of the mistreatment of medieval women.

Katy saw the depiction of gender relations as historically inaccurate because of her suppositions about the strictness of medieval religion:

If you go back to the treatment of women and tie that in with religion, it's probably not what you would expect either with them going off and having affairs and things like that. [In] that you expect them to be really religious and stick religiously to whatever Christianity said, and they weren't doing that.

Katy ties her perception of medieval gender to that of medieval religion (which will be explored more fully below). She held the perception that all medieval people were devout Christians – a common belief that demands complication – and projects her perceptions of the sexual ethics of contemporary Christianity onto the Middle Ages. Thus, she views the casual sexual immorality of the protagonist as an indicator that he is not a good Christian, and, by extension, not very medieval. Hence, the sexual misconduct is not a credible medieval dimension to the film. But she has misremembered; the adulterers (Hrothgar and Beowulf), are not Christians. They are explicitly shown to be non-Christians, making several invocations to Odin. This shows that some participants (like Mark and Dan, above) felt that Christianity is universal and ahistorical, and that it does not change over time. Its moral prescriptions have always been as they are now, and any deviation from this is not 'correct' Christianity. This is incorrect, but also not surprising to hear. Institutions that promote a moral viewpoint (such as religions) often make claims to the universality of their orthodoxies in order to give them a timeless, ahistorical power. God, many claim, does not change. While morality and evil are complex and thorny philosophical and theological questions, the perception that ideas about them – even within the same religion – do not change over time is provably false. Furthermore, just because medieval Christianity differs from contemporary Christianity does not mean that one is 'right' and the other 'wrong'; the seemingly instinctual assumption that modern Christianity is in the 'right' is a problematic, but pervasive, presentist viewpoint.

Shifting focus back to gender, in *Kingdom of Heaven* there is only one significant female character. Princess Sibylla acts primarily as Balian's love interest, providing the romantic sub-plot common in adventure and epic films.[11] Sibylla also plays the role of kingmaker, and is the catalyst for the disaster at the end of the film; she has the power to choose the king when Baldwin IV dies, and by choosing her husband, Guy (after Balian refuses the crown), she indirectly causes the downfall of the Kingdom of Jerusalem. None of the participants in any of the groups discussed the women in *Kingdom of Heaven* or the depiction of Sibylla. While this might imply that they felt the depiction was natural and did not significantly conflict with their expectations, in the absence of evidence, no conclusion can be drawn.

In *The Return of the King*, there are two major female characters, both of whom break the usual social moulds. Arwen rebels against the wishes of her father and, in so doing, ensures a happy romantic ending for the hero. Eowyn, against the orders of the men in her family, dons a man's armaments and becomes a warrior-hero in her own right. The participants' discussion of women in the film centred on Eowyn's role as a heroic rule-breaker. Erica, for example, viewed Eowyn's heroics as a link between two of the films:

> I noticed in the two films, *Kingdom of Heaven* and *Lord of the Rings*, there both was a theme, a little subplot of it doesn't matter where you come from, you can be the hero [. . .] [in *Kingdom of Heaven*] the main guy was a slave.[12] You could be a slave, but you'll still be [able to be] a knight [. . .]. And then *Lord of the Rings*, the little hobbity guy [Merry] and the woman [Eowyn], even though they was told not to go into battle, they still went into battle. And they was the two surviving characters [. . .] if they wasn't there, it could have gone a lot worse.

Erica then tied this equal-opportunity narrative to her understanding of medieval history. When asked if this trope was particularly medieval, she argued that it was, based both upon her knowledge of medieval society and its inclusion in medieval films:

It's shown a lot in those medievally battle films. It's always the underdog that can do it [. . .] I guess it is medieval because people had to fight, [. . .] if you was a blacksmith or something you had to drop your tools and go off to fight – everybody could be a hero.

War in the period was so pervasive *even women* could be heroes.

Women in these films are treated much as the participants expected: abused, considered chattel, or simply ignored. The only times these women rise above this paradigm is when they literally clothe themselves in masculinity and play the man's role. Feminist historians of the Middle Ages seem to have a long way yet to go in order to change the public perception of medieval women's lives. The film industry is complicit in this; a biopic of Eleanor of Aquitaine has yet to be commissioned, and there are very few female-centric medieval films that are not the story of Joan of Arc. Joan stands as the exception that proves the rule due to her gender transgressivity as a woman taking the mantle of a martial, masculine hero. By contrast, the recent spate of superficially 'feisty' love interests in male-centred medieval films (for example, Marian in *Robin Hood Prince of Thieves* (1991) or *Robin Hood* (2013), Jocelyn in *A Knight's Tale* (2001), or Guinevere in *King Arthur* (2005)) has done little to revise ideas about women's place(s) in medieval society. While medieval society was fundamentally unfair to women, surely this does not mean there are no compelling stories to tell; if anything, it should mean the opposite.

Men

By contrast, the protagonists in all three films are men. Even more than this, in many ways each film can be viewed as a parable about what it means to be a good man. *Beowulf* rises because of his prowess, but falls because of his promiscuity and lies. *Kingdom of Heaven* shows that being a good man entails taking on the mantle of knighthood (as both warrior and leader) but using that to fight for peace. Aragorn's narrative in *The Return of the King* requires him to come into his own by discarding his (relatively) safe life as a ranger and taking on the mantle of heroism and kingship. As part of these narratives, each focuses on two medieval social institutions restricted to men: the warrior class (in particular, knighthood) and kingship. It is through these institutions that medieval heroic masculinity is most commonly seen on the screen.

Knights are one of the foremost icons of the medieval past; 'knight' was one of the top two responses in both 'medieval' and 'Middle Ages' word association exercises. As an icon for the period, knights have a dual role: as emblem of the aristocratic warrior class, and a representation of the idealised virtues bound up in the word 'chivalry'. As Katie Stevenson and Barbara Gribling have argued, however, the idea of chivalry is an incredibly malleable concept:

> Chivalry is one of the most elusive ethical and cultural codes to define; it is ever-changing, adapted in the hands of medieval knights, Renaissance princes, early modern antiquarians, Enlightenment scholars, modern civic authorities, authors, historians, and re-enactors. [...] It was regularly reshaped or customised and inevitably developed multiple shades of meaning for different groups, even during its medieval 'heyday'.[13]

The idea was similarly malleable in the films and the minds of the participants. Only *Kingdom of Heaven* addresses knighthood (both the military reality and the moral ideal) directly. It is the only film in which any characters are explicitly called 'knights', and in which a code of chivalry and ideology of knighthood is presented.[14] It could be argued that several characters in *The Return of the King* act as knights (particularly the heavy-cavalry Rohirrim, or Faramir's doomed cavalry charge), though they are never called by that word. In spite of this, some participants saw knights and behaviour that they labelled chivalrous in all of the films – often in unexpected places.

Who should, and should not, be called a knight was often fraught with disagreement. Some went so far as to propose that *every* medieval warrior should be considered a 'knight'. Erica recounted that in *Beowulf*, the 'monster broke through the doors to get in, and that's where all the knighty-kind of heroes went to save the hall'. Stephen, however, did not see the thanes of *Beowulf* as knights. For him to see *Beowulf* as 'medieval', he expected 'knights and castles and things like that; there's none of that'. Sean agreed 'in *Beowulf* no one really stands out as a knight'.

But if thanes were not knights, what constitutes a recognisable knight? Mark felt that the knights of *Kingdom of Heaven* were easily identifiable because they used: 'armour, horseback, and preferably a lance'. Erica said that the knights in *The Return of the King* and in *Kingdom of Heaven* were essentially similar because both had the 'same kind of helmets, same armour, same swords, same catapultey things, [...] had the same flags as well, [...] in a big group, each little mini-group had their own flag and crest'. The inclusion of 'catapultey things' (trebuchets used by the Gondorians in *The Return of the King* and by the Saracens in *Kingdom of Heaven*) is telling. She was not focusing on the cavalry warriors as knights, but on all of the battles' participants – seemingly including the Saracen armies in *Kingdom of Heaven*. The crucial distinction that made them 'knights', as opposed to the warriors in *Beowulf*, was the heraldry. She continued:

> When they were going into battle they had [...] flags and all different types of armour with the [...] crest on them, and the horses in armour. And the fact that they were all sat in a round circle and discussed everything, and they all was responsible, the kings told them what to do – even though there's all different groups of knights there were, they all took orders from the king.

She rapidly switched from what a knight *wears* to what a knight *does*, showing a similar importance in each. But Erica's memory of the knights did not match the film; she has constructed a false memory of *Kingdom of Heaven* which better corresponds with Arthurian archetypes of knighthood. The knights of *Kingdom of Heaven* never 'sat in like a round circle and discussed everything', most were not 'responsible' and only about half 'took orders from the king'. It seems that Erica is misapplying her idea of a virtuous round table of Arthurian knights to the often less-than-virtuous knights of *Kingdom of Heaven*. Perhaps Erica simply did not see *Kingdom of Heaven*'s Templars as knights (though they were frequently described as such in the film) since they did not behave in an expected manner. The Arthurian expectation overrode her memory, even though she had seen the film only days before. For her, evil knights are an oxymoron. Cultural memes like a 'black knight' or 'dark knight' illustrate this point – without the modifier, a knight is expected to be virtuous.

Several others also saw a moral component needed in order to positively identify a 'knight'. These films, particularly *Kingdom of Heaven*, lay a presentist trap for the viewers. The characters in *Kingdom of Heaven* present, and represent, modern-day secular humanist morality as though it were a medieval one. Placing modern morals into historical mouths is one of the most common ways in which historical films promote a presentist perspective. This is, perhaps, to be expected of films attempting to reach a broad audience and bridge the gap between a distant past and a modern-day sensibility. That bridging – whether lamentable or *de rigeur* – has the potential to influence perceptions. But not all participants fell for it. Laura saw knights as paragons of virtue: 'I think you associate knights with honour, though they're generally quite upstanding people. When you imagine a knight you don't get immoral knights going around doing bad deeds.' When asked what she meant by 'honour', she used a speech from *Kingdom of Heaven* to bolster her claim: 'I think the stuff that they listed in that scene in the movie, you know, telling the truth.' Laura is referring to the list of commandments which Godfrey imparts to Balian when knighting him: 'Be without fear in the face of your enemies. Be brave and upright that God may love thee. Speak the truth always, even if it leads to your death. Safeguard the helpless and do no wrong.' But the May group was more critical than Laura was. Even though knights in *Kingdom of Heaven* did not act in the manner they expected, the less virtuous knights were more realistic because they adhered to their more cynical view of the period:

Jake: When you hear legends of knights and things when you're kids [. . .] you always hear {of} this 'shining chivalric' sort of person who does no wrong and always saved the princess and things like that.

Mark: And when you get a little older and a bit more cynical you realise that =

Jake: = Yeah, obviously [they] were like the French =

Mark: = other, French[15] guy who became king [Guy de Lusignan], [. . .] I would imagine most of them probably were like that.

Mark was inclined to believe the depiction of Knights in *Kingdom of Heaven* because his self-professedly 'cynical' view dictated that his childhood image of knights as virtuous warriors was inaccurate. The May group also revised its understanding of knighthood based upon the scene (discussed above) in which Balian helps build a well:

Jake: I like the way, when you saw them go [. . .] to his [Balian's] lands and you saw his knights there, they were just helping out farming and putting [in] wells and things. I thought that was nice. It's not all fighting, and battling, and swords and everything it's . . .

Mark: Much more irrigation-orientated.

Mod: So is being a knight in the same way =

Jess: = I think of knights having their own castle and having to protect their people that live in their castle [and] that live in the village around it. And that's what Orlando Bloom's doing with his 'Ooo, let's irrigate to make crops and stuff'.

Mark: Yes, a good knight is one who would – will get involved in the dirty work.

Here they are using *Kingdom of Heaven* to apply a somewhat Marxist interpretation to the Middle Ages. It seems that they feel that Balian is virtuous because he, as a noble, does not place himself above the proletariat who work his land. Balian creates a classic Marxist 'community of free individuals, carrying on their work with the means of production in common, in which the labour power of all the different individuals is consciously applied as the combined labour power of the community'.[16] Balian is a good knight because he is a good landowner, and to them, being a good landowner means helping his subjects not just by protecting them, but by getting directly involved in the 'dirty work'. In addition to how condescending this scene is towards medieval Arabs (as previously discussed), this scene also presents an unrealistic scene of virtuous social equality. The filmmakers re-establish Balian's virtue, despite his new title, by showing him among the common people. This has become common in popular medievalisms – no longer must the aristocrat (like Shakespeare's Henry V) go amongst his men incognito, but instead is expected to *become them*, if only temporarily. This performed 'averageness' is the same expected of modern politicians; like the political candidate speaking of their humble origins, or posing for photos in a local bar or on a factory floor, the ideal knight must, paradoxically, be a 'man of the people' in order to be deserving of his elite status.

Jess particularly enjoyed the scene in *Kingdom of Heaven* where Balian knights a crowd of militiamen and commoners. For her, this fits better with a view of modern knighthood than medieval knighthood. 'I thought that was cool at the end when he knighted everyone. Because what does it really mean when someone knights you, you know what I mean? In the grand scheme of things, it's just calling someone by a different name.' Dan retorted, 'Usually, when your city's not besieged it'd confer certain actual honours [. . .] like being able to have, [I] think, a few troops.' Jess then replied 'But it doesn't technically make you better than everyone.' For Jess, knighthood is an honorific rather than a way of life, and bristled at the notion that higher social status implied actual improvement – that the phrase 'your betters' should be taken at all literally. For her, the title of knighthood, while a useful motivational tool, neither confers nor confirms greatness or virtue. This relates to a common theme in many contemporary medievalisms: social mobility culminating in knighthood. Extraordinary commoners are plucked from their rural existence by extraordinary circumstances and eventually find themselves knighted in several medieval films, as illustrated by William Wallace in *Braveheart* (1995), William Thatcher of *A Knight's Tale* (2001), the Lancelot of the TV series *Merlin*, or, perhaps more obliquely, Anakin and Luke Skywalker.

When Mark discussed the Rohirrim of *The Return of the King*, he contradicted his earlier claims about the virtue of pacifist knights in *Kingdom of Heaven*. In this context, Mark here saw aggression as one quality of a good knight: 'the king of Rohan, he's obviously a good example of a knight [. . .] he's at the front of his troops, he's charging into battle, he's helping Gondor even when Gondor don't help him'. Theoden is a good knight in this context: he is a good leader, an aggressive warrior, and a loyal ally. Dan agreed that Theoden was a good knight because he:

Took the decision to fight when they didn't need to, and they're fighting for a more just cause than in the last one [*Kingdom of Heaven*]. They were fighting for a place that held very little value [in *Kingdom of Heaven*]; this time they're fighting for their peaceful existence rather than charging off around the world.

A fine moral distinction is at work here. Foreign adventurism in *Kingdom of Heaven* is bad, but not in *The Return of the King*. Dan felt that Jerusalem held very little value. This obviously was not the opinion of most medieval people, whether Christian, Jewish, or Muslim. But this was one of the underlying modern arguments put forward in *Kingdom of Heaven* – that the city of Jerusalem was (and is) not worth the blood spilt over it. On the surface, the Rohirrim and Crusaders in these films are similar – foreign 'knights' called to travel large distances to repel an invasion force of 'others' from a civilisation intent upon the domination of an important city. To both Dan and Mark, context is paramount: aggression is virtuous in *The Return of the King* because the War of the Ring was presented in the film as a just war. In *Kingdom of Heaven*, the Crusades were presented as a fundamentally unjust war and, as a result, aggression there is considered un-chivalric. This shows how malleable perceptions of virtue are; the morality of war and of knighthood (as with anything) is intimately related to its context. The justification of the action presented in the film is a central point, rather than the action in and of itself. It may be interesting to see, in the future, what might be made of a film that presents as virtuous actions that contradict the worldview of the viewers – for example, the celebratory presentation of the crusade in DeMille's *The Crusades* (1935). Would they be swept along with the context of the narrative as presented by the film, or would they reject the moral paradigm they were presented?

Power

Although in the discussions prior to watching the films, the participants often referred to monarchy in gendered pairs (i.e. 'king and queen'), the plots of these films (and hence the discussions of them) centred almost exclusively on kings. Neither Baldwin IV (*Kingdom of Heaven*), Theoden of Rohan, nor the Steward of Gondor (*The Return of the King*) have a queen. Princess Sibylla (*Kingdom of Heaven*) and Queen Wealtheow (*Beowulf*) play minor, mostly passive roles. Therefore it is unsurprising that discussion of the monarchy focused on the figure of the king.

Defining the King

Stephen glibly defined a king as 'a man in a palace who has people killed on a whim'. However, each film meditates upon monarchy and

Figure 6.1   King Beowulf, from Zemeckis' *Beowulf* (Paramount Pictures, 2007).

power in a different way. Guy de Lusignan in *Kingdom of Heaven* plays Stephen's homicidal tyrant, but all of the other kings depicted explore the role and ideology of kingship in a subtler way. *Beowulf* offers an image of how monarchy can fail when bestowing total power on a single, fallible, person. Both *Kingdom of Heaven* and *The Return of the King* can be interpreted as parables about what leadership should and should not be. Both Baldwin IV and Aragorn exemplify the self-sacrifice and wisdom needed in a good monarch. But ideas about monarchy differed widely among the participant groups; everyone had ideas on what makes someone seem kingly, and what attributes make a medieval king good or bad. For example, to Justin, a key difference between Hrothgar and Beowulf was that while Beowulf

Figure 6.2 King Aragorn, from Jackson's *The Return of the King* (New Line Cinema, 2003).

ruled, he fit the expected image: '[Beowulf] was there in his armour on his horse with the red shirt and was, he looked more kingly.' His momentary slip, where he equated looking kingly with being kingly, is telling.

The May group made a different list of the physical or visual attributes of a medieval king: 'beardy' (specifically a 'clean-shaven [trimmed] beard'), 'crown', 'whopping great big sword', 'nice shiny plate mail', 'gold armour', and 'kitted out ceremonially'. The June group listed: 'armour', 'the size [. . .] a tall buff man', 'a massive [. . .] chest', 'distinguished grey hair, no baldness', 'a white horse' and 'a quality crown'. Katy added 'I can see the grey hair bit and the crown, but, in red

Figure 6.3   King Theoden, from Jackson's *The Return of the King* (New Line Cinema, 2003).

as well. I always imagine kings in red' to which Sean added 'It's a noble colour in a way, isn't it?', to which the group agreed. But why red? Red is not necessarily a colour associated with royalty; purple is the more common association. No king but *Beowulf* wears red in these films bar one: Richard the Lionheart. One explanation may be that these participants were all English; the heraldry of the English monarchy (since Henry II) has predominantly featured gold on a red field, and the English national flag, red on white. The royal guards famously wear red, trimmed in gold. So, even their perception of the colours associated with royalty are likely influenced by their national perspective. Their experiences learning of medieval kings seem, even in a subtle way, influenced by the parade of monarchs (whether contemporary or

Figure 6.4   Pseudo-king Balian, from Scott's *Kingdom of Heaven* (20th Century Fox, 2005).

historical) wearing lions on a field of red. It might be revelatory, therefore, to see whether French people associate royalty in general more with 'royal' blue.

Stephen concluded:

> The way that Beowulf was dressed in relation to his life, in relation to the people around him, is much more distinct from the first king and the people around him. The way the first king was dressed was quite similar to how everyone else was dressed. So, it's not the qualities to make a king that you have to have a red shirt and grey hair and stuff. But I suppose it's a quick visual signifier, isn't it? For a Hollywood hero.

Figure 6.5   Queen Sibylla and King Guy from Scott's *Kingdom of Heaven* (20th Century Fox, 2005).

Beowulf was an appropriate and identifiable king not just because he fulfilled their list of visual signifiers, but also because he was visually distinct from those around him.

Instead of the clothing, some participants focused more on the body of the king-as-hero. Dan said: 'It's short-hand isn't it? Someone big, and tall, and with armour, and the buff body walks on screen – you know that he's the hero, rather than having to explain that "This short little fat man, he's going to be the hero. Watch him!"' To John, the stature of the king reflects the state of the kingdom:

> If it's a really peaceful area and there's not that much fighting, the king's going to be fat, basically. But if, for example, if a kingdom's

gone to set up a colony to go and claim land, the king or the leader of that area is going to be a physical guy who can fight, because that's what's needed.

Leaving to one side the unusual comment about medieval colonialism,[17] to John, the king and the kingdom are tied: if the kingdom is prosperous, the king will be fat; if the kingdom is at war, the king will be ready for war. His comments take an Arthurian tone, where, as Perceval discovers of the Holy Grail in Boorman's *Excalibur*, 'the land and the king are one'.[18] The concept of the link between land and monarch is common amongst Arthurian literature and Arthurian medievalisms – either in the figure of the Holy Grail or the Fisher King.

John, Dan, and Mark then continued to explain that, even though they had learned fatness was attractive during the Middle Ages, it would always be prudent for the king to be physically fit:

John: In our eyes it's a bit different, I suppose, because it was quite fashionable to be fat in the past. Because it meant you could afford food; [. . .] you had money. But, I know, I suppose in our eyes we associate fat people with being greedy. And then they'd show the king, like with the scene[s] in the films stuffing their faces, which makes us think [they are] bad. [That] may not be the case. [. . .]

Dan: Fat kings generally get shown as bad or ill-prepared because if there's a change of circumstance to a physically fit king, as in they go from war to peace, that's fine. Then they can get fat. Whereas, if a fat person is suddenly, war is at their doorstep, they're unprepared. They can't fight. They're going to get shown just as this fool who's become lardy and can't do anything.

Mark: While a physically fit king is probably going to want to stay that way.

Their extensive hypothetical questioning led them to the simple answer that a good king is a fit king – a conclusion with which medieval films and television shows typically agree. In *Game of Thrones*, Robert Baratheon is presented as a once-fit king who has grown fat, lazy, and complacent – leading to his, and his kingdom's, downfall. In *Beowulf*, Hrothgar has grown fat and decadent, leading too to his downfall. And in *The Return of the King*, while Denethor, the Steward of Gondor, is not fat, he is shown, to paraphrase John above, stuffing his face. In that moment in the film, his gluttony is contrasted with his son's self-sacrifice on the battlefield, which lends the audience to view him as morally corrupt due to his ravenous indifference. These perceptions of fatness are much more related to contemporary anxieties about weight and anti-fat bias than medieval perceptions of obesity. Medieval romance literature, as Georges Vigarello explores, has a complex relationship with size, where romance heroes are celebrated for devouring massive quantities of food and their strength often linked to their stoutness and voracious appetites.[19] However, there is a limit whereby extreme obesity became an impediment to their martial abilities or their health (as was the eventual fate of William the Conqueror or Louis the Fat), and thus desirable bigness gave way to the undesirable.[20] The ideal became a chimera – a hefty torso atop limber legs, what Vigarello calls 'the alliance of wide and narrow, big and light that becomes the standard way of evoking a condition of adroit heftiness.'[21]

In the end, many participants had a specific physical ideal of kingship that coincided with how kings are presented by the films. A good king should be thin and physically fit, bearded, and mature (but not old). These physical qualities were also linked with more personal ideals of kingship: the king should be an alpha warrior, a paragon of restrained masculinity, and a wise administrator. A king is not just a body wearing a crown, but a ruler. Each film provided examples of good and bad rulership, and participants responded differently to the actions of each.

Dynastic Power

When asked what non-physical qualities implied kingship, Stephen said, 'the logical answer is the qualities that make a king are that he is the son of another king, or has been left the throne. And so, because of genetics, it could be anyone.' John also focused on dynastic succession:

> The king being in a bloodline [...] in the family. I know in *Beowulf*, anyway, [he] kind of became the king just because he saved the town. But [...] in most cases they're predetermined kings, which seems a bit more historically accurate.

In this way, *Beowulf* (and to some degree both of the other films) violates the norm since kingship is passed outside the norms of royal dynasty. But royal succession, and anxieties over this succession, is present in each film. Beowulf takes the throne when the childless Hrothgar dies (and then finds himself unable to sire an heir). Guy de Lusignan is given the crown of Jerusalem when Baldwin IV dies childless. And Aragorn averts disaster by taking the crown of Gondor just as the line of the stewards comes to an end. Royal succession, and its problematic role in terms of governance (leading bad kings to follow good, or kingdoms to be imperilled when royal lines die out) plays a significant role in almost all medieval films that feature royalty. Consider the royal anxieties present in such diverse films as *The Lion in Winter*, *Camelot*, *Braveheart*, and *Robin Hood*. Anxieties about royal succession are not unique to medieval film, but seem to fit most naturally there, and are one of the tools available to those crafting a medievalism's plot. While dynastic monarchy existed prior to the Middle Ages, and continues to this day, it has become centrally, even definitively, associated with the Middle Ages.

The Ideals of the King

Justin felt that the essential qualities of kingship were personal or moral characteristics: 'I think when you see these big castles and these big armies you expect someone at the top to have some kind of qualities [. . .] physical presence [. . .] and a commanding quality.' He then explored other characteristics of kings:

> Nobleness. Power. Ability to command people, I suppose. I don't know. I suppose that's where the story [*Beowulf*] was interesting, I suppose, because Beowulf was the hero, but he turned out to be fallible. So, I suppose it is a film about the nature of what – is a king really elevated above everybody else?

To Justin, a king's elevated social status – which requires, or confers, the ability to command – implies that they must also be morally elevated. Beowulf's fallibility was a significant deviation from the norm, which both led to his downfall and, for Justin, called the whole paradigm of heroic kingship into question. Erica also implied that a king should seem morally *and* physically strong:

most of the kings in these [films] have been weak [...] either physically in last night's movie [*Kingdom of Heaven*] with the leprosy and stuff. In the first one [*Beowulf*] both the weak kings [Beowulf and Hrothgar] were weak because of the temptation of the monster. [...] [Guy de Lusignan] wanted to do and go to battle for his own reasons and [...] didn't think about his kingdom at all, but only for selfish reasons.

Erica's assessment of Guy's failings ties into another commonly expressed metric of good or bad kingship: how and why a king conducts war. Robert saw the two kings of *Kingdom of Heaven* as exemplars of good and bad royal approaches to war. To him, Guy de Lusignan was 'the ambitious sort of king who's greedy, wants power [...] the other king [Baldwin IV] [...] was keeping the peace, intelligent'. Jess, Jake, and John agreed; to them, Baldwin was a good medieval king because 'he didn't want to fight or anything, he just wanted to allow people like Muslims into the city and, he just wanted to live in peace together'. Guy, on the other hand, 'always wanted to have a war and be victorious, and have victories, and be perceived as a hero'. They argued a good king 'shouldn't seek out fighting, should he? He shouldn't go out and just start wars for no reason or [with] just a flimsy excuse.' These participants reacted positively to *Kingdom of Heaven* because they felt that a necessary quality for good kingship was pacifism, and a bad medieval king would, as Jess said, 'just be out for jollies and glory'.

In spite of the fact that they wanted kings with a cautious attitude towards war, when it came to the king's action in battle, they felt differently. It is a common film trope for heroic kings to lead their troops into battle while evil kings watch from afar. Each of the three films shown here uses this trope: each good king (or those, like Balian, who are placed in quasi-royal leadership roles) is shown to be an alpha-warrior who leads from the front, whereas bad kings are either portrayed as incapable warriors or men who lead from the rear. This was noticed by the participants; for example, to Erica, 'A good king is good because he stays and fights with the troops and he leads them all. A bad king is selfish and stays in his little tower, and orders troops, or doesn't order troops, panics, and doesn't order troops, and [...] stays and doesn't really fight.' Erica here was using the Steward of Gondor as her example of bad kingship, but had a similar assessment of Hrothgar because 'he was paying people to do his fighting, battles for him. He never actually went and fought.' John cited Aragorn as good king because in the battle at the Black Gate at the end of the film, 'He's the first one in, isn't he?' He related the concept of a medieval king as alpha-warrior to the alpha-male in the animal kingdom:

> With certain species you'll have two of the strongest males fighting [it] out for the choice of the females and whatnot, and they'll be generally regarded as the leader. [. . .] And it's probably not too dissimilar with some of the early medieval groups I would have thought. Because a lot of the case it was the best fighter, and they'd expect the king to be the best fighter as well I suppose. Obviously it's not the case now because, [we've] kind of got over that stage of everything just being about physical.

For John, the Early Middle Ages was an era of literal strongmen leaders; the difference between medieval and modern is the focus on physicality and personal strength. John is implying that medieval people are literally more animalistic than people today; he sees modern culture as superior because society has 'got over that stage', as if these are childish or immature social behaviours or, worse, animal tendencies, best left behind. This sentiment, the logical extreme of the notion of Whiggish historical progress, is massively problematic. The Middle Ages are no longer just barbaric, backwards, or uncivilised, but *less sapient*. Its people are not just barbarian, but beastly.

This assessment of medieval people echoes the common racist trope whereby racial or cultural 'others' have been compared throughout history to animals. Take for example Edward Long's lengthy excoriation in 1774 of the physical, intellectual and cultural attributes of 'negroes' which ends in an assessment that: 'in many respects they are more like beasts than men', and that 'the organ-outang [*sic*] and some races of black men are very nearly allied',[22] or David Hume's infamous assessment that 'the negroes and in general all other species of men [. . . are] naturally inferior to the whites [. . .] they talk of one negroe as a man of parts and learning; but 'tis likely he is admired for very slender accomplishments like a parrot, who speaks a few words plainly'.[23]

It is worrying to consider how John might approach other less technologically advanced cultures today; would he think Australian aborigines or African tribespeople more like animals than he was? Due to the unacceptability of overt racism in most mainstream contemporary society, it is unlikely John would agree. But why are we safe to do so with our (extremely recent, evolutionarily speaking) medieval ancestors? And what other problems might arise as a result of conceiving of history in this fashion?

The King as Ruler

A king does more than fight. Many participants discussed how a king should reign, and found that the king's relationship with his subjects was of paramount importance. In the April group, Chloe said a good king 'needs the respect from the people and for the people'. The May group instead collectively compiled a list of attributes of good kingship; they focused on this idea as well. To them, an ideal medieval king 'should seek to protect his people', he, paradoxically, 'should be the ultimate servant', and should 'make sure, within the walls of your kingdom, that they [his subjects] are safe'. They defined the primary trait of a bad king as 'selfishness'. A bad king would be 'someone who doesn't look out for his people. If they've got no food, then you're a bad king. If they're dying, you're a bad king.' Carin also felt that the central role of a king was as a protector: 'Orlando Bloom's character [in *Kingdom of Heaven*] was [a king] in a way because he defended the people even though he wasn't a king.'

Their ideas of the king protecting and serving the people stem from *Kingdom of Heaven*. The other films do not feature the 'king as servant and protector' meme, but *Kingdom of Heaven* seems obsessed with the idea. In the film, Godfrey commands his newly knighted son Balian: 'if the King is dead, protect the people'. Balian then serves his people by working alongside them, and justifies an apparently suicidal charge against Muslim cavalry because 'if we withdraw, these people [fleeing civilians] will die'. At the conclusion of his climactic eve-of-battle speech, Balian announces 'We defend this city, not to protect these stones, but the people living within these walls.' *Kingdom of Heaven*'s obsession with 'protecting the people' had a significant impact upon participants' perception of the attributes of a good king, since, in post-viewing discussions, they repeated the film's ideological position almost verbatim. This obviously did not conflict significantly with their previous knowledge; its foregrounding may have caused the participants to repeat the film's perspective as though it were their own.

The May group felt that the most important job of a king was to 'reign well'. When asked how a king might go about doing this, Dan and Mark replied: 'Not [go] around picking fights unless they need to', have 'good administration', and 'keeping promises they make to people who have the power to curse them to living death'.[24] When asked what they meant by 'good administration', Dan referred to Theoden's hierarchy:

Designating specific authorities, like with Theoden we saw that he had several captains which also branched down to various other lower levels who also managed to bring in the men, in order to have his decision carried. A clear hierarchy.

Laura similarly focused on leadership: 'the whole concept of the king is centred around leading people [. . .] the concept of a power-hungry king, that's not really compatible with what a king is'. But to Dan, the essence of a king is that 'he makes the decisions, he has the authority, and the backing of the populace [. . .] kings lose backing, then they very often stop being kings'. Thus, somehow the king must not be power-hungry, but must be powerful. And furthermore, Dan imposed a democratic idea onto medieval kingship where, similar to the prime minister in the British parliament, a vote of no confidence (or, it is presumed for a medieval king, a knife of no confidence) could divest the king of his power. In his mind, true power rests with the populace. He seems to have conflated the aristocracy – who could potentially overthrow a king – with 'the populace' – who never effectively did. While medieval kings were sometimes deposed by rivals, even the large-scale popular revolts during the Late Middle Ages (such as the Jacquerie in France and the Peasants' Revolt of 1381 in England) did not conclude with a change of monarch.[25]

Another feature of medieval kingship, for the participants, was that, in contrast with contemporary British (and European) monarchy, medieval kings were not merely figureheads. Laura defined a medieval kingship as 'in comparison to now, it would be less a symbol and more someone who actually does things. [. . .] I think a medieval king would be more involved in what went on'. But when asked to specify, she had difficulty:

Decision-making so that there weren't people arguing all over the place and there was a final decision and things and, probably, I don't know. And, I don't know, stuff like that. Just generally being a leader in terms of things rather [than], you know, someone at the forefront of everything.

She retained an image of an active, involved king, but like so many other statements by participants, fell short when pressed for details. Her image of medieval kingship is impressionistic – clear in its broader strokes, but with indistinct details.

In short, the participants felt strongly that a medieval king would be an active and able ruler and administrator, and yet had difficulty explaining how a king might do this. They used generic terms to describe their concepts and gave few specific examples. This is unsurprising, considering that most films and popular cultural representations of kingship focus far more upon the king's performance in war than in the details of rule and administration (with the single exception being King John and taxation). Even in strategic medieval video games (like the aforementioned *Medieval: Total War* or *Civilization*), where players must build and maintain infrastructure as well as conduct war, there is little in the game mechanics to indicate how this was accomplished in the medieval world. While warfare is often rendered in excruciating, bloody details, the actions of medieval rulers in peacetime are often limited to preparing for the next war. When the groups did describe details of a king's rule, they seemed to describe a good office manager, supervisor, or CEO: delegating responsibility, establishing workflow and lines of communication, and making firm decisions. In other words, they projected their own experiences and expectations of leadership onto a medieval role that they did not understand well.

These participants had their conception of the archetypal medieval king reinforced by the portrayals of kings in the films. Even when these portrayals seemed contradictory (such as the requirement that a king be both pacifist and bellicose), participants generally accepted both realities with little critical comparison or sense of contradiction. Despite the obvious differences in their stories, these three films present a very similar view of kingship, and very similar kings – especially in terms of their choice of hair and beard (as seen in Figures

6.1–6.5).[26] Taken together, these comprise a 'look' of medieval masculine heroism, particularly royal heroism, during this period. This likely began with *The Lord of the Rings* and was replicated in subsequent films.

The three films, taken together, construct a multi-faceted image of kingship that encompasses both how a king should look and how he should act. Many of these ideas are anachronistic, being either drawn entirely from the three films, or projected from current expectations of military, political, or business leaders onto medieval ones. The king must be reluctant to go to war (except when it is just) but eager to get into the fray (except when it is wrong). He is bearded (but not bedraggled), old (but not wizened) and aggressive (but no barbarian). He at once serves, is one of, and reigns over his people, whose defence is his primary concern. He must be a CEO who is king of the medieval jungle.

The Land

The landscape, both built and natural, often plays a central role in historical films, especially epics. Sweeping panoramas are used to imply the scope of the action and to establish a geographically and/or chronologically distant and distinct setting. An apt example is *Lawrence of Arabia* (1962) in which the desert famously plays a major role in the narrative as context, obstacle, and metaphor. Sweeping shots of a landscape, like those employed in the three films discussed here, make the characters themselves, their struggles and their actions, all seem simultaneously both small and of grand importance. They are dwarfed by the land, but their actions change it.

Second only to the characters, the landscape is often the dominant visual element in a medieval film. It acts as shorthand for the wider world affected by the specific story. Our three films are no exceptions; each makes use of sweeping landscape shots, especially in their battle scenes. The participants often described how the built and natural landscapes in the films related to their expectations of real medieval landscapes. They also reacted strongly to related issues, including their perception of connected geographies, issues of travel, and navigation.

Every natural landscape within these films is, ironically, partially or wholly artificial. *Kingdom of Heaven*'s Middle-Eastern landscape was filmed in Morocco; its cities of the Holy Land rise out of a North Saharan desert. *The Return of the King* was filmed entirely in New Zealand (either on location or in a Wellington sound studio); the land formations and flora of that country are not European, and many were man-made matte paintings and models in long-shot or Weta Workshop creations when in close-up. The dramatic New Zealand landscapes captured (or created) for Middle-Earth lend the story a feeling of exaggerated reality; for audience members not native to the Antipodes, they give it an uncanny feel – plains, hills, forests, swamps, and mountains at once familiar and hyperbolic. *Beowulf*'s landscapes are the most artificial of all: the action does not take place anywhere except within the electrons of the computers that rendered it. As a result, every inch of landscape seen on screen was not scouted, but rather designed quite literally from the ground up.

The participants understood the medieval landscape as often by what it was (and what it contained) as by what it was not. For example, as we have seen, some participants were unsure whether *Beowulf* was medieval at all (believing it to instead be pre-medieval). In some cases, these doubts revolved around the built landscape in the film. Jess felt the Middle Ages began 'when they started building proper castles [...] like the Tower of London, that's when that was built and actual big stone castles. That's what I think of Middle Ages: castles, and then outgoing villages and farming'. For this reason, the wooden hall of Heorot was not properly a part of the Middle Ages. John and Dan defined the period similarly:

John: I always imagine it's whole towns, [with] most buildings made out of wood. Built around a castle, surrounded by a countryside.

Mod: Surrounded by a countryside, okay.

Dan: I imagine that but more woodland rather than countryside.

Mod: More woodland, okay.

Dan: Whenever you look at other countries where they're not especially developed, it's woodland. Whereas here, the woodlands are specific areas, you know. Who's going to cut it down if it's not populated? I think more woodland.

In Dan's mind, the population of the Middle Ages was so low (and land use so sparse) that wildwood would have dominated. This is a common misconception which is a product of (and contributes to) the perception of the Middle Ages as an untamed time before science and industry brought the natural world to heel. In reality, the majority of the wild woodland of Britain had been cleared by the close of the Bronze Age, and most medieval woodland was closely managed for timber or hunting.[27] Contemporary Britain actually has more woodland than medieval Britain did.[28] While the population of medieval Britain was certainly lower, there were not large swathes of unused land; even by the Anglo-Saxon period, the English countryside was blanketed with villages largely within a day's walk from one another.[29] This landscape was crisscrossed with a network of roads, some dating from the Iron Age or the Roman period.[30] The population density was certainly lower than it is now, but the coverage was significant, even by modern standards. Medieval England at its highest had about 3.7 million inhabitants, giving it an average population density of 73.5 people per square mile.[31] This places it between the population densities of West Virginia and Vermont in 2010. It was rural, but hardly an empty wilderness.[32]

The presence of villages strategically situated within a day of one another does raise a question about travel. How was travel perceived, especially considering that all of these films centre upon quests to faraway lands? Beowulf travels from far Geatland to the adventure space of Heorot; *The Return of the King* and *Kingdom of Heaven* are also stories of adventure in foreign climes. The latter two follow a 'there and back again' or 'exile and return' narrative structure, in which heroes venture away from home into the place of adventure, returning once their adventure is complete (though in both they find themselves so changed that they cannot resume their old lives).[33] Both also depict the realities, and difficulties, of medieval travel. Chloe and Erica dwelled on this depiction:

Erica: Yeah, there was no signs to anywhere. Whenever they give directions, it was always 'go to the part where they speak Italian' or =

Chloe: = 'three days gallop away' =

Erica: = yeah. You'd never, nothing's really mapped out, and there's no signs to anywhere. Whereas, if that happened today everybody would just get lost every single time they left the house.

This is a rare moment; Erica seems to have imagined that medieval people had skills and abilities that modern people do not; placed in the medieval world, without our GPS satellites and A-to-Z maps, surely, we would lose our way. This is possibly true until such point as we re-learned how to ask others for directions.

While medieval maps did exist, they were often large and used to conceptualise the world rather than aid travellers.[34] By the later Middle Ages, itineraries came into use,[35] but for the vast majority of medieval people, travel utilised social networks and local knowledge. The films, however, support the view that medieval travel was difficult and treacherous. There are no roads in *Beowulf*. The sea rings the action as a grim barrier, one that is never treated casually; travel on it is shown to be perilous due to ever-present storms and sea monsters. Heroes come from the sea, and they go there when they die. In *Kingdom of Heaven*, the action begins at a crossroads. Balian then is sent out on crusade with a road under his feet, but soon the paths dissolve and the way becomes confused. Balian is given only these directions to the Holy Land by his father: 'You go to where the men speak Italian, then go to where they speak something else' (as paraphrased by Erica above). He endures a shipwreck and finds himself in a trackless desert of a Middle Eastern land where he must make his own path, both literally and metaphorically. *The Lord of the Rings* film trilogy encompasses a journey from the pastoral to the martial epic, from the modern to the medieval. The Shire (where the action begins) is a Victorian pastoral ideal: a land of roads, paths and tamed rural landscape. As the hobbits journey into the unknown, the paths melt away as civilisation disappears and the characters find themselves ranging over endless vistas of medievalesque/Antipodean countryside. By the time the action begins in *Return of the King*, the roads have all but disappeared. As they travel out of Rohan, Gandalf describes the Kingdom of Gondor as being 'three days ride away, as the Nazgul flies' (as Chloe referenced). In this medieval world, people gallop, walk or fly over trackless, open, empty country. They travel as wild animals do – sometimes, in fact, upon them.

When asked whether these depictions of medieval travel were reflective of historical realities, Erica seemed convinced:

Yeah they would have had maps because even at the end of *Lord of the Rings* they showed a map. But it didn't have distances on it [. . .] nobody'd ever studied the land that well to be able to say 'go five miles northeast and you'll get to this certain space', and then you go. It's always, 'travel for a couple of days and if they don't speak Italian you've gone the wrong way'.

Carin agreed in principle, 'In order to have a vague sense of which direction things were in, there would have been maps and, I don't know, some kind of vague idea.' Erica mixed information learned from *Return of the King* and *Kingdom of Heaven* and applied it to her understanding of medieval navigation, and Carin added that people would only have an intuitive sense of the way between places. Thus, the medieval landscape was not just unknown to us, but unknown even by medieval people. The perceived difficulty traversing the medieval landscape seems to have resulted in one of the particular archetypes of a medieval hero: the half-wild/half-civilised hero. They not only live but thrive in wild spaces, and have an almost magical (or actually magical) ability to live in the most liminal landscapes. Robin Hood is the most famous example, but medievalist literature is littered with rangers and pathfinders: Aragorn of *Lord of the Rings*, Beorn of *The Hobbit*, and Prince Gwydion of the *Chronicles of Prydain* series are prime examples.[36]

All three films also included scenes of sea travel. Many participants found this surprising: Jess and Mark reported learning from *Kingdom of Heaven* that many crusaders travelled by ship; Jess said 'I've never thought how they got to Jerusalem on the Crusades. For some reason I just imagined they walked or got on their horse the entire time. So when he got on a boat I was really surprised.' To this, Mark added 'same here [. . .] I was fairly sure they did go by foot.' It is possible that this perception – that crusades were conducted primarily over land – emerged from the history of the First Crusade, which did proceed primarily on land (after forming in Constantinople). However, once Jerusalem was captured and the Kingdom of Jerusalem established (including, importantly here, the port cities of Acre and Ascalon), travel by sea to the crusader states became commonplace. The Second and Third Crusades both had large contingents who travelled by sea.[37]

But it is perhaps more likely that the participants simply did not include sea travel in their understanding of the medieval world. The sea, and by extension sea travel, is not a common part of the historical consciousness of the Middle Ages (except, perhaps, in the specific context of the Vikings), and it did not seem to be part of theirs. This might be due to the fact that navigational science, exploration, and colonisation are some of the features that some historians use to separate the Middle Ages from subsequent periods. For example, David Waters argues that the invention of scientific measurement, developed by navigators to calculate their position at sea, distinguishes the Early Modern period from the Middle Ages.[38] The famous voyages of Vasco de Gama, Christopher Columbus, or Ferdinand Magellan are not just post-medieval, they are definitively so.

Since most participants intuitively felt that the Middle Ages were set on an English or western European landscape, and also felt that the Middle Ages were a time of extremely limited mobility, it is unsurprising that the presence of sea travel was surprising to them. Their (literally) insular viewpoint may have contributed to this: if a person lives on an island and believes – even only intuitively – that the Middle Ages only happened on that island, lack of sea travel is implicit in this worldview. The Vikings arrive and depart (and were not even viewed as part of the Middle Ages by all participants). The Normans invade and stay. But barring that, there is little other sea travel worthy of notice. Even *The Lord of the Rings* (both the novels and films) take place across an unbroken continent. The vast majority of its references to sea travel – excepting perhaps the Corsairs – are as a metaphor for death. This both reflects, and contributes to, the perception that the Middle Ages was landlocked.

However, many participants elected to believe that the representation of sea travel in the films was more reflective of historical reality than their prior knowledge. For example, Jess said: 'It makes sense, travelling by ship is just easier and quicker. Well, except for when you get shipwrecked.' Justin had a similar reaction, 'It made sense in *Beowulf* since the Vikings travelled by ship a lot. Even went to America, right? But I guess I didn't think about other people doing it. But if you're going to Jerusalem, I suppose you should if you could.' This is a place where the films had a definitive positive impact on their perceptions of the Middle Ages. Despite their perceptions of the Middle Ages as featuring trackless, hostile wilderness, the films accurately illustrated that sea travel was not only common, but more widespread than they might have believed, and participants found this depiction believable.

The Built Environment

The dominant feature of the medieval built environment, to most participants, was the castle. To John, the castle is so central that, 'they wouldn't really put a village in a place without castles in it'. To him, castles were not only common, but necessary; any human settlement would have had one. Of course, this was not the case. If anything, castles were built to protect cities, towns, and villages; cities were rarely built around castles. The idea may come from the heritage tourism industry: castles are significant foci for heritage tourism in the UK. Villages, by contrast, are places for living rather than visiting; even in the UK, one does not live in one's medieval heritage, one visits it, either in school, in the movie theatre or on holiday.

Perceptions of the built medieval landscape influenced interpretations of the films as well. Justin felt that the setting of *Beowulf* did not seem medieval, because: 'I've never seen a movie where it has [been set], in that kind of location, completely in the middle of nowhere. I think of somewhere that was more sprawling.' By 'sprawling', he meant dominated by land rather than, as it is in *Beowulf*, the sea. He continued:

Justin: I wouldn't imagine it to be that close to the sea for a start, on the edge of a cliff.
Stephen: Yeah. For some reason that's, I don't know why that surprised me. I just wasn't expecting – everywhere just seemed to be really close to the sea =
Justin: = yeah, and I just expect[ed it] to be more, maybe more agricultural, maybe seeing a bit more [. . .] townsy and more, just great. I don't know. Square mileage. I don't know.
Mod: So, where is the Middle Ages to you?
Justin: I suppose it's everywhere, it's just I've never really seen it though. So when I think of it, I think of it more centralised in the country and stuff.

He knows the Middle Ages is everywhere, but he has never seen it. Or perhaps, he has never been shown a Middle Ages that isn't the fields and forests of his home country.

For several participants, medieval civilisation is a castle surrounded by vast fields. The bleak Scandinavian landscape of *Beowulf* was surprising, not only because of the ever-present sea, but also because the snowy landscape could not be farmed. If *Beowulf* were medieval, Justin concluded, one would expect 'a bunch of agricultural things that you could see, like ploughed fields and things like that. I didn't expect it to be built settlements like I saw in that film. I expected it to be much grander.' On the other hand, these two later agreed that the city of Minas Tirith in *The Return of the King* was not medieval because it was 'too grand':

Justin: I can't imagine that [city] in any medieval world because it's just too, it's too grand.
Stephen: I can see what you mean it's too grand, it's modelled. It seems modelled after some kind of medieval thing. [...] the doors of the city, they look like cathedral doors, and bits looked like [a] church because they've got the panels with the statues of people in them [niches] that look [like it]. Probably, in this movie, they're not saints but they look like [it], it's that, it looks like a church.

They identified that Minas Tirith was designed to look medieval, but their perception of it as clearly having been 'designed' made it problematic. They bristled at the hypermedievalisms they found there – cathedral doors and niches out of place, and a city altogether too medieval to be real. So Heorot was too squalid. Minas Tirith was too grand. Just right, it seems, was Edoras, the city of the Rohirrim in *Return of the King*. Even though they had some trouble identifying it (Sean referring to it as 'the wooden one on the hill'), Justin and Stephen both agreed that 'Yeah, that seems medieval'. This is peculiar considering the depiction of Edoras was based by concept artist Alan Lee upon paintings he had previously done of Heorot.[39] Ironically, *The Lord of the Rings'* version of Heorot was considered more medieval than *Beowulf's*, transplanted, as it is, from the Scandinavian seas to the fields and mountains of Middle Earth.

John also reacted negatively to the Scandinavian setting of *Beowulf*, because to him it did not seem enough like Denmark:

it seemed to be snowing quite a lot. I wouldn't say there was that much in Denmark. Next to the sea as well. So yeah, next to the sea there wouldn't be that much. [. . .] they built a castle as well [. . .] right up against the seafront, and that I know that would never happen. They would never build a castle where they basically back themselves up against a wall.

John felt that the film's landscape was implausible both because it did not correspond with his knowledge of Denmark's landscape and weather, but also because it conflicted with his understanding of medieval battle tactics – where the sea was a wall (since, in their understanding, medieval people did not regularly travel by sea), rather than an escape or source of resupply. He was clearly unfamiliar with a wide range of counterexamples, such as Mont Saint-Michel in France, or any of Edward I's 'ring of iron' castles dotted along the coast of Wales.[40]

The Social Landscape

Some participants also saw the films' built environments as reflective of the social structures of those who lived in them. When Chloe was asked what was particularly medieval about *The Return of the King*, she said:

Big kingdoms with big castles, live in a big building. Big settlements that were together [. . .] everyone lives in the same place. They're all very integrated [. . .] everybody needs each other because everybody has a trade. So you've got the blacksmith, and the carpenter, and everybody has a role, almost. And you've got families, and you all work together and live together, rather than modern day where it's all quite separate.

Chloe added that this compares to the – potentially lamented – individualism of modernity, 'people are more individual now. You work for yourself, whereas before it was, you're . . .' Carin finished, 'Part of the community'. To Carin, the built environment of isolated walled communities was a similarity between *Kingdom of Heaven* and *The Return of the King*:

The two of them [films, seen] today and yesterday, it was all, everything was surrounded by the main walls. Everything, everybody was together. And if they needed help, they called upon it and other sectioned-off communities came and helped. [...] they could get people from outside the walls to help, but yeah. [There is] more [a] sense of doing it for your community than doing it for yourself.

To them, the cities of *Kingdom of Heaven* and *The Return of the King* are models of medieval communalism. Everyone in the local community worked towards common goals, and aid only came from other similarly isolated and insular communities. The built environment is thus both product and cause of social culture: large walled cities imply communal levelling of social strata (presumably amongst those who were not aristocrats), and a closed community requires that collectivist nature and limited individuality in order to survive in a harsh world. Their idea of the medieval social structure seems drawn – intentionally or not – from the socialist medievalism of William Morris who, in his *A Dream of John Ball*, views the Middle Ages as a socialist golden age.[41] Or perhaps they see the Middle Ages like Dennis the peasant from *Monty Python and the Holy Grail*: 'We're an anarcho-syndicalist commune!'

The Agricultural Landscape

Even though communal agrarian society and agriculture seem to epitomise the Middle Ages, *Kingdom of Heaven* is the only film to actually show farmland or farming. *The Return of the King*'s landscape had green fields, and Stephen felt this made it more medieval than *Beowulf*: 'it could just be simply that [...] Beowulf was a snowy waste essentially, but there was greenery in Rohan'. Justin countered, 'but it didn't look like fields that was being harvested in any way. It just looked like a field.' Stephen assumed that there must be some kind of agriculture anyway: 'maybe not advanced agriculture but, I would assume there would be maybe some crops'. To these two, agriculture is *so* necessary for the medieval landscape that they were willing to imagine it into existence. It was not 'advanced', of course, because to them the Middle Ages were not advanced in any way. But it must have been there.

For Katy, the landscape of *The Return of the King* seemed medieval because agriculture is implied by the open, empty spaces:

Mostly, I always think of agriculture and the big churches and buildings and grand – actually I think of grand buildings, but in the middle of nowhere. And that was just fields around. And it's the fields, I think; that's the kind of setting. Not seeing, with it not being built up, I just assume [it is] agricultural. And that was what was in *Lord of the Rings*. In terms of where it was set, [that] would be what I probably expected for medieval.

Katy went on to explain what sort of landscape was *not* medieval:

I don't ever imagine medieval films to be set in big towns and cities. I just always, I think it's because of battlefields. When you think of battle, you think of battlefields and them coming together in the fields and the agriculture. I don't know why.

To Katy, the medieval landscape is defined by grand buildings placed in large swaths of empty fertile land – ripe for battles to erupt. The fields are filled with crops or corpses. Urbanity simply does not exist. The city is a powerful image, it seems, in nearly every European time period barring the Middle Ages. The classical world has Rome, recently articulated in *Gladiator* (2000) and the TV series *Rome* (2005–2007). Elizabeth and Shakespeare have their particular London, as does Dickens, Conan Doyle, and Victoria. Chaucer's version of that city, no matter how distinct and compelling, has not yet taken root in the popular consciousness, despite its presence in *A Knight's Tale*.

This is how the medieval natural landscape is depicted in the three films: there are battles upon wide tracts of land, none of which are used for anything other than battle. Their function outside of warfare is an empty space, rather than filled with the lives and work of people. This is a by-product of the necessities of filmmaking (planting crops and waiting for them to grow only to be trampled by an army of extras seems particularly wasteful). But this peculiarity of filmmaking seems to have shaped, and reinforced, the perception of the medieval landscape as not just rural, but wild and unpopulated. The medieval landscape of their historical consciousness is a barren wilderness, pockmarked only by a castle here or a battle there.

The English Landscape

As discussed previously, many participants overtly or instinctually placed the Middle Ages in England or Britain, and saw it as primarily involving English or British people. However, none of these films is set in Britain. Neither do they have characters who are English or British beyond the scope of their accents.[42] Jess remarked on this in analysing *Kingdom of Heaven*:

> What surprised me was that they were French. That guy – Balian or whatever it was, Orlando Bloom – he was French and they came from France. I don't know why, but I just assumed they'd be English. I mean, I forgot there was others all over the place. It was quite obvious when that German guy turned up as well. That was an initial surprise to me.

Mark agreed, saying, 'I was expecting that, but maybe that's a little stupid.' Even when participants acknowledge that their knowledge is incorrect, the instinct to expect or assume that medieval narratives are English remains. To this group, *Kingdom of Heaven* also revealed a trend where non-English characters in medieval film are typically depicted by actors speaking English with English accents. For example, Jake stated,

> That's more to do with the actual [...] how, more [often], it's English-speaking. You'd, obviously, have more [of] the English being sort of the leads [...] they're obviously French, but they're speaking English. And, they didn't even put on a faux French accent or anything.

Jess agreed, 'except for the stupid names like Guy and Reynard or whatever his name was [Reynald], I forgot they were French'. To these participants, the Middle Ages are set in England partly because characters in medieval films that they have seen do not bear any of the signifiers of foreignness. Their foreignness disappears – though, considering how distracting they found the accents in *Beowulf* as discussed in Chapter 5, this presents a complex problem. The use of English accents perpetuates the idea that the Middle Ages are, by definition, English, but viewers bristle at the use of other accents or languages.

ᴊding further complexity to this question, when asked what aspects of *Beowulf* were not medieval, Robert cited the Danish setting:

Robert: When we'd said medieval, we associate it with Britain, but obviously that was in Denmark. So ...
Chloe: Mmm [in agreement].
Robert: I don't know, it was kind of a mixture.
Chloe: Looking at the Vikings, almost.
Robert: Yeah.
Mod: So, are the Vikings, do the Vikings seem medieval to you, or no?
Robert: They didn't before; I put them under the Middle Ages.

To Robert and Chloe, 'medieval' included Britain but not Denmark, while 'Middle Ages' included both Britain and Denmark. However, Robert's statement 'they didn't before' implies that he may have revised his opinion as a result of what he saw in *Beowulf*.

After viewing the films, Dan was the only participant to disagree with the idea that the 'Middle Ages' are English, seeing the Crusades in *Kingdom of Heaven* as a fundamentally international phenomenon:

I thought it was a good representation of what the Crusades [were]. I didn't think that the Crusaders were predominantly English, so [I looked at it] from the point of view that the Crusades were something that united Europe under Catholicism, generally. So, it was a team effort [laugh] for Europe.

His view was not accepted by all those in his group. For those of the participants who saw the Middle Ages as primarily an English phenomenon, these films offered a revision. It is difficult to ascertain whether that revision was accepted as an exception to the rule or as a new rule altogether. Were the Middle Ages now English *except* for the Crusades, or did this begin to redefine the Middle Ages?

Overall, the participants gleaned a wide range of information (and misinformation) about the medieval landscape from these films, whether that landscape be the natural, built, agricultural, or political. The landscape, in these films, acts as a Barthesian reality effect because it cannot help but be detailed – especially when shot, as it is in epics, in lingering panoramic detail. This makes the landscape a compelling and powerful aspect of historical films, and one from which individuals seem to learn, even subliminally. While a film's budgetary concerns may mean that their medieval landscape is more barren or wild than historical realities, these nuances are taken as historical fact by those who view them.

In terms of its landscape, *Beowulf* was not as believable as the other films. This was not only because it did not meet with expectations – located on the Scandinavian seas far away from castles and agriculture, but also because of the basic ontological question presented by the CGI world. No matter how many details the programmers put in, they could not overcome the fact that they were showing no-place, which undermined the effectiveness of the landscape acting as a reality effect. *The Return of the King* was generally regarded as more believable than *Beowulf*, despite its obvious depictions of a fantasy world rather than our own. That said, participants still bristled at the hypermedievalisms represented by the city of Gondor. Epic films focus on larger-than-life group struggles that play across huge landscapes. But when those landscapes are artificially expanded beyond the realm of reality, it has a noticeable negative effect.

Religion

The final theme discussed by all groups was religion. Each film treated medieval religion differently. In *Beowulf*, religion is used to establish the period and to show cultural and temporal change, with Christianity depicted as taking hold in early-medieval Denmark. *Kingdom of Heaven* brings religion to the fore; religious zeal, which leads to holy war, can be read as the antagonist of the film. In both of these films, Christianity is not seen in a particularly positive light. In *Beowulf*, the antagonistic Unferth becomes a priest (and mistreats his slave, interestingly named Cain). In *Kingdom of Heaven*, Balian's priest in France is avaricious and cruel, the Patriarch of Jerusalem is a religious coward, and the zealous Templars are frothing fanatics. *The Return of the King* deals with religion more obliquely; one of the defining features of medievalist fantasy is its frequent replacement of Christian religion with invented pantheons and magic. Though Gandalf discusses life after death with

Pippin, Christianity (or any form of organised Church) does not exist in Middle Earth.

As could be anticipated, discussions of religion in the films were often shaped by the religious worldviews of the participants themselves. Participants were not sampled by religion, and thus for most of the participants, their religious affiliation (if any) was unknown. Some, like Mark, announced their religion in discussions, but this was the exception rather than the rule. In spite of this, there were occasions where a notably secular perspective on medieval religion was evident when discussing the films.

Disdainful Views of Medieval Religion

William C. Calin rightly points out that:

> Given that this notion – the simple, unproblematic, Christian Middle Ages – did not exist among the medievals [...] it can be deemed an example of medievalism. It is one of the most important medievalism phenomena, for it determines how many academics and the public at large view the Middle Ages – what it means to them.[43]

Many participants held this very view of medieval religion identified by Calin, of it being 'simple, unproblematic, uniform, communal'.[44] To this, the participants may have also added 'universal': the presence of religion – particularly Christianity – was a key marker of medievalness. Congruent with this, they reacted negatively to any point at which medieval people were shown to be religiously unenthusiastic. To them, medieval people were, by definition, devout. For example, Sean commented:

> I was surprised by some of the Christian references [*in Kingdom of Heaven* and *Beowulf*], actually, and that they were kind of negative in a way [...] I tend to think of everyone being really overly [...] religious. And, not really questioning the church in that sense.

To him, medieval people were not just religious but 'overly' so. Religion in the UK is largely a private matter, so overt religiosity, as he expected of medieval people, was socially unacceptable in his eyes.

Chloe also felt that religion in *Beowulf* was 'completely ignored, which I think it probably wasn't back then'. Erica thought, 'you'd think they'd be more focused on that [religion] but it's like "no it's fine", [they] kind of shunned [shrugged] it off, and [...] it wasn't historically correct'. Justin, Stephen, and Sean felt the negative depiction of religion was 'strange':

Justin: [...] with *Kingdom of Heaven* you definitely saw that religions were very, very important and it did dictate a lot. And, if you compare it to *Beowulf*, in that you didn't really see much religion but you saw the growth of one. But, you didn't really see how something [is] really getting its claws into how things run.

Stephen: Yeah, it's really strange though, because in *Kingdom of Heaven* there was really only one priest, or bishop or whatever, solely. There wasn't many.

Justin: And he was a coward as well!

Stephen: And he was a coward, but I don't think ... I may have been forgetting, but I don't think there were any more priests in that. Other than the one he killed right at the beginning.

While they understand the importance of religion in the medieval world, they have little sense of how the medieval church came to be over the course of the Early Middle Ages, how it began and how it grew. Therefore, they thought they would find a hegemonic Latin church with universal adherence even in *Beowulf*, and were disappointed as a result. Moreover, their perspective is not just secular, but occasionally anti-religious – medieval people were 'overly' religious, the Church is a beast with 'claws' – and yet, while Scott's film seems to have been made from a similar perspective (the clergy are corrupt and too-strong adherence to religion is the source of conflict), they labelled that aspect anachronistic. They looked back on medieval religious sentiment with disdain, but did not expect any medieval people to actually agree with them.

In fact, one of the things Erica felt was most medieval about *Kingdom of Heaven* was how alien the Christian religious practices and attitudes seemed:

The way that death was addressed. Like the religion, where they were [said] 'burn the bodies', and the priest saying, 'you can't do that', because it's not the right way to bury them. You wouldn't have got people saying that now. [...] That seemed pretty medieval, [...] when right at the beginning where Orlando Bloom's wife got her head chopped off so she would be headless in hell, and stuff like that. [...] there's a lot more religious aspects to death [then] than you would get now [...] a lot more myth around death and heaven and hell than there is now.

Erica seems to infer that those religious practices that she did not recognise were accurate depictions of medieval religion. The alien-ness of medieval thought and ritual was, itself, a history effect, where ritual and worldview unrecognisable to her were instinctively believed to be medieval. On the one hand, this is an effective technique for depicting historical difference; she recalled those scenes particularly because they offered something unexpected. On the other hand, these rituals and worldviews are seen as alien, cruel, and stupid. Cutting off Balian's wife's head post-mortem (because of her death by suicide) seems, to us, needlessly cruel. Refusing to burn the bodies of the dead is seen as stupid, due to our modern understanding of the vectors for disease. Thus, while *Kingdom of Heaven*'s presentation of medieval ritual presents a moment where viewers can encounter a historical 'other', they come away thinking of that other as stupid and barbaric.

Chloe's feeling of alienation to medieval religious practices included ritual, ceremony, and 'myth' – which she believed to be absent in current Christianity. The word 'myth', as used by her, is telling. While the term can be used neutrally to describe any sacred storytelling, she uses the word to imply that Christian beliefs in the supernatural are 'other', superstitious or false – part of an alien culture or one long dead.[45] For her, death has been divested of ritual in the modern world. That is broadly inaccurate; even secular British people participate in a range of rituals surrounding death. It is likely, then, that much like her perception of 'myth', she does not critically regard the activities of her own culture. Other times and places are full of bizarre 'myth' and 'ritual'. Hers, less so.

Robert also compared medieval religious belief and practice to its modern counterparts. But he took a somewhat more nuanced approach:

> These days it's ... not so black and white. You can believe in
> Christianity, but not believe everything about it. But that
> [medieval Christianity] is more like – they believe that you were
> going to hell, so the practices in their lives were kind of designed
> towards that belief: heaven and hell.

A main difference between the medieval and modern psyche is that, to
Robert, all medieval people believed every aspect of Christianity,
whereas modern people pick and choose the aspects of their religion in
which they choose to believe. Understanding the nature of lay piety
within the Middle Ages is difficult since so many of the sources that
exist were written by clerics. However, Robert assumes that medieval
people were, in essence, fundamentalists, all of whom believed the
same thing. His essentialising seems like a failure of historical
empathy, believing that medieval people were less diverse in their
views than people are today.

Dan and Mark had a very poor opinion of medieval religious
practices, for Mark, stemming in large part from his religious
background. They found that the negative depiction of religion in
Kingdom of Heaven was, thus, accurate:

Dan: I think it displayed a lot of, I'm not sure whether it was
         genuine ignorance from the time, of Christianity, but
         there's a lot of that in there =

Mark: = well, bear in mind that the Latin Bible was in Latin,
         and most peasants couldn't even read their native language.
         So there was a lot of ways for scripture to be misused.

Dan: Well, it didn't even need to be blatantly misused, it was
         just fed to people, and they wouldn't even know most of it
         was =

Mark: = okay, let me rephrase this. They didn't even need
         scripture. Scripture didn't even need to be used, mis- or
         otherwise, to – they could just say what they want to,
         because nobody could contradict them. [. . .]

Dan: Not sure whether that [widespread religiosity in
         Kingdom of Heaven] would have been genuine.
         I couldn't believe that was genuine, in that there was
         very little knowledge of what Christianity was about.

For them, medieval people – particularly the poor – were entirely ignorant, and kept that way by a malicious Church. They thus lauded the film's depiction of malfeasance by the medieval clergy, and miscarriage of what Mark and Dan presumed to be central tenets of Christianity. Thus, medieval Christianity is not a culturally different Christianity from theirs, but rather a 'misused' Christianity, which was fed to a helpless, hapless public. The participants therefore demonstrated an ahistorical view of Christianity. The values they perceive to be central to Christianity and the Christian practices with which they are familiar are the 'correct' ones. Medieval piety is a perversion, or ignorance, of their true church – and they found plenty of evidence to support this in the films.

Religion in The Return of the King

One of the most pronounced differences between *The Return of the King* and the other films is its lack of overt references to religion. Even Tolkien himself received criticism over this, to which he responded:

> The only criticism that annoyed me was one that it 'contained no religion' [. . .] It is a monotheistic world of 'natural theology'. The odd fact that there are no churches, temples, or religious rites and ceremonies is simply part of the historical climate depicted.[46]

The June focus group agreed both with Tolkien's unnamed critics *and* with Tolkien's rebuttal: they argued that there was no explicit religion, however there was 'the sense of a higher power', 'not a creator god, but something', and 'there was a belief that there was more. But there wasn't so much of a structure to focus that belief.' For the participants, religion existed in *The Return of the King*, even without churches or the Church.

Justin and Stephen saw the magic in the film as religiously oriented: 'because you had all these small players like Gandalf who did these amazing things. And you had that Orb thing [the Palantir] that, you know what I mean. There's a very spiritual–' Stephen then interrupted with 'and the miracles, but I don't think it's a very religious link'. To them, Gandalf's spells are 'miracles' and the Palantir is a sort of relic. Mark also felt that 'Gandalf is both priest and wizard', because:

You had him crowning Aragorn, and traditional[ly] that's a role
the Archbishop of Westminster would do. [...] He's also one of
the messengers of the gods. And he's also got all these mystical
names associated with him, which is very medieval priest [...]
[Priests] would have been normally the only one in the village who
could read [...] Words certainly have power, and if you can
understand the words then you might be able to use some of that
quote-unquote power.

To Mark, Gandalf's power is directly related to that of the priest because
both of them have a ceremonial role within secular institutions, act
as divine intercessors, and are seen to have mystical power. This is a
remarkably sophisticated reading of medieval priesthood, despite it
being laced with his typical negative attitudes about medieval religion
and people.

Erica was one of the few to take the opposite viewpoint, not seeing
religion at all in the film. To her, in *The Return of the King:*

They didn't go into it [religion], whereas the other two films was
very, really strongly focused on religion; that was the main aspect
of life. Probably everybody went to church, everybody had a
religion and a faith and they would go to battle for that faith.
Whereas nowadays, most people is atheist.

To her, one of the defining differences between *The Return of the King* and
modern society on the one hand, and the Middle Ages on the other, is
religious belief. She even misremembered *Beowulf* as being 'strongly
focused on religion' in line with her knowledge that religion was a
significant cultural element of the age. This shows the importance of
religion to these participants' view of the Middle Ages: if something
is considered medieval, religion must play a part. Even if it is not
addressed explicitly in a medieval film, viewers will find — even
misremember — religion as a potent force in the story.

These perspectives are illuminating. No matter whether coming from
a Protestant or secular perspective, all of the participants focused on the
inescapable 'otherness' of medieval religion. Historical empathy did not
seem to extend to religious practice whatsoever. Medieval people
were seen universally as zealots and fundamentalists who believed in

'myths' and participated in antiquated rituals. Their church had clawed its way into power and, once there, became abusive and corrupt. Its followers were impossibly gullible, or simply ignorant. This intensely negative reaction to medieval religion – is an obstacle impeding historical empathy and understanding. Religion is a contentious issue in contemporary society, and at the beginning of the twenty-first century remains a key source of conflict and division. If we separate ourselves from our historical forebears by this metric, seeing them as 'other' or even 'lesser' for their religious beliefs, there is little stopping us from doing the same to those of other religions today.

Conclusion: How Did the Participants Learn?

In several ways, the participants saw these films as more alike than different. The films presented three medieval worlds with marked similarities in terms of gender norms, power structures, landscapes, and religious practices. Through each of these lenses, the world the viewers saw is fundamentally different from the one experienced today. This is, of course, one of the things that makes historical films so compelling: they offer the opportunity to imagine, and have imagined for the viewer, a completely different world. But this world is not just different. The medieval world presented in these films was viewed as worse than the contemporary world in almost every conceivable way.

This raises a number of concerns from an educational perspective. Observing the participants' reactions to the films, it was rare for those films to fundamentally differ from their previous perceptions of the past. In many of those instances, the gulf between their expectation and the film was explained away as a deviation from reality by the film. Far more commonly observed were instances where the information provided in the films added nuances to their already existing ideas. Both of these are classic examples of Piaget's *assimilation* process (as discussed in Chapter 3).

As perhaps expected (but nevertheless important for historians and educators to remember), these individuals brought themselves to their interpretations of these films. Perspectives of the treatment of women in films were assessed not just against their knowledge about the period, but their experience as a woman or man, and their perception of gender norms today. Their judgements of medieval religion were not solely based on their knowledge of medieval religious practices, but also on their experience of living in a largely secular society and their personal religious beliefs. Even the landscape is not immune to personal perspective. Despite the likelihood that at least a few participants grew up in towns and cities with medieval origins, castles were regarded as far more medieval because of their iconic status. The medieval world – in general and in these films – was English because these participants were.

Overall, though each participant reported learning different things from these films, most reported learning from the experience of watching films, discussing them and sharing their ideas about the past. As they viewed more films, their ideas became more sophisticated as they combined ideas drawn from each film. This demonstrates how viewers of medieval films learn. Little learning seems to occur from one film in isolation. But far more learning was observed when examining several films in conversation with each other, such as in their ideas about medieval sea travel. This learning process became most apparent when they discussed these emerging ideas in conversation with the broader context of their educations, their other experience with the period, and their worldviews. It is through the repetition of these consonant ideas and images – whether in films or through other medievalisms – that new intellectual frameworks are created, by way of Piaget's *accommodation* learning process.

Ultimately films can, and do, have a profound impact upon the broader public's historical consciousness of the Middle Ages. However, the way in which they affect that consciousness varies from individual to individual. After viewing the films, participants often reported understandings of the Middle Ages which were strikingly similar to how they had been depicted in the films, acting as a prosthetic memory; sometimes they were self-aware that the films were the source of their interpretation, but often this process seemed to be acting at an unconscious level.

CHAPTER 7

DISCUSSION, CONCLUSIONS, AND LOOKING FORWARD

People rarely behave in exactly the ways anticipated by even the most sophisticated theories. But one of the greatest benefits of qualitative research is in revealing the surprising, nuanced, and often unpredictable ways that people actually think and behave. This study was no exception. While some of the results surely confirm what medievalists and educators have found in their anecdotal experiences with their students or the wider public, there were several illuminating surprises where the participants said things that were, at least for me, entirely unexpected.

This final chapter reflects upon the results of the study, drawing out some of the implications of the most significant findings. At the end, it will look down some avenues for research that this line of inquiry opens – both those avenues revealed by the substance of this study specifically, and also the potential applicability of the methodology used in this study to other areas. This study does not offer the definitive scholarly foray into the popular historical consciousness of the Middle Ages, but instead, hopefully, marks a beginning.

Before delving into the conclusions, it is important to recall, first, the limits of what can be drawn from this study (as well as others like it). As described in Chapter 1 (and more fully in the appendices), qualitative research provides an in-depth view of a phenomenon and/or the perspectives of particular research participants. Its intent is to deepen our understanding of events, ideas, and behaviours, not to enable broad conclusions that can be definitively generalised to mathematically circumscribed proportions of the broader population.[1] The nineteen participants in this study held particular perspectives on the past as they understood it, the films they were shown, and the questions they were asked. Since knowledge is determined and influenced socially, it is vanishingly unlikely that they are the only ones to hold such views, especially amongst people like themselves. However, without further research, we cannot say what proportion of people like them (along, for example, the demographic axes of age, class, education, gender, religion, race/ethnicity, etc.) hold the same views. This is both a limitation and an opportunity. How do views of the Middle Ages change from childhood to adulthood and old age? How do ideas about the period vary amongst Christians and Muslims, or among men and women? What effect might participation in a re-enactment group, or a particular political party have on perceptions of the past? The avenues for further exploration are legion.

Another limitation to empirical research such as this is that it was conducted at a particular point in time. Research involving human subjects means, by definition, chasing a moving target. The historical consciousness of British young people is constantly evolving as they have new experiences; while perhaps not *fundamentally* different from those studied here, today's young people have surely been influenced by more recent medievalisms in addition to the ones studied here. This does not render the present research obsolete (certainly no more so than any other published research), but it is important to recognise that it is present research – meaning research in, and on, a particular present moment. Thus, there are ever more avenues for similar research to be considered.

And though it may seem obvious, another limitation to the conclusions drawn here is that this study was conducted by a person. Significant effort was expended to ensure that the data were collected and analysed in a systematic and neutral manner. For example, I never revealed to the participants that I am a medievalist (though some may have guessed so, either based on the topic of the research or with the aid of even rudimentary Googling). As described in Chapter 3, a constructivist approach was used to develop the interview prompts and questions. This meant that the questions and prompts were open-ended, and that in moderating the sessions I consciously tried to avoid influencing the participants' responses, or asking questions that might steer the conversation (such as not asking why they thought Marie

Antoinette or Henry VIII were medieval). I audio-recorded and transcribed all of these groups verbatim. When analysing the data, I read each transcript at least three times in order to ensure, as best possible, that I had understood the full meanings of what was said. It is these precautions, and the other rigorous ways in which this research was conducted, that causes the participants' statements to be considered sound qualitative data rather than simply a collection of anecdotes. Yet, in spite of these precautions, no researcher – especially in the social sciences – can fully remove themselves from their research. All data are interpreted by individuals with a perspective. Thus, the conclusions here may not be the only valid ones that can be drawn from these data. These conclusions are all open to critical engagement.

The Utility of Qualitative Research

The most important conclusion in this book, one that I hope the previous chapters have thoroughly illustrated, is the utility of qualitative research methods for exploring public perceptions of the past. The open-ended nature of this research approach encouraged the participants to grapple with complex issues for which they may not have ready, simple answers. It was the complexity and nuance of their answers that this research sought most to capture. Because of its research methods, this book offers empirical evidence more reliable and useful than anecdotes, surveys of historical ignorance or 'man on the street' interviews. And the most revelatory findings plumbed deep psychological territory inaccessible through quantitative methods like surveys. These methods allowed the participants to express how meaningful the Middle Ages had been made for them, such as Katy's reminiscences of her grandfather teaching her about the Crusades through the art on his wall. They revealed how the Middle Ages had become part of the participants' identity, such as Mark's defining his own Evangelical Protestant Christianity against 'papist' medieval Christianity. And they revealed complex cognitive dissonances, such as the problematic revelation by Justin and Stephen that the medieval Muslim world felt, to them, both cultured and barbaric. This research offers a window into how their historical consciousness affected their perceptions of themselves, their ideas about the world, and their prejudices about others. In short, it revealed how the medieval past was important to these people.

Some historians may not much concern themselves with popular perceptions of the past. But I agree with Richard Utz, who, quoting the late, great medievalist Norman Cantor, said that 'the "ultimate task and obligation of a historian" was to make history "communicable to and accessible by the educated public at large"'.[2] For those academic medievalists, public historians, and educators who believe, like Utz, Cantor, and I do, in the importance of effective history communication, understanding the nuances of the public's understanding of the past – and that *these nuances exist* – is a crucial first step.

The Shape of Knowledge of the Middle Ages

Those readers who opened this book hoping to find participants with detailed and sophisticated understandings of medieval history, or knowledge that neatly matches current academic thinking, are likely disappointed. Most of the participants were tentative in their statements and insecure in their knowledge. When they did assert themselves, they had many misperceptions of the period and were prone to anachronistic thinking. Presentism was rife in their statements, as was a condescending view of both the past and the people in it.

Alienation and Condescension

In the pre-film discussion, several of the participants invoked an idea of the Middle Ages as a place of adventure, romance, and idyllic fantasy. This arose particularly in conversations about the medievalisms they consumed as children: Disney films, tales of Robin Hood and King Arthur, or school trips to heritage sites. However, this view of the medieval world was not generally reflected either in the films they were shown, or their interpretations of those films. Far more common, particularly in their post-film discussions, was an overriding sense of negativity towards the Middle Ages in general, and medieval people in particular.

They derided the Middle Ages for its perceived barbarity, lack of scientific advancement, and outmoded religious practices. There was consistent focus on the period as bloody, disease ridden, poverty-stricken, backward, and marked by oppressive rulership. This is consistent with a common thread in many medievalisms, as described by Louise D'Arcens: 'The first kind of presentism subscribes to a progressivist model of history, in which the medieval past has been superseded by modernity; the Middle

Ages is depicted using the standards of the present and found wanting.'[3]
L.P. Hartley famously wrote, 'The past is a foreign country: they do things
differently there.'[4] To these participants, the Middle Ages were not just a
foreign country, but a developing one. This allowed them, sometimes
explicitly, sometimes implicitly, to indulge in a presentist, Whiggish
schadenfreude, feeling smugly confident of their position at the ever-
improving apex of human progress.

The consistent presentist condescension amongst the participants
towards historical 'others' is a problem, and exposes an area where
medievalists should seek to shift popular views. For many of these
participants, medieval people were not just different, but worse. As a
result, they were worthy of casual derision. Justin's offhand assertion
(discussed in Chapter 5) that England has always been culturally 'advanced'
on the world stage can be viewed as part of a wider problem: not only did
several participants hold a sense of British (or Western) cultural superiority,
but they judge other cultures negatively if they do not measure up to an
imagined bar of 'advancement'. This raises worrying implications for these
young adults' ability to encounter other cultures – particularly ones with
different religious and cultural practices or standards of living – while
maintaining a sense that the 'others' they encounter are worthy of respect.

Despite film's noted potential as an art form that can inspire or teach
historical empathy, these films did not particularly help to rectify the
participants' feelings of alienation from medieval people. This was
especially true of *Beowulf* and *Kingdom of Heaven*. *Beowulf* offers only
caricatured portraits of medieval people as drunken, brawling fornicators.
Its hero is a case in point – he becomes heroic through his abilities as a
brawler, but is brought low due to his fornicating. *Kingdom of Heaven* posed
people with stereotypically 'medieval' perspective – one which regarded
Crusade positively – as the antagonists, and, according to the participants,
offered only a weak, unrealistic hero to counterpoint them. This reveals one
of the paradoxes inherent in this issue: on the one hand, it is important not
to render medieval people as caricatures that act according to stereotype, as
occurred in *Beowulf*. But in offering a different sort of hero, as *Kingdom of
Heaven* attempted to do, filmmakers risk the character not being seen as
believable. Piaget's theory of learning argues that individuals are far more
likely to disregard information that conflicts with their preconceptions.
That makes it remarkably difficult for filmmakers to present medieval
characters that buck stereotypes but remain believable.

One way to thread this needle might be the use of the 'true story' history effect; by presenting real historical stories, viewers might be more inclined to see a different sort of medieval person as real. None of the films presented in this study were effective at this. *Beowulf* in particular failed to engage the participants empathetically, likely exacerbated by its CGI rendering techniques. The participants pointed out that the CGI became an interfering layer, where they were continually reminded of the film's technological artifice – an artifice that seemed antithetical to the Middle Ages. Further complicating this was that the characters were rendered semi-realistically, falling into the 'uncanny valley'.

This 'uncanny valley' was first described by Masahiro Mori in his article 'Bukimi no tani'. In it, Mori explains the discomfort felt by humans viewing facsimiles of humanity that are almost, but not quite, lifelike.[5] His theory has since been applied to computer-generated renderings of humans in visual media, like the characters in *Beowulf*.[6] For Mori, as robots (and CGI facsimiles of people) are made more and more human-like in appearance and movement, they elicit greater empathetic responses from the people who view or use them. However, when human facsimiles become almost, but not quite human the response flips to one of revulsion (Figure 7.1). Mori explains:

> The prosthetic arm has achieved a degree of human verisimilitude on par with false teeth. But this kind of prosthetic hand is too real and when we notice it is prosthetic, we have a sense of strangeness. So if we shake the hand, we are surprised by the lack of soft tissue and cold temperature. In this case, there is no longer a sense of familiarity. It is uncanny.[7]

The uncanny valley is that sharp switch from empathy to revulsion and back again. It is felt most when a character skirts along the right edge of the graph in Figure 7.1 – a character that, like some in *Beowulf*, looks real when still, but when moving is not quite normal, or whose skin has beautifully detailed pores, but whose eyes seem cold and dead.

The difficulty many of the participants had empathising with *Beowulf*'s characters can be explained, at least in part, by the revulsion evoked by their place in the uncanny valley.

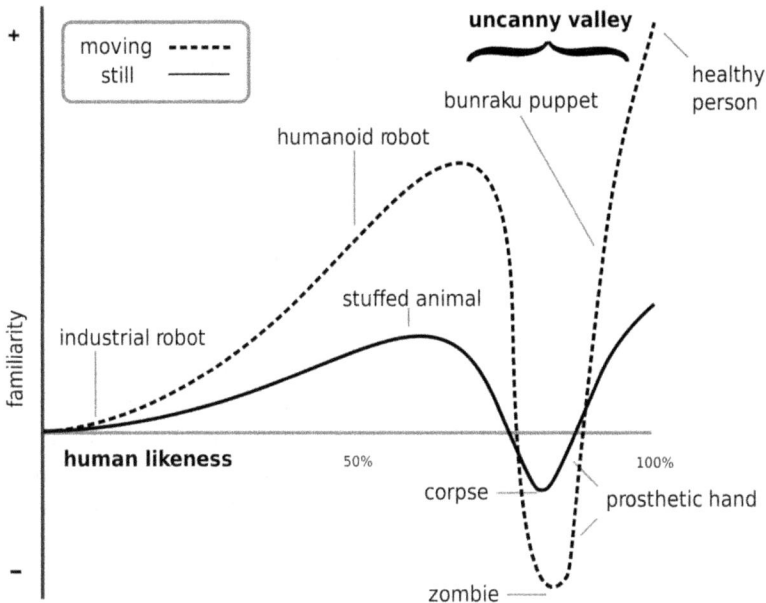

Figure 7.1 Masahiro Mori's 'uncanny valley', graphed on axes of familiarity and lifelikeness.

But even in the live-action *Kingdom of Heaven*, there was no consensus among study participants about whether the characters were based on real people. This is astute of them, and belies their media-savviness, considering how many characters in 'based on a true story' films are amalgamations or outright fabrications. But it reveals a deeper issue. Larger-than-life characters presented in heroic narratives and epic films (such as the ones shown in this study) represent power fantasies rather than people with whom audiences can easily empathise.

The Middle Ages are presented far more often through the medium of heroic epics and fairy tales than through complicated stories featuring real, nuanced people. Robin Hood and King Arthur, for example, were the most commonly cited people in the stream of consciousness exercises, despite being entirely fictional. This mixing of fiction and reality – even leaving the fantasy genre aside – makes it natural to approach reality claims in medieval films like *Kingdom of Heaven*, and in other films like it, with suspicion. Might this be changed? It would require a concerted effort by medievalists to present compelling stories of real medieval people who do not fit the mould of the warrior-hero. This push will likely not originate in the entertainment industry, which currently seems content to recycle past successes rather than offer true novelty and nuance in its medieval narratives. Medieval films seem to be an obstacle to, rather than a facilitator for, truly empathetic connections with historical people. This means that medievalists seeking to create innovative narratives for the public may find their efforts best directed towards other media.

The light and dark interpretations of the Middle Ages are fundamentally similar to the ongoing popular historiographical debates about the period. The Middle Ages were first defined as a backward time by Italian humanists and Enlightenment-era thinkers, but re-forged as an era of adventure, spirituality, light, and beauty by the romantics and fantasists of the nineteenth and twentieth centuries.[8] However, to the participants in the current study, the darker, dirtier image of the age was far more commonly expressed. This clearly relates to larger trends in popular culture, where the film industry currently favours so-called 'gritty realism', particularly in its big-budget epics and franchise films. But this is a trend; it will be fascinating to see whether filmic depictions of the Middle Ages swing back towards the romantic adventures of the 1930s, 40s and 50s, or take some new form in the future – and what effect that will have on popular perceptions.

All of these contradictions in the participants' thinking were understandable considering their backgrounds. By design, the partici-pants of this study had not studied the Middle Ages beyond GCSE level. Most said they had not studied the period – at least academically – since primary school. Furthermore, they frequently looked back with scorn on how history had been taught during that primary school education and, by proxy, the history they had been taught at that time. Despite all this, many of their ways of thinking about history – particularly medieval history – are consistent with the ways history was presented (during their tenures in school) by the English National Curriculum. The strict compartmentalisation of history into discrete periods such as 'The Tudors', 'The Vikings and Saxons', 'The Middle Ages', or 'The Second World War' is one example. Their insular perspectives, in which they frequently defined the Middle Ages as exclusively English or British, is another.

These perspectives instilled sharp borderlines in their historical consciousness – between places and between periods – that do not exist in a medieval context (or, for that matter, in any historical context). Additionally, perhaps as a result of encountering history largely through a 'national' lens, there was very little sense of a local, regional, or personal identification with the medieval past or medieval people; they took little personal ownership of the Middle Ages. None of the participants discussed the medieval features or medieval histories of their home town or region. No one discussed the Middle Ages as personally relevant to their lives, and no one seemed to identify the Middle Ages as a past inhabited by their own ancestors. Despite being surrounded by medieval heritage, the Middle Ages were seen as *a* past, or *the* past, but even to those who found great interest or meaning in it, not *their own* past.

The Silver Lining

Even bearing the misconceptions held by the participants in mind, this study should not be construed as a 'survey of public historical ignorance' such as those discussed in Chapter 1. Those approaching this study expecting to see a populace of know-nothings, entirely ignorant and undiscerning about medieval culture, or caring little about history and believing everything they see on screen, may be surprised.

Although few participants recounted specific persons, events, or dates (barring those related to Robin Hood or King Arthur) in their pre-film discussions of the period, several revealed areas in which their perceptions of the Middle Ages were remarkably detailed, and in which they had a passionate interest. Encouragingly, many of the participants seemed genuinely to *care* about the Middle Ages. Despite not relating the medieval to their ancestors, their locality, or their region, the Middle Ages were clearly meaningful for many of these participants. Strong viewpoints were common. Many recalled with delight those instances they remember learning about the Middle Ages, either from participatory experiences in school, trips to historical sites, learning with and from their families, or consuming medievalisms in their spare time.

These individuals are ideal audiences for well-crafted public engagement with historical scholarship. Over the past decade, publicly engaged scholars have found audiences hungry for good content on the internet. For example, the popular YouTube video series 'Crash Course' offers entertaining, well-produced history lessons at a high-school level.

At the time of writing, their video on the Crusades has been viewed over three million times; their video exploring the myth of the 'Dark Ages' has been viewed over 3.5 million times.[9] Blogs, podcasts, and twitter feeds featuring medieval content have achieved successes in direct public engagement as well.[10] And while the age of free content on the internet offers its own set of challenges, it proves that there are audiences hungry for rigorous historical scholarship presented in an approachable, entertaining manner.

Additionally, many of these participants were voracious consumers of popular culture; much of their knowledge of the Middle Ages originated there. This may elicit concerns, since popular culture's images of the Middle Ages are often divorced from historical reality. Even more concerning was the fact that most participants simply could not remember the sources of their knowledge, making it more difficult for them to critically examine their own knowledge. All that being said, however, their consumption of popular medievalisms shows a powerful potential for education, particularly for medievalists who can positively engage with the entertainment industries. Doing so has been notoriously difficult, as several disenchanted historical advisors for TV and film have reported.[11] The entertainment industries engage their audiences in vastly different ways than do the writers of academic histories; adaptation to a new medium (and the needs of a commercial enterprise) are necessary, and seem to be more difficult than it may first appear. The question remains whether best practices can be established whereby academics and entertainers can work together productively, rather than at odds with one another.

Perhaps a more realistic goal would be for historians to engage directly with interested groups of fans; as Richard Utz recently implored,

> Knowing what we know now about our own academic and other non-academic selves' enthusiasm for the medieval past, I think we should pursue more lasting partnerships with so-called amateurs and enthusiasts for the sake of a sustainable future engagement with medieval culture.[12]

In his book, *Medievalism: A Manifesto*, from which that quotation is drawn, Utz outlines several 'interventions' – ways in which scholars of the Middle Ages could productively engage with popular medievalisms.[13] As another positive example, the popular computer game series *Total War* (mentioned by some of the participants as a favourite), spawned a community of amateur programmers who released a number of overhauls of these games (called 'mods'). One of these was titled *Medieval: Total Realism*.[14] As part of the project, a team of historians and programmers modified core elements of the game that they felt did not fit with the historical record, and removed what they considered to be deviations from history made for the purposes of game balance or excitement. Many other games (including but not limited to those depicting the Middle Ages) have had similar 'modding' projects, for example *Crusader Kings II*, the *Civilization* series, *Mount & Blade Warband: Napoleonic Wars*, and *World of Tanks*.

This illustrates the importance that some fans and players place on 'getting it right', since creating these mods takes considerable effort by a community, and several of the mods have been downloaded frequently. Furthermore, Helen Young, in her study of the debates around diversity among players of the *Dragon Age* fantasy game series, found 'Players on both sides of the diversity debate place a high level of value on the game-world representing the Middle Ages in ways they consider historically authentic.'[15] That such concerns are present even among fans of fantasy medievalisms shows the degree to which there is a hunger for the authentic within the gaming community. While deviations from history in popular culture are perhaps inevitable, historians can, and should, engage and collaborate more fully with interested fans as mediators and co-creators of their own versions – not by only decrying historical inaccuracies, but by proposing and programming their own compelling versions. But this need not be limited to historical games. While working directly with Hollywood may be impossible for many historians, the internet is rife with venues – through podcasts, blogs, videos, and more – where historians can collaborate with those seeking to bring history to life for the public.

Implications for the Classroom

Educators reading this study may have much to consider as well. On the one hand, it was clear that many of the 'facts' that these individuals had been taught about the Middle Ages in their childhood history classes had not been retained. This is likely no surprise to most teachers.

However, this should not be construed as a reinforcement of the perennial call for so-called 'facts-based' history education, which Michael Gove emphasised in the 2011 revisions to the English National Curriculum.[16] The finding that most of the participants had forgotten many of the 'facts' they may have learned in school does not necessarily mean they were never taught them, but instead that there was no continuing need to remember, or that they were not taught in an engaging manner. Those historical facts they did recall were those that were relevant to their interests and reinforced by later consumption of medievalisms – whether the medieval martial history offered in computer games, or the social history depicted in historical fiction films and novels.

On the other hand, the broad paradigms about the past established by the English National Curriculum, such as the focus on national history and the (often confused) sense of periodisation, were retained. Similarly, some lessons imparted by favourite teachers were remembered vividly and fondly: Justin and Stephen's teacher's lessons on Beowulf, or the multisensory, experiential living-history lessons recounted so passionately by Eleanor, Elizabeth, and Jane. This clearly illustrates the lasting effect that good history education can have, and its power to shape frameworks for understanding the past. The participants' patchy knowledge about the basics of the Middle Ages (such as when the period was, what its defining features were, and what distinguished it from what came before and after) may demand a shift of emphasis. It implies a need for context, and a better understanding of larger narratives of cultural establishment and change from which children (and adults) may then hang their knowledge.

Most of the learning observed in this study was done through the mechanism Piaget called *assimilation*, where new information was reshaped or misremembered in order to fit prior frameworks of understanding. This reveals the critical importance of childhood learning in establishing broad historical consciousness, since it is at this early stage that these resilient schematic frameworks are established. For academic medievalists looking to shift and shape popular ideas about the past, collaborating with early education systems – whether to help shape curricula, write textbooks, or work with individual teachers – could be a fruitful endeavour. The participants' vivid memories of school and family trips to heritage sites also highlight the importance, for academics, of rigorous engagement with public historians and the heritage industry and the effectiveness, for teachers, of these field trips.

Learning from Medieval Film

Another major finding of this study for educators is that the participants actually learned from viewing these films. What they learned, and its relationship with academic understandings of the past, varied. But, *they did learn*. This learning occurred despite many of the participants' cynicism about the validity of the historical content in the films. Such cynicism is certainly understandable in the case of *The Return of the King*. But interestingly, despite their initial protestations about the fictional nature of *The Return of the King*, many participants readily used what they were shown in that film when discussing the Middle Ages in the plenary discussion – some even going so far as to see *The Return of the King* as a superior depiction of the Middle Ages by contrast with the other films. This shows that learning often happens unconsciously. There is enough visual, narrative, and iconic similarity between fantasy films like *The Return of the King* and medieval historical films that fantasies can become part of the popular historical consciousness. This can occur despite any apparent cognitive dissonance.

The participants' cynicism about films correlates neatly with the findings from *The Presence of the Past* study, in which, as explored in Chapter 3, historical films were ranked very low in terms of the trustworthiness of the historical information they presented, but, despite this, were still consumed extensively. This seeming paradox sheds some light on what may be an obvious point: many, perhaps most, people do not view historical films primarily to learn historical facts. Neither *The Presence of the Past* nor the study at the centre of this book asked why people choose to watch historical films. But the answer seems to lie somewhere within the interpersonal, emotional, empathetic, and affective pleasure of a good film, coupled with the magnifying effect offered by the knowledge that they are viewing something which is, at least to some degree, *real*. And even those who do come for the history find many good reasons to opt for a film over a text. Unlike an academic text, films are easily consumed over a relatively short period of time, and require little or no foreknowledge of the subject (or specialist vocabulary). And, a factor not to be underestimated, they are designed to be enjoyable.

Participants' perceptions of a film's realism or 'historical accuracy' were often not based on an overall impression of the film, but upon dissection of particular scenes, objects, characters, and narratives.

This contrasts what William Woods wrote in his article 'Authenticating realism in medieval film':

> When viewers argue the authenticity of a film or the lack of it, they usually mean realism based upon decorum or fittingness. [...] What is interesting is not how seldom Hollywood makes such a mistake [...] but how unusual it is that a lapse of authenticity tears the fabric of the viewer's sense of the authentic.[17]

Several of the viewers found the 'fabric of [their] sense of the authentic' torn, though more often by a deviation from their expectation of historical realities or a deviation from their expectations of a film of this type, rather than deviations from any externally validated historical authenticity. For these viewers, the line between reality effects and history effects often blurred in their judgements of a particular scene, narrative, or character.

However, this does not mean that judgements of individual elements and overall impressions were not linked; an overall judgement that the film was poorly made often had repercussions on their judgement of the rest of the film. For example, Jess felt that *Beowulf* was a bad film (and said so repeatedly). As a result, she often judged it to be historically inaccurate. This judgement seems to have been based upon her displeasure with the film rather than independent of it. In other words, an entertaining, well-made film is far more likely to be accepted as historically accurate than one that is poorly made, no matter its actual relationship to the historical record.

Evidence for this comes from the fact that participants often couched their negative reactions to the film in historical terms, even when their criticisms were not about history-related elements. For example, many criticised the accents in *Beowulf* or Orlando Bloom's effete manner in *Kingdom of Heaven* as not reflective of historical realities. But these were more violations of their expectations of historical films and medievalisms than deviations from history. It is possible that this opinion was influenced by the focus group setting: since the topic was *historical* film they may have felt that their criticisms should centre on history (though they often did not). However, it is also possible that a film's adherence to historical film genre tropes acts as a history effect. This adherence, in turn, can lend a film credibility as a type of historical text. Thus, deviations from genre can be misconstrued by viewers as a deviation from history. This may imply that people conflate their expectations of media histories with their understanding of history in general; this warrants further study. Do people really believe that medieval people spoke with RP English accents, and that historical heroes conformed to current standards of masculinity? These expectations may be limited to the context of medieval film, but they may also be transferred to depictions of the medieval in other media. The public's ideas about medieval culture or behaviour in film may be related more to their ideas about what makes a 'good' medieval film than any professed concerns about historical accuracy – but this requires further exploration.

Contradictorily, however, those moments in the films that seemed to evoke the most excitement among participants (and which were recalled most readily in the discussions) were those which both confirmed an aspect of their prior knowledge of the Middle Ages and also were perceived to violate 'Hollywood' conventions. There was a common perception that 'Hollywood' (as a stand-in for the financial concerns of the producers, or filmic and generic tropes) has a negative impact on films – despite the unacknowledged fact that, in a very real way, films could not be made without them. But bucking those concerns and trends in a limited fashion was, itself, a type of history effect.

Participants' previous knowledge of the period was often a greater influence on their interpretation of the film than what they saw. This shows that viewing each film seemed to be largely an exercise in Piaget's *assimilation* (as explored previously) – meaning that the information that was retained was that which corresponded to prior expectations, and deviating information was either explained away or discarded. Participants sometimes constructed false memories of the film – even mere moments after the film's credits rolled – that better matched their expectations. Thus, individual films promoted learning, but primarily by reinforcing rather than revising ideas about the Middle Ages. This cuts both ways; on one hand, it offers a way for filmmaker-historians to make the historical content in their films be more impactful. The content simply needs to correspond with prior ideas already held about the Middle Ages, ideally shown as a contravention of generic tropes. The negative aspect of this, of course, is that real learning – meaning the establishment and acceptance of new paradigms and schematic structures in their historical consciousness – is far harder to accomplish.

The few times that those larger paradigms and structures about the Middle Ages were observed changing (via *accommodation*) seemed to be during the conversations at the end of the third day in which they compared and contrasted the three films. During these conversations, it became apparent that aspects common to each film – for example, a focus on the isolated city in a barren medieval landscape – were far more likely to shift paradigms. One individual film, viewed in isolation, may have relatively little impact beyond further entrenching existing views. But several films – or films acting in concert with other sources of information – can offer a foundational shift, at least for regular consumers of medievalisms. Efforts among historians to change popular narratives about the period thus require a broad-based approach, focusing not just on one film, but many – and not just on films, but on every form of medievalism. And most importantly, it requires repeated, concerted effort over the long term.

Teaching with Medieval Film

Though this study was done outside of school hours, it has implications for educators looking to use medieval films within their classrooms. The student participants were shown films without any sort of curricular or pedagogical scaffolding. As a result, as explored above, the learning that they achieved from these films was extremely provisional, and relied heavily on their existing historical consciousness. The conclusions that they came to about the past were as often incorrect as they were correct. This reinforces the conclusions of the studies of historical films cited in Chapter 3, which found that students learn far more effectively from historical films when there is pedagogical scaffolding, where a teacher guides students through the processes of understanding what was invented by the filmmakers and what is reflective of historical realities. This is a crucial part of acquiring media literacy.

Much has been written, particularly in the wake of the political upheavals of 2016 (and the proliferation of 'fake news'), of the need for improved media literacy education.[18] Teaching historical films can play an important part of this. As discussed in Chapter 3, Scott Alan Metzger argued that historical films should not simply be used in the classroom to help teach historical content, but to teach important aspects of historical literacy like cultural positioning, narrative analysis, and an understanding of presentism; essentially, these films should be taught as texts. However, historical films are not just historical texts, but media texts as well, and the self-same lessons that teach cultural positioning and narrative analysis can be applied when critically analysing any piece of media. In essence, fictionalised histories are not so dissimilar from 'fake news'. Learning to critically engage with historical films could help students critically engage with other mediated narratives.

That having been said, as discussed above, the true educational power of historical films is not just that they can be entertaining conveyors of historical content, or texts for critical dissection. Rather, they can – and should – be used as a way to promote excitement about the past that may put them on a path towards a life of learning. They can be part of a curriculum that seeks not just to teach historical 'facts', but helps them better understand themselves and their world.

Onward

This book, focusing as it does on the historical consciousness of nineteen British university students, is admittedly only the beginning of the empirical exploration of public medievalism. The field of research using qualitative methods to study public medievalism, and historical consciousness more widely, should be expanded. Further avenues of exploration could be geared towards different age groups – of particular interest is the presentation to and reception of the medieval past by children (both within and outside school). It could also be fruitful to examine the historical consciousness of the Middle Ages among people of different demographic (national, racial/ethnic, class, religious) backgrounds. This study was limited to British-identified people in higher education, who were likely to have had middle- or upper-class upbringings. Hence, the results cannot be generalised to people of other backgrounds; it is very likely that Italians would feel different about medieval religion, or that Egyptians would feel differently about the Crusades. It might be that Americans, who consume much of the same media that these English people did, would likely have some similar responses to these British participants. However, America's non-medieval heritage, coupled with the medievalisms offered in popular carnivalesque 'renaissance faires', might render vastly different interpretations. As has been the guiding principle of this research, it is important to test their hypotheses rather than assume their accuracy. If this study is any indication, there will be a range of differences among ostensibly similar groups that could provide fascinating insights. It would also be helpful to take account of different class, ethnic, religious, or educational backgrounds, to more thoroughly explore how historical consciousness is informed by social context.

Film is only one of many popular-cultural influences on historical consciousness. The participants of this study named a number of sources for their understandings, including novels, video games, TV shows, museum trips, and more. With some adaptation, the methods used in this study could be employed to study the effects of any encounter with medievalism. This research framework could also be used to study the historical consciousness of other periods. The English media have a perennial love affair with Regency and Victorian narratives; the American media have seen a recent resurgence of the depiction of the Classical world and the World Wars. These all merit vigorous study.

A research programme involving just a few of these various permutations could comprise a life's work, or many, and it is my hope that the approach outlined in this book will be taken up by others. The work is valuable because it allows academics to understand better what people – whether their incoming students or the public with whom they are increasingly encouraged to interact – think about the past, and why. This information could help scholars, public historians, and educators to invent better ways to meet the public on their own terms, rather than condescending or overshooting the mark. A related lesson awaits politicians responsible for education and curriculum content.

The results of sociological studies, located as they are in one time and place, are doomed always to obsolescence – or, perhaps more generously, are a snapshot of an historical moment. As each new piece of imaginative medievalism is released, and as each generation is introduced to our collective imaginary Middle Ages, the historical consciousness shifts. Each subsequent study done will be another cultural snapshot: not of the present, but of a present culture that quickly becomes the past. That does not mean that such studies should be done less, but instead, more, and with greater frequency. If many such snapshots are taken, they can give a better and better image of how and why cultural ideas of the Middle Ages (or indeed of any historical period) change. Once assembled, a sort of 'moving image' emerges, an image of how and why the historical consciousness evolves over time, one that is constantly changing and being changed by the cultures and minds in which it resides.

APPENDIX A

USING SOCIAL SCIENCE METHODS TO STUDY HISTORICAL CONSCIOUSNESS

To build theories about past events and cultures, historians rely on the evidence to hand coupled with some logical or imaginative speculation.[1] This is the necessary default since the people in question are no longer alive. By contrast, studying the current public's historical consciousness provides a rare opportunity to use empirical data-gathering methods in order to develop, test, and refine theories. Instead of deducing or imagining what people may have thought, felt, or understood, a researcher of the current public's historical consciousness can simply ask them. However, in order to have any validity this needs to be done in a rigorous, systematic manner.

Social scientists in a number of cognate disciplines have developed an array of methods for this very purpose. Since these methodologies have been so well described elsewhere, what follows will be a brief overview of the methodological possibilities available to a researcher interested in conducting studies of this sort, with references to relevant volumes on the topic for further reading.

Quantitative Methods

Broadly speaking, there are two types of method for this type of research: *quantitative* and *qualitative*. Quantitative methods are those wherein numbers are counted; the classic example is a census, where a large number of people report on their various personal attributes. Data are gathered through multiple-choice or fill-in-the-blank questions and analysed using statistics – ideal for very large data sets. Most surveys, questionnaires and polls are fundamentally quantitative. Modern elections, in theory, bestow their resulting governments with validity and authority based upon the power of a quantitative survey. As a result of the mathematical basis of these methods, studies of this sort strive for statistical verifiability. Without delving into the mathematical details, this rests upon the idea that a smaller number of people *truly randomly selected* from a desired population (a sample) will respond in the same way as the whole group, within a relatively small percentage margin of error.[2]

This statistical verifiability bestows 'external generalisibility' – that the properties and opinions of the few can, roughly speaking, be assumed to also be the properties and opinions of the many. When this external generalisibility is coupled with a good research design, it can offer to the results the weight of significance – if a study is backed by true external generalisiblity, then the value of the claims and conclusions drawn from it increases.[3]

This is the ideal scenario. It is easy to think of occasions where this can go wrong. Election results can fail to match public opinion polls ('Dewey defeats Truman'). A product, despite vigorous market research, may fail to sell. This mismatch of research and reality could be for many reasons: a research instrument which does not address the relevant issues, has a skewed sample, offers leading (or misleading) questions, or simply reflects the changes between the time of the survey and the present. Simply put, surveys cannot predict the future; at their best they can only reveal the present.

With these considerations in mind, a well-designed quantitative study can answer interesting questions about how the public engages with the past. These methods have been most often used in the past to study the proportion of the population who correctly answer a series of questions about history (which, in Chapter 1, I term 'surveys of historical ignorance') – but this is hardly the best use of these methods. These methods could be used, for example, to study how frequently people participate in certain history-related activities (such as viewing historical films or participating in re-enactments). A study could be done to track the degree to which studying history in high school or at university relates to students' later lives, such as in their careers, or their religious or political orientations. Visitors to historic sites could be surveyed to show which aspects of the site's interpretation are most effective. Or, grander surveys could be devised which may help us answer whether public interest in and engagement with history is actually in decline, as is so often opined in the media.

Further Reading: Quantitative Methods

Many useful volumes exist which describe the uses of quantitative methods and how to go about designing studies using them in depth. The most recent editions of the ones I have found most useful are:

Black, Thomas R., *Doing Quantitative Research in the Social Sciences: An Integrated Approach to Research Design, Measurement and Statistics* (London: Sage Publications, 1999).

Fink, Arlene., *How to Conduct Surveys: a Step-by-Step Guide*. Fifth Edition (London: Sage Publications, 2012).

Fowler, Floyd J., *Survey Research Methods*. Fourth Edition. Applied Social Research Methods Series 1 (Thousand Oaks: Sage Publications, 2009).

Groves, Robert M., Floyd J. Fowler Jr, Mick P. Couper, James M. Lepkowski, and Eleanor Singer, *Survey Methodology* (Hoboken, NJ: John Wiley & Sons, 2009).

Schonlau, Matthias, Ronald D. Fricker, and Marc N. Elliott, *Conducting Research Surveys via E-mail and the Web* (Santa Monica, CA: Rand, 2002).

Qualitative Methods

Quantitative methods are excellent at counting numbers of people, establishing long-term trends and establishing mathematical certainty in results. But they are not as effective at exploring subjective matters of opinion with nuance. Quantitative surveys often measure matters of opinion along a rubric that can be rendered into numbers – rating reactions to a political candidate or a brand of soda on a scale of one to five. While this makes the results easily comparable to one another, it can flatten any subtlety or complexity. It is in exploring these shades and nuances that qualitative methods shine.

Qualitative research methods are used to analyse data not easily rendered into numbers or statistics, such as interviews (whether individual or group), observations, or documents. Some quantitative surveys will have free-response sections where the respondents are allowed to voice their opinions with fewer restrictions than with strict multiple choice; these data are often analysed with qualitative methods. Whereas quantitative methods are used to gather a relatively small amount of data from a large number of people, qualitative methods specialise in gathering in-depth data from individuals or small groups. Furthermore, qualitative research that includes interviews or focus groups allows for the interrogation of ideas; the researcher can ask follow-up questions, explore subtleties of meaning or even press a participant for a difficult answer. Qualitative methods specialise in addressing different sorts of research questions than quantitative ones. Quantitative methods can help answer 'who' or 'how many'. Qualitative methods are better at answering questions regarding 'how' a person thinks or feels, and – most compellingly – 'why'. Furthermore, while quantitative methods seek to answer questions already well-defined by the researchers, qualitative methods excel at exploring less well understood areas of knowledge. Because of the discursive nature of qualitative methods, the researcher can ask open-ended questions that allow the participants to respond in their own words, rather than according to the metrics provided by a survey.

However, qualitative research does have its pitfalls. Even short interviews, when converted from recording to transcript, can quickly become a large amount of data. For this reason, sampling sizes for qualitative research are much smaller than in quantitative studies. It is not unusual to see studies conducted with fewer than twenty people, or even as few as one. The fewer the people, the more data is required from each. However, as the saying goes, 'the plural of anecdote is not data'. So what is to prevent qualitative research from merely being a collection of anecdotes? With such a small data set, how does the researcher counter claims of insignificance? One solution can be in gathering particularly meaningful data through 'purposeful sampling'; while qualitative research may not be able to speak for large populations, it may be able to speak for a smaller population which has a unique or important perspective, or provide an in-depth view of a complex phenomenon.[4] Attitudes on the HIV virus amongst the general populace are interesting, but even more interesting may be in-depth studies of the attitudes about the virus amongst people immediately after being diagnosed with it.

Another at least partial solution to the question is repetition. One qualitative study will not be able to say what exact percentage of the population believes a certain thing – and will not try to do so. However, if the researcher has the resources to conduct interviews until the point where few novel responses emerge with each new transcript, it is possible to say that the range, if not proportion, of ideas has been explored. Or, another tack that is sometimes taken is to use the data gathered by qualitative methods to develop and deploy subsequent quantitative studies. However, researchers rarely have the time, funding and support to comprehensively explore ideas on a certain topic, especially if it is a broad one. In those scenarios, it may be necessary for the qualitative researcher to accept that their data may not necessarily be comprehensive, but neither is it insignificant. Archaeologists rarely have the time or funding to excavate an entire site, but they make educated guesses about where to dig that may yield productive finds. In archaeology, this is called a 'grab sample' technique – in qualitative research it is called 'purposive sampling'.[5] Just because the findings do not tell the entire story of a dig site, or a population, does not mean that they have nothing to say. Similarly, so long as they are treated with some caution in terms of the breadth of the conclusions reached about them, even non-exhaustive qualitative research can present tentative findings, point to new areas of research or unearth theories that can be confirmed with further investigation. And even limited external generalisibility may still be garnered from the results; it is almost assured that the participants who believed them are not alone – especially those ideas which recur frequently in the research.[6]

So what questions might qualitative studies be able to answer about the public understanding of the past? First, these methods are well-equipped to explore the basic question 'What does the public understand about the past', especially if 'the public' is defined in a meaningful way; a study exploring how survivors of the Blitz interpret history, or how historical re-enactors view the period they (re)create could be compelling. Well-designed qualitative studies could also explore and add nuance to the various ways in which the public engages with the past. How do people relate history – both the recent and distant past – to their gender, racial/ethnic, national, or religious identity? Why do people participate in modern-day pilgrimages to historic sites? How does consuming popular-cultural escapist historical fantasies affect an individual's understanding of the past? How might historical narratives contribute to prejudice and hatred in the contemporary world? Qualitative methods could also be used to explore how primary, secondary, or higher history education influences interpretations of present events. In sum, studies of this type could help us to begin to answer the question 'Why is the past important to us?'

Further Reading: Qualitative Methods

Many volumes exist which are useful for designing and implementing qualitative research studies. The most recent editions of the ones I have found most useful are:

Berg, Bruce L., *Qualitative Research Methods for the Social Sciences*. Sixth Edition (Boston: Pearson, 2007).

Maxwell, Joseph Alex., *Qualitative Research Design: An Interactive Approach*. Third Edition (Thousand Oaks, CA: Sage Publications, 2012).

Merriam, Sharan B., *Qualitative Research: A Guide to Design and Implementation* (San Francisco, CA: John Wiley & Sons, 2009).

Morrison, David E., *The Search for a Method: Focus Groups and the Development of Mass Communication Research* (Luton: University of Luton Press, 1998).

Strauss, Anselm L., and Juliet M. Corbin., *Basics of Qualitative Research: Techniques and Procedures for Developing Grounded Theory*. Second Edition (Thousand Oaks: Sage Publications, 1998).

APPENDIX B

METHODOLOGY OF *THE MIDDLE AGES IN POPULAR IMAGINATION* STUDY

The purpose of this study was to explore how the public understanding of the Middle Ages is shaped by big-budget films. This study set out to answer these research questions:

(1) How do British undergraduates (with no GCSE or higher academic qualifications in history) describe their understanding of the Middle Ages?
  a. Is there a difference between their understanding of the term 'medieval' and 'Middle Ages' and, if so, what?
  b. What experiences in their lives, past or present, do participants describe as influencing their understanding of the Middle Ages?
(2) What role do medieval films play in these students' understanding of the Middle Ages?
  a. Specifically, what role do recent (defined as released during the period 2000–9), popular medieval films have on participants' understanding?
  b. How do these films compare to participants' previous understanding of the period?
  c. What occurs when the film coincides with or conflicts with participants' previous knowledge?

Data were collected from four groups of undergraduates from the University of Leeds. These four groups were recruited from the general campus population (not as part of an in-class activity) using campus mailing lists and flyers, and met after-hours in a room on campus. Each group met three times (meaning twelve sessions were done in total), and each group had between 3–6 participants, with nineteen participants in total.

Upon recruitment, potential participants were sent a demographic questionnaire which screened out anyone who had studied the Middle Ages at GCSE level or above, those who did not self-identify as 'British', those who had not studied exclusively in the UK, and individuals who had not seen at least three recent films which portray the Middle Ages.

A pilot of the study was conducted in November of 2008. The pilot group consisted of five women. This group met once for a ninety-minute discussion that focused exclusively upon research questions 1a and 1b. The group began with a word-association exercise, where each participant was given a page with either the word 'medieval' or the words 'Middle Ages' at the top. They were then asked to write down anything they associated with the words beneath it. Half the participants were first given 'medieval' and half were first given 'Middle Ages', and after they completed the exercise, they then repeated the exercise for the other word. The point of this exercise was threefold. Firstly, it served as an icebreaker, to prompt participants' thinking about the topic and to give them reference points upon which they could base their later discussions. Secondly, it provoked a consideration of the semantic differences between 'medieval' and 'Middle Ages'. Finally, it produced individual responses before any group interaction and discussion. These responses were therefore free from the inclinations towards consensus or conflict which commonly occurs during group discussions.

Next, participants were split into two groups. They were provided with another sheet containing an oval with the words 'medieval' or 'Middle Ages' in the centre, and asked to create 'concept maps' based upon their responses to the word association and rank how important each element was to the central concept.[1] Each group then shared its scheme and ranking system. This exercise was meant to allow participants to express how they believed they organise their schemata, and to explore the nuances of how they defined their ideas based upon their own understanding rather than imposing external definitions. A discussion of these words and their relationship followed, as well as a general discussion about the participants' understanding of the period and the sources of their knowledge. The results of this pilot study were then used to refine the methodology used with subsequent groups.

The subsequent three groups were conducted during the spring of 2009, each with between four and six participants. Each group met on three occasions. For all of these groups, on the first day participants were first interviewed as a group about their understanding of the medieval past (similarly, though in abbreviated form, to the November 2008 group). During this interview, they completed and discussed the above-described word-association exercises. They were then shown the film *Beowulf*.[2] They were next invited to participate in a follow-up discussion. While participants were allowed to raise any issues related to the film, in all groups the researcher also asked questions related to the film's authenticity to the source material, its 'realism' and 'medievalness', and how its depiction of the period compared to participants' expectations.

On the second day, participants were first asked to produce another word-association exercise, this time for the word 'crusade', and discuss what the word meant to them. They then were shown the film *Kingdom of Heaven*. Afterwards, their discussion focused on the medieval aspects of the film and whether they felt it portrayed 'crusade' in a way they expected. The discussion also often included the depiction of knighthood and kingship and how this film compared with *Beowulf*.

On the final day, participants were shown *The Lord of the Rings: The Return of the King*.[3] Due to the length of this film (with a three and a half hour running time), there was no preliminary discussion. Instead, after the film, there was an hour-long discussion focusing on whether the film was realistic, to what degree participants believed the film to be 'medieval', whether the fantastical elements seemed believable, and possible relationships between the fantasy genre and the Middle Ages. This final discussion also included a plenary discussion of all three films, their landscapes, depictions of kingship and knighthood, the role of heroes, the role of women, or any other emergent issues when comparing them.

Each group was asked a similar set of semi-structured interview questions in order to gauge whether, what, and how they had learned from each film. The questions included:

(1)   What about the film seemed particularly medieval to you?
(2)   What about the film seemed less medieval to you?

(3)   What would you change in order to make this film more medieval?

(4)   Do you feel like you learned anything from this movie?

These open-ended questions were designed to allow participants to express themselves freely. Follow-up questions were drawn from the participants' responses. As a result of the open-ended nature of the questions, topics ranged widely, and as a consequence the results reflect this broad scope of interpretations. Also, because of the semi-structured nature of the interview, some spontaneously arising topics were only discussed by one or two of the groups. This does not necessarily mean that other participants would not have felt similarly had these topics been discussed – or that they would have disagreed.

Qualitative Data Analysis Procedures

These data, including the word associations and focus group interviews, were analysed using qualitative thematic analysis methods as described by Joseph Maxwell in *Qualitative Research Design: An Interactive Approach* and Bruce Berg in *Qualitative Research Methods for the Social Sciences*.[4] An inductive approach was used, the aims of which, as David Thomas writes, are 'to aid an understanding of meaning in complex data through the development of summary themes or categories from the raw data', and to thus derive conclusions and theory from those emergent themes and categories.[5] In aid of this, the audio recording of the interviews were transcribed and read at least three times to identify common themes. While reading, the statements had 'codes' applied according to these themes. After this the coded data were organised into substantive thematic categories.[6] Initially, stand-alone themes were identified. The transcripts were then re-read and hierarchical relationships drawn out among the data and thematic categories.

The word-association exercises were also examined for common responses, and a frequency count done of the responses. All responses were then sorted by category in order to explore and identify any emerging sub-themes, contradictions or subtleties. Those themes and subthemes that emerged were then used to make sense of the data.

While it is impossible, and arguably even undesirable, to completely eliminate the influence of the research setting or the researcher from the results of the study, this study relied upon semi-structured, open-ended questions and probes primarily formulated from the participants' previous responses. The interview questions were 'semi-structured' in that, though they were structured by the research design to keep the participants on a particular topic of interest, they were not designed to elicit short-answer responses, and were open-ended enough to allow the respondents to respond freely, structuring their responses however they saw fit.

Research Design Rationale

As discussed, qualitative methods, like those used in this study, have advantages in studies about individual experiences, opinions, or complex social phenomena. They can explore a sociological phenomenon or process in more depth than a poll or survey.[7] Speaking with a participant at length allows the researcher to explore the meaning of what a participant said, to ask follow-up questions and fully to explore the meaning that may be loaded in hesitancy, confusion or other subtle linguistic cues. This may shed further light on a complex issue.[8] Additionally, qualitative methods are useful for exploring new areas of research such as the one present here; at the current stage of research, qualitative methods are required in order to develop the theory that may underpin any further research. Though quantitative data gathering methods, such as surveys, can offer statistical verifiability and reproducibility, they cannot provide the depth of understanding required by this field of enquiry.

This study utilised focus group interview methods; focus groups are a type of moderator-led group interview in which participants are asked to react to and discuss various stimuli. Developed during World War II to evaluate mass response to radio programmes, their employment has since become a useful tool for social-science inquiry.[9] Though there is no set formula for focus groups, they typically have between four and twelve participants, depending upon the demands of the research.[10] For the purpose of this study, focus group research methods offer a few notable advantages over other research methodologies. Firstly, focus groups can acquire data from a larger group of participants in a much more time-

and cost-effective manner than individual interviews. The open-ended format of a focus group also allows the researcher to gather, as Stewart and Shamdasani assert, 'large and rich amounts of data *in the respondents' own words*' (my emphasis).[11] Additionally, the open-ended nature of focus groups allow participants more free rein to, as Barbour and Kitzinger assert, 'generate their own questions, frames and concepts and to pursue their own priorities on their own terms, in their own vocabulary'.[12] Because this study is focused upon a social activity, movie watching, it is well-served by a methodology that is conducted in a social atmosphere which can best replicate the experience of watching and discussing a film.

Watching a film is, at the basic level of interaction between viewer and image, an individual activity. With that said, it is typically done (at least in the context of the cinema) in groups as a social activity. The vibrant discussion after, or even during, the film, is an important way for people to formulate and voice their opinions and structure their interpretation of what they saw. It is thus ripe for exploration within the context of the sociology of knowledge. Though the interaction between the film and the individual is unique to each person, the interpretive discussion that inevitably occurs after the film helps viewers to negotiate the meaning and value of what they have just seen with others. It is this phenomenon into which this research hopes to tap.[13]

Another advantage to using focus groups is the synergistic responses that groups naturally evoke. One participant often prompts a response from their peers, allowing them to 'react and build upon the responses of other group members'.[14] Differences of opinion or agreement can then be brought to the fore and explored within the group, rather than simply left to the analysis of the researcher. Also, the interactive nature of focus groups allows synergy between subjects; when done well, subjects will prompt each other to offer up more thorough input than would be achieved using an individual interview.

In conducting focus groups, certain group behaviours must be discouraged during the session and taken into account in analysis. Firstly, any group interaction provokes the natural sociable desire to form a consensus. Individuals may agree, especially if merely in brief verbal assents, with opinions that they may or may not themselves hold. At times it can be difficult for a researcher to distinguish truly assenting opinions from those which are generated by the group's desire to be agreeable, or the simple 'yeah' or 'uh-huh's which acknowledge polite comprehension rather than true agreement. For this reason the moderator thoroughly explored agreement, and encouraged dissent wherever appropriate during the discussion.

Additionally, for every researcher there exists the problem of group dynamic. As any teacher can attest, often in-group interaction sessions one or two members of any group may dominate the conversation. If this is taken as representative of the larger group opinion, it might over-represent the ideas of those more talkative members. It was important for the moderator, then, to encourage all members to contribute as equitably as possible.

There is always the question of whether or not the respondents are accurately reporting their own thoughts and to what degree the researcher should believe what is said. The researcher must tread a fine line between accepting all which they are told at face value and treating the respondent as if they were a hostile witness to their own experience. It is important for the analysis to explore those internal contradictions that are found in the transcript in order to explore respondents' unconscious ideas. However, it must be taken on faith that if a participant expresses an opinion, unless there is compelling evidence to believe the contrary, they are the best reporters of their own experience.

Selecting Which 'Public': The Sampling Rationale

There is not one 'public'. When 'public history' or 'the public understanding of the past' is discussed academically, there is sometimes an implicit assumption that 'public' is simply defined as those who are not historians. To some degree, this study defines the public similarly. The sample excluded anyone with academic credentials that would give them specialist knowledge. This included any academic study of the period at GCSE level (age 14–16) or higher.[15] In addition to calcifying understanding of the topic, the authority conferred by academic study or qualification might have caused their presence to influence the group.

However, the public are not only those who are not historians, and so I winnowed the field further. This study is also focused on the public who are interested in this type of film. It would be possible to conduct focus groups comprised of persons who never go to the movies or watch TV, but doing so would not provide any insights into how the larger public who are more familiar with visual culture are influenced by the films in question. It would also be less fruitful to study individuals who never see films set in the Middle Ages.[16] Therefore, the screening questionnaire included a list of twenty-two popular medieval or fantasy films. Anyone who had seen fewer than three of these was excluded.[17]

The sample for this study was also limited to persons who self-identified as British and who went to school exclusively in the UK. All participants spontaneously further specified that their nationality was English and had studied exclusively in England (meaning most had similar curricula at school).

Using undergraduate students from the University of Leeds makes certain demographic characteristics implicit in the sample. Students from the University of Leeds are all academically successful enough to gain entry (though departmental requirements vary). All completed GCSEs and A Levels to a high standard. Members of the student body are, on average, from middle-class backgrounds, and students from the north of England predominate. With that said, region of origin and economic class were not considered in the sampling strategy. Thus, further assumptions about this would be inappropriate.

Volunteers were not precluded from participating if they had already seen the films that were to be screened during the groups; this was decided largely because of the difficulty in finding students who had not seen *The Lord of the Rings*. However, their memories of previous experiences with the film were acknowledged and addressed during the interviews.

NOTES

Introduction

1. Henry Augustin Beers, *A History of English Romanticism in the Eighteenth Century* (London: Kegan Paul, Trench, Trübner, 1899), p. 281.
2. Quentin Tarantino, *Pulp Fiction* (Miramax Entertainment, 1994).
3. Conrad Rudolph, *A Companion to Medieval Art: Romanesque and Gothic in Northern Europe* (Malden, MA: Wiley-Blackwell, 2006), p. 4.
4. For a seminal view of the concept of medievalism, see: Tom Shippey and Richard Utz, 'Medievalism in the modern world: Introductory perspectives', in *Medievalism in the Modern World: Essays in Honour of Leslie J. Workman* (Turnhout: Brepols, 1998), 1–14. For a broad view of the current state of medievalism studies and a history of the discipline, see Chapters 1–9 in Karl Fugelso (ed.), 'Defining medievalism(s)', *Studies in Medievalism* 17 (2009).
5. Leslie Workman, 'Preface', *Studies in Medievalism* 8 (1996): 1–2, p. 1.
6. Elizabeth Emery, 'Medievalism and the Middle Ages', *Studies in Medievalism* XVII (2009): 77–85, p. 85.
7. For an excellent translation of Halbwachs' work on collective memory, see: Maurice Halbwachs, *On Collective Memory*, Lewis A. Coser (ed. and trans) (Chicago: University of Chicago Press, 1992).
8. The best compilation of scholarship in memory studies currently available is: Jeffrey K. Olick, Vered Vinitzky-Seroussi, and Daniel Levy (eds), *The Collective Memory Reader* (Oxford: Oxford University Press, 2011).
9. For a fuller exploration of the development of 'historical consciousness', see: Peter C. Seixas, 'Introduction', in Peter C. Seixas (ed.), *Theorizing Historical Consciousness* (Toronto: University of Toronto Press, 2004), pp. 3–20.
10. Peter C. Seixas, 'What is historical consciousness?', in Ruth Sandwell (ed.), *To the Past: History Education, Public Memory, and Citizenship in Canada* (Toronto: University of Toronto Press, 2006), pp. 11–22.

11. There are two significant exceptions to this rule. The first is the recent interesting volume *Memory and Myths of the Norman Conquest* by Siobhan Brownlie, in which the author explores the complex reception of the Norman Conquest in the UK. She does this with particular focus on how it has been reimagined by popular culture and the media, and through the deployment of a quantitative survey of popular views of the event. The second is an ongoing project by a few scholars of medieval literature, Helen Young for example, that touch upon their reception by contemporary audiences. While each of these explores a particular event or instance of medievalism in culture, they do so by grappling with the larger pool of public medievalism. Siobhan Brownlie, *Memory and Myths of the Norman Conquest* (Woodbridge: Boydell Press, 2013); Helen Young, *Constructing 'England' in the Fourteenth Century: A Postcolonial Interpretation of Middle English Romance* (Lewiston, NY Mellen Press, 2010).

12. 'Medieval, adj. and n.', *OED Online* (Oxford: Oxford University Press, 1989). Available at http://www.oed.com/view/Entry/115638?redirectedFrom= medieval (accessed 24 August 2016).

13. Alison Landsberg, *Prosthetic Memory: The Transformation of American Remembrance in the Age of Mass Culture* (New York: Columbia University Press, 2004).

14. Robert A. Rosenstone (ed.), *Revisioning History: Film and the Construction of a New Past* (Princeton: Princeton University Press, 1995), p. 3.

15. See, for example, Helen Young, 'Approaches to medievalism: A consideration of taxonomy and methodology through fantasy fiction', *Parergon* 27/1 (2010): 163–79; Helen Young (ed.), *The Middle Ages in Popular Culture: Medievalism and Genre* (Amherst: Cambria Press, 2015), particularly the introduction, and; Andrew B. R. Elliott, *Remaking the Middle Ages: The Methods of Cinema and History in Portraying the Medieval World* (Jefferson, NC: McFarland, 2011).

Chapter 1   The Public Understanding of the Past

1. To use Great Britain as an example, in 2007, Oxford Economics estimated that the British heritage industry generates approximately £7.4 billion for the UK economy every year. Heritage Lottery Fund and VisitBritain, *Investing in Success: Heritage and the UK Tourism Economy* (London: Heritage Lottery Fund, 2010), p. 8. Available at http://www.hlf.org.uk/aboutus/ howwework/Documents/HLF_Tourism_Impact_single.pdf (accessed 22 August 2016).

2. This is an oversimplification for the sake of brevity. For the current shape of this international debate, see: Irene Nakou and Isabel Barca (eds), *Contemporary Public Debates over History Education* (Charlotte, NC: Information Age Publishing, 2010), and Peter N. Stearns, Peter Seixas, and Sam Wineburg (eds), *Knowing, Teaching and Learning History: National and International Perspectives* (New York: NYU Press, 2000).

3. Sam Wineburg, *Historical Thinking and Other Unnatural Acts: Charting the Future of Teaching the Past* (Philadelphia: Temple University Press, 2001), pp. vii–viii.

4. J. Carleton Bell and David F. McCollum, 'A study of the attainments of pupils in United States history', *Journal of Educational Psychology* 8 (1917): pp. 257–74.

5. Wineburg, *Historical Thinking and Other Unnatural Acts*, p. vii.

6. Ibid.

7. Peter N. Stearns, 'Why study history?', *American Historical Association*, 1998. Available at https://www.historians.org/about-aha-and-membership/aha-history-and-archives/archives/why-study-history-(1998) (accessed 21 August 2016).

8. 'Essential history survey results (Internet archive)', *Osprey Publishing*, 18 January 2001. Available at http://web.archive.org/web/200102031935/http://www.ospreypublishing.com/features/5 (accessed 22 August 2016).

9. Amanda Kelly, 'What did Hitler do in the war, miss?', *Times Educational Supplement*, 19 January 2001. Available at https://www.tes.com/news/tes-archive/tes-publication/what-did-hitler-do-war-miss (accessed 1 June 2017).

10. This statistic may seem bad. However, it is important to remember that it is unknown how the question was worded, and the ages of the respondents. It seems probable that a proportion – likely a significant one – of that 4 per cent misunderstood the question to mean that Hitler fought Britain in World War II. Thus, this statistic relates as much to quiz-question comprehension as it does to historical knowledge.

11. 'Essential history survey results (Internet archive)'.

12. Ibid.

13. Ibid.; Kelly, 'What did Hitler do in the war, miss?'.

14. According to the 2001 UK census, there were five million three hundred and ninety-three thousand two hundred and forty-one children between the ages of 10 and 17 at that time. Calculating a margin of error with 95 per cent confidence from a sample of 200 gives us a margin of error of 6.93 per cent. London Datastore, 'Census 2001 key statistics 02: age structure', 2003. Available at http://data.london.gov.uk/dataset/census-2001-key-statistics-02-age-structure (accessed 22 August 2016).

15. BBC, 'Press releases: Alexander the Great won the Battle of Hastings', *BBC Press Office*, 5 August 2004. Available at http://www.bbc.co.uk/pressoffice/pressreleases/stories/2004/08_august/05/battlefield.shtml (accessed 22 August 2016).

16. Ibid.

17. Press Association, 'Gandalf finds a place in British history', *Guardian*, 5 August 2004. Available at https://www.theguardian.com/education/2004/aug/05/schools.highereducation (accessed 1 June 2017).

18. Chris McGovern, 'The new history boys', in Robert Whelan (ed.), *The Corruption of the Curriculum* (London: Civitas, 2007), p. 59.

19. Derek Matthews, *The Strange Death of History Teaching (Fully Explained in Seven Easy-to-Follow Lessons)* unpublished report, January 2009. Available at http://bit.ly/2bRZwKS (accessed 22 August 2016).

20. Ibid., p. 1.

21. Jeevan Vasagar, 'Michael Gove accuses exam system of neglecting British history', *Guardian*, 24 November 2011, sec. Education. Available at http://www.guardian.co.uk/education/2011/nov/24/michael-gove-british-history-neglected (accessed 22 August 2016).

22. Michael Gove, 'I refuse to surrender to the Marxist teachers hell-bent on destroying our schools: Education Secretary berates "the new enemies of promise" for opposing his plans', *Daily Mail*, 23 March 2013. Available at http://www.dailymail.co.uk/debate/article-2298146/I-refuse-surrender-Marxist-teachers-hell-bent-destroying-schools-Education-Secretary-berates-new-enemies-promise-opposing-plans.html (accessed 22 August 2016).

23. Alex Hern, 'Michael Gove revealed to be using PR-commissioned puff-polls as "evidence"', *The New Statesman*, 13 May 2013. Available at http://www.newstatesman.com/politics/2013/05/michael-gove-revealed-be-using-pr-commissioned-puff-polls-evidence (accessed 22 August 2016). The survey by Ashcroft had a more thorough methodology, studying 1,000 school-aged children in the UK. However, it has the same flaw as the others, in that its framing and reporting was all explicitly negative. It very clearly was designed to 'prove' how limited the children's understanding of history was, rather than understand its totality. Lord Ashcroft, 'How much do children know about the Second World War?', *Lord Ashcroft Polls*, 25 June 2012. Available at http://lordashcroftpolls.com/2012/06/how-much-do-children-know-about-the-second-world-war/ (accessed 28 August 2016).

24. The trend of politicians and pundits using badly constructed research to bolster attacks on history educators and public historians is hardly exclusive to the UK. For the Australian context, see: Anna Clark, *Teaching the Nation: Politics and Pedagogy in Australian History* (Carlton, Vic.: Melbourne University Press, 2006). For the US context, among others, see Gary B. Nash, Charlotte Crabtree, and Ross E. Dunn, *Culture Wars and the Teaching of the Past* (New York: Vintage Books, 2000); Edward T. Linenthal and Tom Engelhardt (eds), *History Wars: The Enola Gay and Other Battles for the American Past* (New York: Henry Holt and Company, 1996).

25. Rosenzweig and Thelen's work can be compared with similar studies done involving school-aged children, such as one conducted in the early 1990s that surveyed over 32,000 students in 27 European countries. This survey was expansive and touched on 15- and 16-year-old students' historical consciousness and their political attitudes – and examined the causative links between those two things. Where Rosenzweig and Thelen's work (as well as their successors') differed was on focusing on adults rather than children, integrating limited qualitative methods into their studies, and focusing on questions other than the political. Magne Angvik and Bodo von

Borries (eds), *Youth and History: A Comparative European Survey on Historical Consciousness and Political Attitudes among Adolescents* (Hamburg: Körber-Stiftung, 1997).

26. Roy Rosenzweig and David Thelen, *The Presence of the Past: Popular Uses of History in American Life* (New York: Columbia University Press, 1998).

27. Ibid., p. 3.

28. Ibid., p. 12.

29. Ibid.

30. Ibid., p. 13.

31. Rosenzweig and Thelen, *The Presence of the Past*. The sister website offers a more comprehensive presentation and analysis of the data of the survey than would be possible in the book. Roy Rosenzweig and David Thelen, *The Presence of the Past survey website*, 1998. Available at http://chnm.gmu.edu/survey/ (accessed 22 August 2016).

32. Rosenzweig and Thelen, *The Presence of the Past*, pp. 210–11.

33. Ibid., p. 6.

34. Ibid., p. 211.

35. Paul Ashton and Paula Hamilton, *History at the Crossroads: Australians and the Past* (Sydney: Halstead Press, 2010).

36. Margaret Conrad, et al., *Canadians and Their Pasts* (Toronto: University of Toronto Press, 2013).

37. Rosenzweig and Thelen, *The Presence of the Past*, p. 237.

38. Conrad et al., *Canadians and Their Pasts*, p. 36.

39. This assumption of Chang's is based upon a truly random mating chance, which is historically unlikely. However, despite this, the probability of this common medieval ancestor rises significantly if considered within smaller regions, or extending the time frame back only a few hundred years into the Middle Ages. Joseph T. Chang, 'Recent common ancestors of all present-day individuals', *Advances in Applied Probability* 31/4 (December 1999), 1002–26; p. 1005.

40. Steve Olson, 'The royal we', *The Atlantic*, May 2002. Available at http://www.theatlantic.com/magazine/archive/2002/05/the-royal-we/2497/ (accessed 22 August 2016).

41. For more on nation-formation and the Middle Ages, see: Patrick J. Geary, *The Myth of Nations: The Medieval Origins of Europe* (Princeton, NJ: Princeton University Press, 2002).

42. One might add a further category, of undifferentiated 'Celtic', in contradistinction to 'English' – however that term is also historically problematic.

43. Eric Weiskott, 'Feeling "British"', *The Public Medievalist*, 28 March 2017. Available at http://www.publicmedievalist.com/feeling-british/ (accessed 30 May 2017).

44. For concepts of race and ethnicity in the Middle Ages, see: Robert Bartlett, 'Medieval and modern concepts of race and ethnicity', *Journal of Medieval and Early Modern Studies* 31/1 (2001), pp. 39–56.

45. The *Canadians and Their Pasts* survey asked whether there were any 'other' histories they found important beyond the six offered options. One third of people did, and cited the past of Canadian Aboriginal peoples, the past of friends, immigrant pasts, and a few others. None of the categories offered by participants seemed to include medieval history. Conrad et al., *Canadians and Their Pasts*, p. 37.

46. A significant number of students who study medieval studies at the postgraduate level in the UK are from the US, Canada or Japan, outside the usual boundaries of the medieval world and thus with little obvious national connection to the period. Aside from the logical conclusion that it is sensible to study the Middle Ages in a country where it existed, there has been no rigorous exploration of why there is such a fascination with the medieval in places where it did not exist, particularly in places like Japan that were not European colonies.

47. Rosenzweig and Thelen, *The Presence of the Past*, p. 237. My emphasis.

48. For a fuller exploration of qualitative and quantitative research methods, see Appendix A.

49. Conrad et al., *Canadians and Their Pasts*, p. 166; p. 168.

50. For an introduction to how to conduct a study of the public understanding of the past using these research methods, see Appendix A.

51. General Certificate of Secondary Education (commonly known as GCSE) is an academic qualification taken by British students between the ages of fourteen and sixteen. GCSE also refers to the secondary school courses that prepare students for those exams (comprising their education between fourteen and sixteen). The only GCSEs required for students are those in English, Mathematics and Science (with Welsh and Irish also compulsory in some schools in Wales and Northern Ireland). It is roughly analogous with grades nine through eleven in the USA.

52. It should be noted that the highest-grossing cinematic medievalisms of that period were, in fact, the three *The Lord of the Rings* films. But it was decided that this study should not focus solely on *The Lord of the Rings*, and so took the highest grossing of those films (*The Return of the King*) and the two next-highest grossing medieval films.

Chapter 2   Their Understanding of the Middle Ages

1. Anaïs Nin, *Seduction of the Minotaur* (London: A. Swallow, 1961), p. 124.

2. One *caveat*: since the goal of this research was to explore popular knowledge of the Middle Ages, the participants were young adults chosen precisely because they had *not* studied history at an advanced level. There are many gaps in their knowledge, many vaguely understood theories, and many ideas that are simply incorrect. The purpose of this book is not just to point out where the participants get the medieval past wrong; if anything, those instances when people go awry with their historical thinking are far more fascinating than

when they are correct. In theory, if the participants' knowledge of the topic is perfectly in tune with the best of contemporary scholarship, this only indicates that they studied exceptionally well, that their teachers deserve a pat on the back, and that the dissemination of information from the academy to the public is working perfectly and with shocking speed.

3. Some of the data pertaining to the differences between 'medieval' and 'Middle Ages' have been expanded upon and published as Paul B. Sturtevant, 'Medievalisms of the mind: Undergraduate perceptions of the "medieval" and the "Middle Ages"', *Studies in Medievalism* 26 (Martlesham: Boydell and Brewer, 2017), pp. 213–37.

4. David Matthews argues that the word 'medieval' was first popularised in scholarly circles by Thomas Fosbroke starting about 1817. That being said, it does not necessarily mean earlier speakers did not have an adjectival term for 'Middle Ages' – they simply used 'of the Middle Ages', or terms like 'gothic' and 'feudal'. David Matthews, 'Middle', in Elizabeth Emery and Richard Utz (eds), *Medievalism: Key Critical Terms* (Cambridge: D. S. Brewer, 2014), pp. 144–5.

5. Explained more fully in Appendix B.

6. Since participants often used similar terms to describe a single idea, terms that were obviously synonyms were collapsed together. For example, 'black death', 'black plague' and 'plague' were combined into 'disease' (though if a person wrote more than one of these, it was only counted once). Other terms did not require collapsing because word choice amongst participants was more consistent (e.g. 'castles' or 'jesters'). The idea was to count the frequency of schematic concepts rather than specific verbiage.

7. Depending upon academic periodisations, the reign of Henry VIII is more often placed in the Early Modern than the medieval period (or occasionally on the border of the two).

8. The statements of the study participants have been edited for clarity and to remove filler words and sounds.

9. Square brackets across two lines indicate that two participants were talking at the same time. Additionally, for clarity words used as linguistic fillers have been removed.

10. The equals sign indicates that one participant interrupted another.

11. 'Medieval, adj. and n.' *OED* Online (Oxford: Oxford University Press, 2016). Available at: http://www.oed.com/view/Entry/115638?redirectedFrom = medieval (accessed 8 August 2016).

12. Umberto Eco, 'Dreaming of the Middle Ages', in William Weaver (trans), *Travels in Hyperreality: Essays* (London: Picador, 1987), p. 68.

13. David Williams, 'Medieval movies', *The Yearbook of English Studies* 20 (1990): 1–32, p. 10.

14. Elliott, *Remaking the Middle Ages*, p. 1.

15. Claire A. Simmons, 'Romantic medievalism', in Louise D'Arcens (ed.), *The Cambridge Companion to Medievalism* (Cambridge: Cambridge University Press, 2016), 103–18, pp. 112–14.

16. Williams, 'Medieval movies', p. 10.

17. Elliott, *Remaking the Middle Ages*, p. 2.

18. The participants did not make clear distinctions between the concepts of myth, legend, fantasy, and fairy-tale.

19. The latter two are a clear reference to Helgeland's 2001 film *A Knight's Tale*, a favourite among these participants. Jane felt this film fits in this category of myth and legend, despite its inclusion of historical figures like Edward the Black Prince and Geoffrey Chaucer.

20. Leonardo Bruni, *History of the Florentine People: Books 1–4 V. 1*, James Hankins (ed.) (Cambridge, MA: Harvard University Press, 2001), pp. xvii–xviii.

21. The most significant detractor to this view of the beginning of the Middle Ages is historian Henri Pirenne, who proposed that the end of the Roman world (and thus the beginning of the Middle Ages) came with the Islamic expansion in the eighth century. For a critical examination of the Pirenne thesis, see: Richard Hodges and David Whitehouse, *Mohammed, Charlemagne, and the Origins of Europe* (Ithaca, NY: Cornell University Press, 1983).

22. Bruni, *History of the Florentine People*, pp. xvii–xviii.

23. 'Middle age, n. and adj', *OED Online* (Oxford: Oxford University Press, 2016). Available at http://www.oed.com/view/Entry/118142 (accessed 13 October 2016).

24. The 'Renaissance' is difficult to define temporally because it spread variably across Europe, bringing the 'Middle Ages' to a close in different countries at different times. Hence, while Geoffrey Chaucer's late fourteenth-century opus *The Canterbury Tales* is regarded as one of the great pieces of medieval English literature, Giovanni Boccaccio's earlier *The Decameron* (*c*.1350–3), on which some of Chaucer's *Tales* are based, is generally regarded as a work of the Italian Renaissance.

25. Angus A. Somerville and R. Andrew McDonald, *The Viking Age: A Reader* (Toronto: University of Toronto Press, 2010), pp. xiv–xv; Peter H. Sawyer, 'The age of the Vikings, and before', in Peter H. Sawyer (ed.), *The Oxford Illustrated History of the Vikings* (Oxford: Oxford University Press, 1997), p. 1.

26. Theodor E. Mommsen, 'Petrarch's conception of the "dark ages"', *Speculum* 17/2 (April 1942): 226–42, p. 227.

27. Wallace K. Ferguson, 'Humanist views of the Renaissance', *The American Historical Review* 45/1 (October 1939): 1–28, p. 28.

28. Fred C. Robinson, 'Medieval, the Middle Ages', *Speculum* 59/4 (October 1984): 745–56, pp. 750–1.

29. Ibid., p. 751.

30. For the most recent research on some of the spectacular archaeological finds from early-medieval England, see: Martin Carver, *Sutton Hoo: A Seventh-Century*

Princely Burial Ground and Its Context (London: British Museum Press, 2005); Stephen Dean, Della Hooke, and Alex Jones, 'The "Staffordshire hoard": The fieldwork', *The Antiquaries Journal* 90 (2010): pp. 139–52.

31. For more on this changing idea of where the Middle Ages were, see the work of the scholars of the Global Middle Ages project. For an introduction to the project, see Geraldine Heng, 'The global Middle Ages: An experiment in collaborative humanities, or imagining the world, 500–1500 C.E.' *English Language Notes* 47/1 (2009): pp. 205–16. For the research publications of this collaborative, see the Global Middle Ages website. Available at http://globalmiddleages.org/research-and-teaching (accessed 29 May 2017).

32. Christopher Tyerman, *England and the Crusades* (Chicago: University of Chicago Press, 1988), p. 15.

33. Tyerman, *England and the Crusades*, p. 6. Tyerman goes on to describe a variety of interesting ways in which England *did* contribute to the First Crusade, despite being a relatively minor player by comparison with France or the Holy Roman Empire.

34. The five films are: DeMille, *The Crusades*, 1935; David Butler, *King Richard and the Crusaders*, 1954; Chahine, *El Naser Salah Ad-Din*, 1963; Scott, *Kingdom of Heaven*, 2005; Flinth, *Arn: The Knight Templar*, 2007. *Arn: The Knight Templar* is the only film that does not depict Richard I; since *Arn* was made primarily for the Scandinavian market it may have seemed less important to include the English monarch.

35. This is particularly ironic as the guillotine, at its invention, was considered a more humane way to execute than the methods that had been used previously.

36. Michael Hirst, *The Tudors* (Showtime/BBC, 2007–10).

37. Charismatic Baptists are a neo-Pentecostal sect of Baptists who believe that miracles, glossolalia and prophecy can be, and are, experienced in the modern day.

38. 'British Social Attitudes information system: Variable analysis, "Do you regard yourself as belonging to any particular religion?"'. Available at http://www.britsocat.com/BodySecure.aspx?control=BritsocatMarginals&var=RELRFW&SurveyID=346 (accessed 26 May 2011). This overall rise can largely be attributed to a significant shift away from the Church of England towards the 'no religion' and 'Christian – no denomination' categories, rather than a marked fluctuation in any other religion. The relatively static age factor indicates perhaps that if there is an overall secularisation of British society, it may be attributed to fewer people coming to religion later in life than before.

39. For an overview of the relevant historiographical issues in terms of defining 'crusade', see Giles Constable, 'The historiography of the Crusades', in Angeliki E. Laiou and Roy Parviz Mottahedeh (eds), *The Crusades from the Perspective of Byzantium and the Muslim World* (Washington, DC: Dumbarton Oaks, 2001), pp. 1–22. Available at http://www.doaks.org/resources/publications/doaks-online-publications/crusades-from-the-perspective-of-byzantium-and-the-muslim-world/cr01.pdf (accessed 6 October 2016).

40. Ibid., p. 12.
41. Kate Mosse, *Labyrinth* (London: Orion, 2005); Kate Mosse, *Sepulchre* (London: Orion, 2007); Kate Mosse, *Citadel* (London: Orion, 2012).
42. Edward Peters (ed.), *The First Crusade: The Chronicle of Fulcher of Chartres and Other Source Materials*, Second Edition (Philadelphia, PA: University of Pennsylvania Press, 1998), p. 31.
43. A.J. Pollard, *Imagining Robin Hood: The Late-medieval Stories in Historical Context* (London: Routledge, 2004), p. 15. For more on the development of the Robin Hood legend, especially in the sixteenth century, see: Peter Stallybrass, '"Drunk with the cup of liberty": Robin Hood, the carnivalesque, and the rhetoric of violence in Early Modern England', *Semiotica* 54/1–2 (January 1985): pp. 113–46; Helen Phillips (ed.), *Robin Hood: Medieval and Post-medieval* (Dublin: Four Courts Press, 2005); Stephen Knight, *Robin Hood: A Mythic Biography* (Ithaca, NY: Cornell University Press, 2003).
44. Allan Dwan, *Robin Hood* (United Artists, 1922); Reynolds, *Robin Hood: Prince of Thieves* (Warner Bros., 1991); Mel Brooks, *Robin Hood: Men in Tights* (20th Century Fox, 1993); Ridley Scott, *Robin Hood* (Universal Pictures, 2010). In addition, two recent popular British TV series include the 'Robin as crusader' narrative: *Robin of Sherwood* (ITV, 1984–6) and *Robin Hood* (BBC, 2006–9).
45. 'Little Englander' is a dismissive term in British English that refers to English people perceived to be xenophobic or overly nationalistic.
46. See, for example: Samuel P. Huntington, *The Clash of Civilizations and the Remaking of World Order* (New York: Simon & Schuster, 1996); Niall Ferguson, *Civilization: The West and the Rest* (New York: The Penguin Press HC, 2011).
47. Laurie A. Finke and Martin B. Shichtman, *Cinematic Illuminations: The Middle Ages on Film* (Baltimore: The Johns Hopkins University Press, 2010), p. 196. Finke and Shichtman are quoting James Carroll, *Crusade: Chronicles of an Unjust War* (New York: Metropolitan Books, 2004), p. 4.
48. As much as possible, the moderator avoided using the term 'learning', since it was expected that this would steer the participants to talk about academic learning rather than informal learning.
49. Richard C. Anderson, 'Role of the reader's schema in comprehension, learning, and memory', in Robert B. Ruddell, Martha Rapp, and Harry Singer (eds), *Theoretical Models and Processes of Reading*, Fourth Edition (Newark, DE: International Reading Association, 1994), pp. 469–75.
50. Due to the lack of a national curriculum in some other countries (such as the USA), it would be more difficult to perform a similar analysis in those places.
51. The current National Curriculum for England was introduced in 2014 and is not significantly better in terms of its approach to medieval history. For the full statutory programmes of study in the current curriculum, see: Department for Education, 'National curriculum in England: History programmes of study', Gov.uk (2013). Available at https://www.gov.uk/government/

publications/national-curriculum-in-england-history-programmes-of-study (accessed 10 October 2016).

52. National Curriculum Council, *History in the National Curriculum (England)* (London: Department of Education and Science, 1991), pp. 19–45.

53. Ibid., p. 39. Whether this contributed in some part to Britons' general feelings of separateness from Europe (and the political ramifications thereof) is beyond the scope of this study.

54. National Curriculum Council, *National Curriculum Council Consultation Report: History* (York: National Curriculum Council, 1990), p. 51.

55. Brownlie, *Memory and Myths of the Norman Conquest*, p. 197.

56. Department of Education and Science and the Welsh Office, *National Curriculum History Working Group: Final Report* (London: HMSO, 1990), p. 177.

57. The round table bearing an image of King Arthur on the wall of the great hall of Winchester Castle has inspired much popular interest and scholarly debate, best explored in: Martin Biddle (ed.), *King Arthur's Round Table* (Woodbridge: Boydell & Brewer, 2000).

58. An excellent guide for using re-enactment and living history as an educational tool for children is: Ronald Vaughan Morris, *History and Imagination: Reenactments for Elementary Social Studies* (Plymouth: Rowman & Littlefield Education, 2012).

59. Géza Gárdonyi, *Eclipse of the Crescent Moon*, George F. Cushing (trans), Sixth Edition (Budapest: Corvina, 2002). This book was first published in 1899. The major historical events depicted in the book are the occupation of Buda in 1541 and the siege of Eger by the Ottoman Empire in 1552, well beyond the crusading period. Additionally, this novel does not portray events from the Ottoman (Islamic) perspective, but the Hungarian one. The Hungarians are presented as nationalistic heroes.

60. More of the results of the focus groups pertaining to the films of Disney have been adapted into: Paul B. Sturtevant, '"You don't learn it deliberately, but you just know it from what you've seen": British understandings of the medieval past gleaned from Disney's fairy tales', in Tison Pugh and Susan Aronstein (eds), *The Disney Middle Ages: A Fairy-Tale and Fantasy Past* (New York: Palgrave McMillan, 2012), pp. 77–96.

61. For more on the powerful ubiquity of Disney (in particular, its 'princess' narratives), see: Claire Bradford, 'Where happily ever after happens every day', in Tison Pugh and Susan Aronstein (eds), *The Disney Middle Ages: A Fairy-Tale and Fantasy Past* (New York: Palgrave McMillan, 2012), pp. 171–88.

62. W. George Scarlett and Dennie Wolf, 'When it's only make-believe: The construction of a boundary between fantasy and reality in storytelling', *New Directions for Child and Adolescent Development* 1979/6 (1979): 29–40, p. 37.

63. Ibid.

64. Claudine Beaumont, 'Call of Duty: Modern Warfare 2: Why video games can't be ignored', *Telegraph*, 13 November 2009, sec. Technology. Available at http://www.telegraph.co.uk/technology/video-games/6562828/Call-Of-Duty-Modern-Warfare-2-why-video-games-cant-be-ignored.html (accessed 12 October 2016).

65. *Age of Empires 2: Age of Kings* (Microsoft, 2001); *Medieval II: Total War* (Creative Assembly, 2008); *Sid Meier's Civilization IV* (2K Games, 2005).

66. For a typical opinion piece on video games and violence, see: Dave Grossman, 'Video Games as "murder simulators"', *Variety, Special Issue: Violence & Entertainment*, p. 45. Available at http://variety.com/violence/ (accessed 12 October 2016).

67. James Paul Gee, *What Video Games Have to Teach Us About Learning and Literacy*, Second Edition (Basingstoke: Palgrave MacMillan, 2003); Richard E. Mayer, *Computer Games for Learning: An Evidence-Based Approach* (Cambridge, MA: The MIT Press, 2014).

68. Matthew Wilhelm Kapell and Andrew B.R. Elliott (eds), *Playing with the Past: Digital Games and the Simulation of History* (New York: Bloomsbury, 2013).

Chapter 3   Learning History from Film

1. Peter Biskind, *Seeing is Believing* (New York: Pantheon, 1983), p. 2.

2. Margaret Conrad et al., *Canadians and Their Pasts*, p. 142.

3. The *Canadians and their Pasts* survey asked three questions about 'movies, videos, DVDs or TV programs' about the past: (1) whether they had seen one in the past twelve months (2) how many they had seen, and (3) the name of the last one they watched. Unlike other past-related activities such as old photographs, internet, books, historic sites, and museums, films were not included in their deeper assessment of past-related activities (such as asking how connected to the past a past-related activity made them feel or how trustworthy they found them). This omission is not explained. Margaret Conrad et al., *Canadians and Their Pasts*, pp. 165–8.

4. On this scale, one was low and ten was high. Rosenzweig and Thelen, *The Presence of the Past*, p. 248.

5. The full rankings were: Museums: 8.4, Personal accounts from grandparents or relatives: 8.0, Conversation with someone who was there: 7.8, College history professors: 7.3, High school history teachers: 6.6, Non-fiction books: 6.4, Movies or television programmes about the past: 5.0. Ibid., p. 244.

6. There are a variety of important works which introduce the concept of the active rather than passive audience, but the two most seminal in this topic are: Stuart Hall, 'Encoding/decoding', in Stuart Hall (ed.), *Culture, Media, Language: Working Papers in Cultural Studies, 1972–79* (London: Hutchinson in association with the Centre for Contemporary Cultural Studies, University of Birmingham, 1980), pp. 128–38; John Fiske, *Television Culture* (Abingdon: Taylor & Francis, 2011).

7. Sam Wineburg and Daisy Martin, 'Reading and rewriting history', *Educational Leadership* 62/1 (2004): 42–5, p. 44.

8. Rosenzweig and Thelen, *The Presence of the Past*, p. 98.

9. Ibid.

10. Ibid.
11. Ibid.
12. Watching films and TV was only surmounted in the survey of how often people feel they participate in a historical activity by taking photographs and looking at photographs. Ibid., p. 234.
13. Ibid., pp. 100–1.
14. Ibid., p. 101.
15. Scott Alan Metzger, 'Pedagogy and the historical feature film: Toward historical literacy', *Film & History: An Interdisciplinary Journal of Film and Television Studies* 37/2 (2007): 67–75, p. 68.
16. Peter L. Berger and Thomas Luckmann, *The Social Construction of Reality: A Treatise in the Sociology of Knowledge* (Harmondsworth: Penguin, 1991).
17. Ibid., p. 15.
18. Ibid., p. 27.
19. Ibid., p. 15.
20. John Fiske, *Understanding Popular Culture*, Second Edition (London: Routledge, 2010).
21. Berger and Luckmann, *The Social Construction of Reality*, p. 48.
22. David E. Morrison, *The Search for a Method: Focus Groups and the Development of Mass Communication Research* (Luton: University of Luton Press, 1998); David E. Morrison, *Defining Violence: The Search for Understanding* (Luton: University of Luton Press, 1999).
23. Morrison, *Defining Violence*, p. 1.
24. Ibid., p. vii.
25. I use the term 'medievalness' to describe the subjective degree to which something is understood to be a part of the Middle Ages. This term was used regularly by participants in my study.
26. Immanuel Kant, *Critique of Pure Reason*, Norman Kemp Smith and Gary Banham (trans), Revised Second Edition (Basingstoke: Palgrave Macmillan, 2007), pp. 182–3.
27. Frederic C. Bartlett, *Remembering: A Study in Experimental and Social Psychology* (Cambridge: Cambridge University Press, 1932).
28. Richard C. Anderson, Rand J. Spiro, and William Edward Montague (eds), *Schooling and the Acquisition of Knowledge* (London: Lawrence Erlbaum, 1977); Richard C. Anderson, 'The notion of schemata and the educational enterprise: General discussion of the conference', in Richard C. Anderson, Rand J. Spiro, and William Edward Montague (eds), *Schooling and the Acquisition of Knowledge* (London: Lawrence Erlbaum, 1977): pp. 415–31; David E. Rumelhart and Andrew Ortony, 'Representation of knowledge in memory', in Richard C. Anderson, Rand J. Spiro, and William Edward Montague (eds), *Schooling and the Acquisition of Knowledge* (London: Lawrence Erlbaum, 1977), pp. 99–135.
29. Rumelhart and Ortony, 'Representation of knowledge in memory', p. 101.

30. Ibid.
31. Ibid.
32. Ibid.
33. Ibid., p. 109.
34. William F. Brewer and Glenn V. Nakamura, 'The nature and functions of schemas', in Thomas K. Srull and Robert S. Wyer (eds), *Handbook of Social Cognition* (Hillsdale, NJ: L. Erlbaum Associates, 1984), p. 123.
35. Richard C. Anderson, 'The notion of schemata and the educational enterprise: General discussion of the conference', in Richard C. Anderson, Rand J. Spiro, and William Edward Montague (eds), *Schooling and the Acquisition of Knowledge* (London: Lawrence Erlbaum, 1977), pp. 418–19.
36. Rumelhart and Ortony, 'Representation of knowledge in memory', p. 106.
37. David E. Rumelhart, 'Schemata: The building blocks of cognition', in Rand J. Spiro, Bertram C. Bruce, and William F. Brewer (eds) *Theoretical Issues in Reading Comprehension: Perspectives from Cognitive Psychology, Linguistics, Artificial Intelligence and Education* (Hillsdale, NJ: Lawrence Erlbaum, 1980): 33–58, p. 34.
38. Robert Axelrod, 'Schema theory: An information processing model of perception and cognition', *The American Political Science Review* 67/4 (December 1973): 1248–66, p. 1248.
39. For more on Piaget's theory of accommodation, see: Jacques Montangero and Danielle Maurice-Naville, *Piaget, or, The Advance of Knowledge* (Mahwah: Lawrence Erlbaum Associates, 1997), pp. 63–7.
40. Jean Piaget, *The Origin of Intelligence in the Child* (London: Routledge, 1998), p. 416.
41. For more on Piaget's theory of assimilation, see: Montangero and Maurice-Naville, *Piaget*, pp. 73–7.
42. Ron Briley, 'Teaching film and history', *OAH Magazine of History* 16/4 (Summer, 2002): 3–4, p. 3.
43. Metzger, 'Pedagogy and the historical feature film', p. 70.
44. Ibid., pp. 70–1.
45. Ibid., p. 71.
46. Ibid.
47. Scott Alan Metzger, 'Maximizing the educational power of history movies in the classroom', *The Social Studies* 101 (2010): 127–36, p. 135.
48. Briley, 'Teaching film and history', p. 4.
49. Andrew C. Butler, Franklin M. Zaromb, Keith B. Lyle, and Henry L. Roediger, III, 'Using popular films to enhance classroom learning: The good, the bad, and the interesting', *Psychological Science* 20/9 (September 2009): pp. 1161–8.
50. Ibid., p. 1161.
51. Ibid., pp. 1164–5.

52. Alan S. Marcus and Jeremy D. Stoddard, 'Tinsel town as teacher: Hollywood film in the high school classroom', *The History Teacher* 40/3 (May, 2007): pp. 303–30.

53. Ibid., pp. 314–17.

54. Ibid., pp. 318–19.

55. Alan S. Marcus, '"It is as it was": Feature film in the history classroom', *The Social Studies* 96/2 (2005): 61–7, p. 61.

56. Melvyn Stokes, *D.W. Griffith's* The Birth of a Nation*: A History of 'The Most Controversial Motion Picture of All Time'* (Oxford: Oxford University Press, 2007), pp. 111–12.

57. Peter Seixas, 'Confronting the moral frames of popular film: Young people respond to historical revisionism', *American Journal of Education* 102/3 (May 1994): pp. 261–85.

58. Alan S. Marcus, Richard J. Paxton, and Peter Meyerson, '"The reality of it all": History students read the movies', *Theory and Research in Social Education* 34/3 (Fall 2006): 516–52, p. 517.

Chapter 4   The Medieval Film

1. Kevin J. Harty, *The Reel Middle Ages: American, Western and Eastern European, Middle Eastern, and Asian Films About Medieval Europe* (Jefferson, NC: McFarland, 1999).

2. Ibid., pp. 265–6.

3. For an exploration of the twenty-first century renaissance of the epic film, see: Andrew B. R. Elliott, *The Return of the Epic Film: Genre, Aesthetics and History in the 21st Century* (Edinburgh: Edinburgh University Press, 2014).

4. Williams, 'Medieval movies', p. 1.

5. Well-known film studies journals like *Cineaste, Cinema Journal* and *Film History* occasionally publish articles about medieval film. Examples are Tony Pipolo's comparative study of the aesthetics of Joan of Arc films and Greta Austin's polemic on medieval film's typical lack of historical accuracy. Tony Pipolo, 'Joan of Arc: The cinema's immortal maid', *Cineaste: America's Leading Magazine on the Art and Politics of the Cinema* 25/4 (September 2000), pp. 16–21; Greta Austin, 'Were the peasants really so clean? The Middle Ages in film', *Film History* 14/2 (2002): pp. 136–41.

6. Rick Altman, *Film/Genre* (London: BFI Publishing, 1999), p. 14.

7. Mel Gibson, *Braveheart* (Paramount, 1995); Zack Snyder, *300* (Warner Brothers, 2007); Jean-Jacques Annaud, *The Name of The Rose* (20th Century Fox, 1986); Gil Junger, *Black Knight* (20th Century Fox, 2001).

8. John Aberth, *A Knight at the Movies: Medieval History on Film* (London: Routledge, 2003).

9. The output of these historians (and others in the same vein) has been considerable. The foundational text in this study is the special forum published in the *American Historical Review* in 1988. This special forum

featured five articles that introduced many critical issues in studying historical films, and also served to validate the historical fiction film as an object of serious consideration by academic historians. Much of the subsequent work done in this field has focused on defining what makes a 'historical film' – what should or should not be included in that category. A general consensus has emerged that winnows out 'bad' films, derided as either 'nostalgia', 'costume' or 'heritage' films (by Frederick Jameson, Pierre Sorlin, and Andrew Higson respectively). Fredric Jameson, *Signatures of the Visible* (New York: Routledge, 1992), p. 137; Pierre Sorlin, *The Film in History: Restaging the Past* (Oxford: Blackwell, 1980), p. 116; Andrew Higson, *Waving the Flag: Constructing a National Cinema in Britain* (Oxford: Clarendon Press, 1995), p. 113. To these scholars, true 'historical' films, by contrast, are those which engage with history seriously or take innovative approaches in (re)presenting it. Robert Rosenstone labels these 'postmodern histories'. Rosenstone strictly limits his classification of 'postmodern history'. His classification excludes 'mainstream' and 'standard' films, and focuses only on 'experimental' or 'postmodern' films, or films lauded as 'innovative' during their time as objects of study, such as *Reds* (1981), *JFK* (1991), *Walker* (1987), or *October* (1928). Robert A. Rosenstone, *Visions of the Past: The Challenge of Film to Our Idea of History* (Cambridge, MA: Harvard University Press, 1995), pp. 83–151; Robert A. Rosenstone, *History on Film/Film on History* (Harlow: Longman/Pearson, 2006), pp. 50–69; Robert Brent Toplin, *History by Hollywood: The Use and Abuse of the American Past* (Urbana: University of Illinois Press, 1996); Robert Brent Toplin, *Reel History: In Defense of Hollywood* (Lawrence: University Press of Kansas, 2002).

10. As an example of work in this vein, Susan Aronstein examines the Americanisation of the Arthurian legend in film in *Hollywood Knights*, and Kevin Harty has recently published three collections of essays which also explore film adaptations of Arthuriana. Susan Aronstein, *Hollywood Knights: Arthurian Cinema and the Politics of Nostalgia* (New York: Palgrave Macmillan, 2005). Kevin J. Harty, *King Arthur on Film: New Essays on Arthurian Cinema* (Jefferson, NC: McFarland, 1999); Kevin J. Harty, *Cinema Arthuriana: Twenty Essays*, Second Revised Edition (Jefferson, NC: McFarland, 2002); Kevin J. Harty (ed.), *The Holy Grail on Film: Essays on the Cinematic Quest* (Jefferson, NC: McFarland, 2015).

11. For example, Queer Theory provides a focus in *Queer Movie Medievalisms. Race, Class and Gender in 'Medieval' Cinema* deploys postcolonial, Marxist, and feminist dialogues. Nickolas Haydock's *Movie Medievalism* uses Lacanian psychoanalysis and Deleuze's theory of the time-image to analyse seven medieval films. Much of *Hollywood in the Holy Land* engages with postcolonial discourses (especially using Edward Said's *Orientalism* and its antecedents). And *Cinematic Illuminations* brings a number of political theories to a large corpus of medieval film. Kathleen Coyne Kelly and Tison Pugh (eds), *Queer Movie Medievalisms* (Farnham: Ashgate, 2009); Lynn Tarte

Ramey and Tison Pugh (eds), *Race, Class, and Gender in 'Medieval' Cinema* (New York: Palgrave Macmillan, 2007); Nickolas Haydock, *Movie Medievalism* (Jefferson, NC: McFarland, 2008); Nickolas Haydock and Edward L. Risden (eds), *Hollywood in the Holy Land: Essays on Film Depictions of the Crusades and Christian–Muslim Clashes* (Jefferson, NC: McFarland, 2009); Laurie A. Finke and Martin B. Shichtman, *Cinematic Illuminations: The Middle Ages on Film* (Baltimore: The Johns Hopkins University Press, 2010).

12. For example, many scholars consider the original *Star Wars* trilogy to be a neo-Arthurian romance. *The Medieval Hero on Screen: Representations from Beowulf to Buffy* includes chapters that discover the medieval in *E.T.*, *Buffy the Vampire Slayer*, and *Dirty Harry*. A recent paper at the International Congress on Medieval Studies in Kalamazoo even found the medieval in *Sex in the City*, and sessions there regularly occur on *The Lord of the Rings* (both books and films). Robert G. Collins, 'Star Wars: The pastiche of myth and the yearning for a past future', *Journal of Popular Culture* XI/1 (1977), pp. 1–10; Kathryn Hume, 'Medieval romance and science fiction: The anatomy of a resemblance', *Journal of Popular Culture* XVI/1 (1982), pp. 15–26; Martha W. Driver and Sid Ray (eds), *The Medieval Hero on Screen: Representations from Beowulf to Buffy* (Jefferson, NC: McFarland, 2004), p. 240; Driver and Ray, *The Medieval Hero on Screen*, p. 240; pp. 73–90; pp. 133–44; pp. 156–64; Julie Nelson Couch, '"I couldn't help but wonder ... ": Sex and the City a Medieval Romance?' (presented at the International Congress on Medieval Studies, Kalamazoo, MI, 2010).

13. Abraham H. Maslow, *The Psychology of Science: A Reconnaissance*, The John Dewey Society Lectureship Series no. 8 (New York: Harper & Row, 1966), p. 15.

14. Anke Bernau and Bettina Bildhauer (eds), *Medieval Film* (Manchester: Manchester University Press, 2009), p. 2.

15. After making this statement, they turn away from this astute line of questioning toward a critical-theoretical examination of 'temporality', which forms the core of their book. Ibid., p. 2.

16. Ibid.

17. Andrew B.R. Elliott's *Remaking the Middle Ages* begins a serious exploration of the *topoi* of the medieval film; in it he analyses the depiction of the stock figures of the knight, king, priest, and peasant. This is, of course, not comprehensive, but a very productive start to this line of inquiry. Elliott, *Remaking the Middle Ages*.

18. Rosenstone, *Revisioning History*, p. 3.

19. Nineteenth-century medievalism is a complex subject that has been studied by scholars too numerous to list here. For a recent overview of the field, see Clare A. Simmons, 'Romantic medievalism', in Louise D'Arcens (ed.), *The Cambridge Companion to Medievalism* (Cambridge: Cambridge University Press, 2016), pp. 103–18.

20. During this period, film versions of Gounod's 1859 opera *Faust* were the most common medieval opera films, perhaps due to *Faust's* extreme popularity in America during the late nineteenth century. Medieval opera films during the silent cinema era include: *Parsifal* (1904), *Faust and Marguerite* (1904), *Faust* (1909), *Mephisto and the Maiden* (1909), and *Tannhauser* (1913).

21. Michael Curtiz and William Keighley, *The Adventures of Robin Hood* (Warner Brothers, 1938); Henry Hathaway, *Prince Valiant* (Twentieth Century Fox, 1954); Melvin Frank and Norman Panama, *The Court Jester* (Paramount, 1956); Joshua Logan, *Camelot* (Warner Brothers, 1967).

22. Clyde Geronimi, *Sleeping Beauty* (Walt Disney Studios, 1959); Wolfgang Reitherman, *The Sword In The Stone* (Walt Disney Studios, 1963); Wolfgang Reitherman, *Robin Hood* (Walt Disney Studios, 1973). The fourth that does not follow this formula is: Gary Trousdale and Kirk Wise, *The Hunchback of Notre Dame* (Walt Disney Studios, 1996) – which is remarkable for its dark tone. When listing only three medieval Disney films here, I am only counting those that are *explicitly* medieval, in that they are adaptations of medieval legends, or are explicitly set in the Middle Ages. Disney's other fairy tale films, though in some ways recognisably or implicitly medieval, are not explicitly so and thus are not counted here. For more on Disney's medievalisms, see: Tison Pugh and Susan Aronstein (eds), *The Disney Middle Ages: A Fairy-Tale and Fantasy Past* (Basingstoke: Palgrave Macmillan, 2012).

23. Peter Glenville, *Becket* (Paramount, 1964); Franklin J. Schaffner, *The War Lord* (Universal Pictures, 1965); Anthony Harvey, *The Lion in Winter* (Avco Embassy Pictures, 1968).

24. Robert Bresson, *Lancelot du Lac* (Artificial Eye, 1974); John Boorman, *Excalibur* (Warner Brothers, 1981); Kenneth Branagh, *Henry V* (MGM, 1989); Sam Raimi, *Army of Darkness: Evil Dead 3* (Universal Pictures, 1993); Mel Gibson, *Braveheart* (Paramount, 1995); John McTiernan and Michael Crichton, *The 13th Warrior* (Touchstone Pictures, 1999); Trousdale and Wise, *The Hunchback of Notre Dame*.

25. Terry Gilliam and Terry Jones, *Monty Python and the Holy Grail* (EMI Films, 1974).

26. Brian Helgeland, *A Knight's Tale* (Sony Pictures, 2001).

27. Snyder, *300*; see also: Jesse Warn, Michael Hurst, and Rick Jacobson, *Spartacus: Blood and Sand* (Starz, 2010) and a host of subsequent pulp iterations of the classical world, most recently including: W. S. Anderson, *Pompeii* (TriStar Pictures, 2014).

28. Currently, hypermedievalism is far more common than hyperclassicism, hypervictorianism or any other. That having been said, hypervictorianisms, such as the goth or the steampunk pop/sub-culture movements, have become steadily more popular over the course of the twenty-first century.

29. Frank Frazetta, *Testament: A Celebration of the Life & Art of Frank Frazetta*, Arnie Fenner and Cathy Fenner (eds) (Nevada City, CA: Underwood Books, 2008); Mark Kidwell et al., *The Fantastic Worlds of*

Frank Frazetta, Volume 1 (Portland, OR: Image Comics, 2008); Boris Vallejo and Julie Bell, *Boris Vallejo and Julie Bell: The Ultimate Collection* (London: Paper Tiger, 2005).

30. Even when not adhering to the grotesque distortions of the human figure or the 'dark' aesthetic commonly seen in Frazetta and Vallejo's work, the genre of fantasy art follows many of the models they set. This includes the use of extreme detail and vividly saturated colours – ironically rendering these fantasy scenes in a 'hyper-real' way. For examples, see: Dick Jude, *Fantasy Art Masters: The Best Fantasy and Science Fiction Artists Show How They Work* (New York, NY: Watson-Guptill, 1999), pp. 12–60; Bruce Robertson, *Techniques of Fantasy Art* (London: Macdonald Orbis, 1988); Jane Frank and Howard Frank, *Great Fantasy Art: Themes from the Frank Collection* (London: Paper Tiger, 2003).

31. 'Barbarians' is not an uncontroversial term in an academic context. While in an academic context, 'barbarians' only denotes those groups which invaded the Western Roman Empire towards its demise, contemporary medievalist popular culture often amalgamates many distinct groups (separated by centuries) under that overarching title, including: Vikings, Anglo-Saxons, Huns, Vandals, Goths and more. The term was originally used by Romans to describe pejoratively those on the edges of their empire, but has subsequently become a catch-all generally referring to a hairy, fur-wearing sort of 'uncivilised' (another problematic term) person.

32. Kevin Reynolds, *Robin Hood: Prince of Thieves* (Warner Brothers, 1991); Gibson, *Braveheart*; McTiernan and Crichton, *The 13th Warrior*; Antoine Fuqua, *King Arthur* (Buena Vista, 2004).

33. Philip Vilas Bohlman, *The Music of European Nationalism: Cultural Identity and Modern History* (Santa Barbara, CA: ABC-CLIO, 2004), pp. 183–6; Hans A. Pohlsander, *National Monuments and Nationalism in 19th Century Germany* (Peter Lang, 2008), pp. 32–5; Paul Robinson, *Opera & Ideas, from Mozart to Strauss* (Ithaca, NY: Cornell University Press, 1986), pp. 155–74.

34. Clare A. Simmons, *Reversing the Conquest: History and Myth in Nineteenth-Century British Literature* (New Brunswick: Rutgers University Press, 1990), p. 11.

35. Examples include *The Crusades* (1935), *The Seventh Seal* (1957), *Braveheart* (1995), and *Kingdom of Heaven* (2005).

36. This homogenisation has been argued to be the by-product of the many protests and boycotts of Hollywood films called in the 1980s and 1990s by special interest groups. Francis G. Couvares, 'The paradox of protest: American film, 1980–1992', in Frances G. Couvares (ed.), *Movie Censorship and American Culture*, Second Edition (Boston, MA: University of Massachusetts Press, 2006), pp. 277–318.

Chapter 5   The Middle Ages They Watched

1. David L. Hamilton, *Cognitive Processes in Stereotyping and Intergroup Behavior* (Hillsdale, NJ: L. Erlbaum Associates, 1981), p. 137.

2. Kevin Harty (ed.), *The Vikings on Film: Essays on Depictions of the Nordic Middle Ages* (Jefferson, NC: McFarland, 2011), p. 3.

3. 'The Viking Age' is generally dated between the eighth and eleventh centuries. For dates of 'the Viking Age' in Scandinavian history (and the invention of the term), see: Eric Christiansen, *The Norsemen in the Viking Age* (Malden, Mass: Blackwell Publishers, 2001), pp. 4–9; Peter Sawyer, 'The age of the Vikings, and before', in Peter Sawyer (ed.), *The Oxford Illustrated History of the Vikings* (Oxford: Oxford University Press, 1997), pp. 1–18.

4. One strategy employed by these three participants in their decision-making about the dragon was questioning me (as a perceived authority on the subject), asking, 'Do you know, do you know the original poem?' I only answered, 'A little, yeah', which they interpreted, correctly, was a way of communicating that I could not participate in the discussion and that they would have to decide for themselves.

5. For dragons in Classical literature, see: Daniel Ogden, *Drakon: Dragon Myth and Serpent Cult in the Greek and Roman Worlds* (Oxford: Oxford University Press, 2013). For the figure of the dragon in *Beowulf*, see: R. D. Fulk, Robert E. Bjork, and John D. Niles, 'Bēowulf's fight with the dragon' in R. D. Fulk, Robert E. Bjork, and John D. Niles (eds), *Klaeber's Beowulf and the Fight at Finnsburg*, Fourth Edition (Toronto, University of Toronto Press, 2008), pp. xlv–xlviii; Christine Rauer, *Beowulf and the Dragon: Parallels and Analogues* (Cambridge: D.S. Brewer, 2000).

6. Rauer, *Beowulf and the Dragon*, p. 4.

7. Participants often used the terms 'mythology' and 'fantasy' interchangeably. In this instance, Erica used mythology to refer to the familial and social relationships between the supernatural creatures (all bound together with the film's 'sins of the father' narrative).

8. Martha Carlin, 'Feast', in Elizabeth Emery and Richard Utz (eds), *Medievalism: Key Critical Terms* (Woodbridge: D.S. Brewer, 2014): 63–9, pp. 63–4.

9. Gwendolyn Morgan, '*Beowulf* and the Middle Ages in Film', *The Year's Work in Medievalism* XXIII (2009): 3–15, p. 10.

10. Hugh M. Thomas, *The Norman Conquest: England After William the Conqueror* (Lanham: Rowman & Littlefield Publishers, Inc., 2008), p. 64.

11. Ibid., p. 129.

12. Morgan, '*Beowulf* and the Middle Ages in Film', pp. 10, 13.

13. Neil Gaiman, 'The monarch of the glen' in *Fragile Things: Short Fictions and Wonders* (New York: Harper, 2006), pp. 284–340; Graham Baker, *Beowulf* (Miramax Films, 1999); Les Landau (dir), 'Heroes and demons', *Star Trek: Voyager.* (Paramount Network Television, 24 April 1995).

14. Robert Zemezckis, *A Hero's Journey: The Making of Beowulf* (Paramount Pictures, 2008); William Brown, 'Beowulf: The digital monster movie', *Animation* 4/2 (July 1, 2009): pp. 153–5.

15. The credit to Mr Stephens for the role of 'Beowulf Physique' has been removed from his IMDB listing and the IMDB listing of the film for reasons unknown, though probably in order to cover up the potentially unnerving truth that Beowulf's head and body were not provided by the same person. However, this credit (and Mr Ritchson's) can be seen by accessing an archived IMDB page using the Internet Archive. All of the complete relevant credits can be found at: 'Internet Archive: IMDB Beowulf (2007)', 10 February 2007. Available at http://web.archive.org/web/20070905003741/www.imdb.com/title/tt0442933 (accessed 1 May 2010).

16. Neil Gaiman and Roger Avary, *Beowulf: The Script Book* (New York: Harper Collins, 2009), p. 140.

17. John H. Fisher, *The Emergence of Standard English* (Lexington: The University Press of Kentucky, 1996), p. 145.

18. M.J. Toswell, 'Lingua', in Elizabeth Emery and Richard Utz (eds), *Medievalism: Key Critical Terms* (Woodbridge: D.S. Brewer, 2014): 117–24, p. 118.

19. Roland Barthes, 'The reality effect', in Richard Howard (trans), *The Rustle of Language* (Oxford: Blackwell, 1986), pp. 141–8.

20. Ibid., p. 141.

21. Roland Barthes, 'The Romans in films', in Annette Lavers (trans), *Mythologies* (London: Vintage, 1993), pp. 26–8.

22. Vivian Sobchack, '"Surge and Splendor": A phenomenology of the Hollywood historical epic', *Representations* 0/29 (Winter, 1990): 24–49, pp. 26–7.

23. The only exception is a final cameo appearance of King Richard I – and even he should be speaking French. Richard I, despite his lasting reputation in English popular culture, famously spent most of his time in France, spoke French primarily and seems to have had little affinity for the land over which he ruled. The best recent biography and assessment of Richard I's reign is: John Gillingham, *Richard I*, English Monarchs (New Haven, London: Yale University Press, 1999).

24. While Hollywood medieval films tend to exaggerate the efficacy of swords (and tend to de-emphasise the efficacy of armour), they were never the glorified clubs that Mark seems to believe they were. This idea seems to fit as part of his larger idea that the Middle Ages were un-technological and barbaric.

25. Steven Spielberg, *Saving Private Ryan* (DreamWorks, 1998); Doug Liman, *The Bourne Identity* (Universal Studios, 2002); Christopher Nolan, *Batman Begins* (Warner Brothers, 2005); Martin Campbell, *Casino Royale* (Columbia Pictures, 2006); Miguel Sapochnik (dir), 'Battle of the bastards', *Game of Thrones* (HBO, 19 June 2016).

26. Roger Ebert, 'Movie reviews: *The Hurricane*', *The Chicago Sun-Times*, 7 January 2000. Available at http://rogerebert.suntimes.com/apps/pbcs.dll/article? AID=/20000107/REVIEWS/1070302/1023 (accessed 14 November 2016).

27. For a thorough examination of the changes to the historical story made in *Kingdom of Heaven*, see: Jeffrey Richards, 'Sir Ridley Scott and the rebirth of the historical epic', in Andrew B.R. Elliott (ed.), *The Return of the Epic Film: Genre, Aesthetics and History in the Twenty-first Century* (Edinburgh: Edinburgh University Press, 2014), pp. 25-9.

28. Ambroise, *The History of the Holy War: Ambroise's Estoire de la Guerre Sainte*, Marianne Ailes (trans) and Malcolm Barber (ed.) (Woodbridge: The Boydell Press, 2003), p. 149.

29. For medieval sources on Balian of Ibelin, see: William of Tyre, *A History of Deeds Done Beyond the Sea*, Records of Civilization, Sources and Studies 35 (New York: Columbia University Press, 1943); *La Continuation De Guillaume De Tyr, 1184–1197*, Documents Relatifs à l'Histoire Des Croisades 14 (Paris: Librairie Orientaliste P. Geuthner, 1982); William of Tyre, *The Conquest of Jerusalem and the Third Crusade: Sources in Translation*, P. W Edbury (ed.) (Brookfield, VT: Scholar Press, 1996).

30. In the extended 'director's cut' version of the film, in France Balian is shown to have been a siege master as well as a blacksmith. The companion guide to the 'history behind the film' calls him 'an artificer', as Scott describes him, 'who in another era would be a talented engineer'. This makes his use of sophisticated anti-siege tactics (such as range-markers and counterweighted *ballistae*) during the siege of Jerusalem more plausible. However, participants were shown the theatrical release of the film in which his previous experience with siege technology is never made clear. This may have contributed to their feeling that the arc of the hero was unrealistic. Ridley Scott, Diana Landau, and Nancy Friedman, *Kingdom of Heaven: The Ridley Scott Film and the History Behind the Story* (London: Newmarket Press, 2005), p. 17.

31. Finke and Shichtman, *Cinematic Illuminations*, p. 233.

32. Frank Capra, *Mr. Smith Goes to Washington* (Columbia Pictures, 1939).

33. The phenomenon of the 'pretty boy' in popular culture also has a long history in Japanese culture as the figure of the Bishōnen (literally 'beautiful boy'), a beautiful, androgynous, highly sexualised young male. However, unlike the common Western perception of the 'pretty boy' type being ineffectual, effete and weak, Bishōnen commonly are often depicted with extreme sport or martial arts prowess. Sandra Buckley (ed.), *Encyclopedia of Contemporary Japanese Culture* (London: Routledge, 2001), pp. 45-6.

34. Harry M. Benshoff and Sean Griffin, *America on Film: Representing Race, Class, Gender, and Sexuality at the Movies*, Second Edition (Malden, MA: Wiley-Blackwell, 2009), p. 255.

35. L.M. DeBruine et al., 'The health of a nation predicts their mate preferences: Cross-cultural variation in women's preferences for masculinized male faces',

Proceedings of the Royal Society B: Biological Sciences 277/7 August (March 2010): 2405–10, p. 2405.

36. Finke and Shichtman, *Cinematic Illuminations*, p. 182; Susan Jeffords, *Hard Bodies: Hollywood Masculinity in the Reagan Era* (New Brunswick: Rutgers University Press, 1994).

37. Susan Aronstein, *Hollywood Knights: Arthurian Cinema and the Politics of Nostalgia* (New York: Palgrave McMillan, 2005).

38. This reference is in relation to a statement by Justin and Stephen that Richard Gere, though silver-haired, would *not* have the appropriate gravitas to play a medieval hero. Stephen postulated this is 'because we haven't seen him [Gere] in a suitable role'. Obviously, these participants had not seen *First Knight*, in which Gere is cast as Lancelot. It is unknown whether they would revise their opinion after having seen the film. Jerry Zucker, *First Knight* (Sony Pictures, 1997).

39. Scott, Landau, and Friedman, *Kingdom of Heaven: The Ridley Scott Film*, p. 68.

40. Finke and Shichtman, *Cinematic Illuminations*, p. 197.

41. Stephen is here incorrect in his labelling of Saladin as being depicted as someone who was a 'baddie' and who 'wanted to make war'. Immediately afterwards, both Sean and Justin questioned this statement. Stephen then recanted, saying Saladin 'was a bit of a mysterious character'. Stephen's original interpretation (or slip of the tongue) puts him in line with some depictions of Saladin, like DeMille's *The Crusades* (1935). For a further examination of the character of Saladin as depicted in cinema and television, see Lorraine K. Stock, 'Now starring in the Third Crusade: Depictions of Richard I and Saladin in films and television series', in Nickolas Haydock and Edward L. Risden (eds), *Hollywood in the Holy Land: Essays on Film Depictions of the Crusades and Christian-Muslim Clashes* (Jefferson, NC: McFarland, 2009), pp. 93–122.

42. For an exploration of why Azeem is such a problematic depiction of Muslims, see: Lorraine K. Stock, 'Now starring in the Third Crusade', pp. 117–19.

43. Jack Shaheen, *Reel Bad Arabs: How Hollywood Vilifies a People* (Northampton, MA: Olive Branch Press, 2009), p. 4.

44. For more on modern historiography of the Crusades and Riley-Smith's contribution, see: Christopher Tyerman, *The Debate on the Crusades* (Manchester: Manchester University Press, 2011), pp. 224–32.

45. Jonathan Riley-Smith, 'Crusading as an act of love', *History* 65/214: pp. 177–92. Available at http://dx.doi.org/10.1111/j.1468-229X.1980. tb01939.x (accessed 7 November 2016).

46. Evelyn Alsultany, *Arabs and Muslims in the Media: Race and Representation after 9/11* (New York: New York University Press, 2012), pp. 10–11.

47. Pronouncing Saladin's name this way was clearly a tactic, by Mark, of asserting himself as an authority on the subject within the group.

48. Jonathan Riley-Smith, *The Crusades, Christianity and Islam* (New York: Columbia University Press, 2011), pp. 63–9.

49. Thomas F. Madden, *The Concise History of the Crusades* (Lanham: Rowman & Littlefield, 2014), pp. 200–4.

50. For more on British Imperialism and the origins of the phrase 'make the desert bloom' see: Robert S. G. Fletcher, *British Imperialism & 'The Tribal Question': Desert Administration & Nomadic Societies in the Middle East, 1919–1936* (Oxford: Oxford University Press, 2015), p. 184.

51. To accurately illustrate how uncomfortable this conversation became, this section has been transcribed verbatim without editing.

52. Two compelling collections on the depiction of the Middle East in the media are: Peter van der Veer and Shoma Munshi (eds), *Media, War, and Terrorism: Responses from the Middle East and Asia* (London: Routledge, 2004); Yahya R Kamalipour (ed.), *The U.S. Media and the Middle East: Image and Perception*, Contributions to the Study of Mass Media and Communications 46 (Westport, CN: Greenwood Press, 1995). Of particular interest in this context is part VI of the latter volume (pp. 199–230), which describes three different studies of the effects that depictions of Arabs and the Middle East have upon children and students' perceptions of them.

53. For example, throughout the Middle Ages it can be argued that England was something of a cultural backwater by contrast with France or the Holy Roman Empire. For more, see: John Gillingham and Ralph A. Griffiths, *Medieval Britain, A Very Short Introduction* (Oxford: Oxford University Press, 2000), pp. 26–7.

54. Whereas *Beowulf* would be considered medieval fantasy (since it is based on the fantasy of a medieval imagination), *The Lord of the Rings* is a work of medievalism, and thus a *medievalist* fantasy. This term seems particularly apropos since Tolkien himself was a medievalist. Since I consider creators of historical films to be historians (in that they create histories, just in a different medium), the term seems appropriate even for those without Tolkien's pedigree.

55. Tolkien occasionally asserted that *The Lord of the Rings* is a fantastical pre-history set in our own world: 'The theatre of my tale is this earth, the one in which we now live, but the historical period is imaginary.' While this may have been the author's intention, to the casual reader (and viewer), Tolkien seems to be building a world entirely unlike and separate from our own. J. R. R. Tolkien, *The Letters of J.R.R. Tolkien*, Humphrey Carpenter (ed.) (New York: Houghton Mifflin Company, 2000), p. 220; p. 239.

56. In the books (and also in the films), the Rohirrim speak Old English and have a culture similar to the Anglo-Saxons. However, some scholars have drawn apt comparisons between the Rohirrim and the Germanic tribes described by Tacitus as well. Sandra Ballif Straubhaar, 'Myth, Late Roman history, and multiculturalism in Tolkien's Middle-Earth', in Jane Chance (ed.), *Tolkien and the Invention of Myth* (Lexington-Fayette, KY: University Press of Kentucky, 2004), pp. 101–18.

57. Rick Lyman, 'Movie marketing wizardry; "Lord of the Rings" trilogy taps the internet to build excitement', *New York Times*, 11 January 2001, sec. Movies.

Available at http://www.nytimes.com/2001/01/11/movies/movie-marketing-wizardry-lord-rings-trilogy-taps-internet-build-excitement.html (accessed 15 November 2016).

Chapter 6   The Medieval Worlds They Found

1. Daphne Du Maurier, *Rebecca* (London: Arrow, 1992), p. 15.
2. Edward Morgan Forster, *A Room With a View/Where Angels Fear To Tread* (New York: Alfred A. Knopf, 2011), p. 44.
3. The UK's 12A rating is roughly analogous to a PG-13 rating in the US. Australia does not have a rating that is truly equivalent – but for context, *Beowulf* was rated M, meaning it was only for audiences over 15.
4. Joseph M. Sullivan, 'Silly Vikings: Eichinger, Hickox, and Lorenz's Anglo-German-Irish Production of Hal Foster's *Prince Valiant* (1997)', in Kevin J. Harty (ed.), *The Vikings on Film: Essays on Depictions of the Nordic Middle Ages* (Jefferson, NC: McFarland, 2011): 56–71, p. 61.
5. In *Kingdom of Heaven*, Balian murders a priest in his home in France, which precipitates his departure on Crusade. On the road to Jerusalem, he and his father encounter, and kill, several men attempting to bring Balian to justice. At the end of the film, Balian then returns to his home in France (albeit briefly), seemingly without consequence.
6. Mark then endured teasing from the rest of the group because poison ivy in a glass would not be lethal.
7. Though medieval law enforcement differed in its methods from those of today, the period was hardly lawless: see John Briggs, Christopher Harrison, Agnus McInnes, and David Vincent, 'The medieval origins of the English criminal justice system", in *Crime and Punishment in England: An Introductory History* (London: UCL Press, 1996), pp. 1–14; Anthony Musson and Edward Powell (eds), *Crime, Law and Society in the Later Middle Ages: Selected Sources* (Manchester: Manchester University Press, 2009); Barbara A. Hanawalt and David Wallace (eds), *Medieval Crime and Social Control* (Minneapolis: University of Minnesota Press, 1999).
8. Slavery was common in the place and time in which *Beowulf* is set, and is subsequently recorded by contemporaries in England from the seventh century to the eleventh. Stephen's potential misunderstanding of medieval Norse slavery fits with Ruth Karras' assertion in her book *Slavery and Society in Medieval Scandinavia* that, 'The existence of slavery in medieval Scandinavia comes as a surprise to many historians who are not medievalists and to many Scandinavians who are not historians [...] the institution does not often appear in any detail in discussions of medieval European social history'. Ruth Mazo Karras, *Slavery and Society in Medieval Scandinavia*, Yale Historical Publications 135 (New Haven, CT: Yale University Press, 1988), p. 1. For slavery in Anglo-Saxon England, see: David A.E. Pelteret, *Slavery in Early Mediaeval England: From the Reign of Alfred Until the Twelfth Century*, Studies in Anglo-Saxon History 7 (Woodbridge: Boydell, 1995).

9. The Bechdel test is a test invented in 1985 by Alison Bechdel (author of the long-running comic 'Dykes to Watch Out For') to highlight the institutional problems in the depiction of women by the filmmaking industry. In order to pass the Bechdel test, a film must have three simple things: 'One, it has to have at least two women in it who, two, **talk** to each other about, three, something besides a **man**. [*sic*]' This test is not an assessment of a film's quality, or even a judgement of whether it can be considered feminist (though it would be difficult for a film to be considered feminist *without* passing this test). However, it is a simple way of highlighting how relatively insignificant the representation of women and women's stories is in cinema. Alison Bechdel, 'The rule', *Dykes to Watch Out For*, 16 August 2005. Available at http://dykestowatchoutfor.com/the-rule (accessed 22 December 2016).

10. The women of the poem *Beowulf* have been reassessed by Jane Chance, Dorothy Carr Porter, and others. Arguments have been made that interpret the women in Beowulf as central to the poem, either as hostesses, peace-weavers or warmongers. Wealtheow and Hyrd represent the Anglo-Saxon female ideal of hostess and peace-weaver, Grendel's mother and Thryth represent the monstrous inversion of that ideal. However, this does not lessen the point that the role played by women in the *Beowulf* poem is limited. For more see: Jane Chance, *Woman as Hero in Old English Literature* (New York: Syracuse University Press, 1986); Gillian R. Overing, 'The women of Beowulf: A context for interpretation' in Peter S. Baker (ed.), *The Beowulf Reader*, Basic Readings in Anglo-Saxon England 1 (London: Garland, 2000), pp. 219–60; Dorothy Carr Porter, 'The Social Centrality of Women in Beowulf: A New Context', *The Heroic Age* 5 (Summer/Autumn 2001). Available at http://www.heroicage.org/issues/5/porter1.html (accessed 22 December 2016).

11. Sibylla's character is much expanded in the 'Director's Cut' edition of the film: Ridley Scott, *Kingdom Of Heaven – Definitive Edition DVD* (20th Century Fox, 2005). For more on the real Sibylla of Jerusalem, see: Bernard Hamilton, 'Women in the crusader states: The queens of Jerusalem (1100–1190)', in Derek Baker (ed.), *Medieval Women*, Studies in Church History 1 (Oxford: B. Blackwell, 1978), pp. 143–74; Bernard Hamilton, *The Leper King and His Heirs: Baldwin IV and the Crusader Kingdom of Jerusalem* (Cambridge: Cambridge University Press, 2000).

12. In *Kingdom of Heaven*, Balian is not a slave but a free blacksmith. Erica's false memory of his bondage may imply she sees all medieval poor as slaves, or there may have been something in the blacksmithing scene that implied slavery to her.

13. Katie Stevenson and Barbara Gribling, 'Introduction: Chivalry and the medieval past', in Katie Stevenson and Barbara Gribling (eds), *Chivalry and the Medieval Past* (Woodbridge: Boydell Press, 2016), 1–14, pp. 2–3.

14. The film's interest in defining knighthood could spring from the fact that this was Ridley Scott's first film after he himself was knighted in 2003.

15. This is another example of some of the insular attitude held by some of the participants. Almost all of the Christians in this film – including the

protagonist – are explicitly French. To pick out the antagonist as 'the French guy' implies they instinctually saw the protagonist – and perhaps by association, all virtuous characters, as, if not necessarily English, then definitely not French.

16. Karl Marx, *Capital: A Critique of Political Economy*, Ben Fowkes and David Fernbach (trans) (Harmondsworth: Penguin, 1976), p. 90.

17. While colonies existed during the Middle Ages, it was fundamentally different from the European colonialism witnessed in the seventeenth through nineteenth centuries. It is difficult to know from this brief mention how John envisages colonialism, but it seems likely that he projected the type of colonialism witnessed in the later period onto the Middle Ages. Perhaps he thought it was a historically universal phenomenon, which may cause a number of errors in thinking – but it is difficult to say only from this evidence. For more on specifically medieval colonisation, and the differences between it and that of other periods, see: Robert Bartlett, *The Making of Europe: Conquest, Colonization and Cultural Change, 950–1350* (Harmondsworth: Penguin, 1994), pp. 292–315.

18. Richard W. Barber, *The Holy Grail: Imagination and Belief* (Cambridge, MA: Harvard University Press, 2004), p. 332.

19. Georges Vigarello, *The Metamorphoses of Fat: A History of Obesity* (New York: Columbia University Press, 2013), pp. 3–6.

20. Ibid., p. 8.

21. Ibid., p. 21.

22. Edward Long, *The History of Jamaica*, vol. 2 (London: T. Lowndes, 1774): 351–65, pp. 364–5.

23. David Hume, 'Of national characters', in *Essays: Moral, Political and Literary* (New York: Cosimo, 2007), p. 213.

24. This is in reference to the King of the Dead in *The Return of the King*.

25. Claire Valente, *The Theory and Practice of Revolt in Medieval England* (Aldershot: Ashgate, 2003), pp. 1–14.

26. King Baldwin IV and Hrothgar are the only kings that are physically dissimilar from the others in the films. Notably, this could be because both are seen as impaired in some way – Hrothgar is old and fat, and Baldwin IV is so deformed by his leprosy that he wears a mask.

27. Tony Brown, 'Clearances and clearings: Deforestation in Mesolithic/Neolithic Britain', *Oxford Journal of Archaeology* 16/2 (July 1997), pp. 133–46. cf. Christopher Taylor, *Village and Farmstead: A History of Rural Settlement in England* (London: George Philip, 1984).

28. Leonard Cantor, 'Forests, chases, parks and warrens', in Leonard Cantor (ed.), *The English Medieval Landscape* (London: Croom Helm, 1982): 56–85, pp. 56–65; Oliver Rackham, *Trees and Woodland in the British Landscape*, Revised Edition (London: Phoenix Giant, 1996).

29. Carenza Lewis, Patrick Mitchell-Fox and Christopher Dyer, *Village, Hamlet and Field: Changing Medieval Settlements in Central England* (Manchester:

Manchester University Press, 1997), pp. 77–118; Brian K. Roberts and Stuart Wrathmell, *Region and Place: A Study of English Rural Settlement* (London: English Heritage, 2002).

30. Many of these ancient roads still exist today. Francis Pryor, *The Making of the British Landscape: How We Have Transformed the Land, from Prehistory to Today*, First Edition (London: Allen Lane, 2010), pp. 170–4.

31. J.C. Russell, 'Late Ancient and Medieval population', *Transactions of the American Philosophical Society* 48/3 (1 January 1958): 1–152, p. 105.

32. France was even more populous and dense than England – at around 17.6 million inhabitants in 1346 (on the eve of the Black Death) – its density would be 83.8 people per square mile, just under the average density of the USA in 2010 (88.08 people per square mile). Ibid.; United States Census, 'Resident population data – 2010 Census'. Available at http://www.census.gov/2010census/data/apportionment-dens-text.php (accessed 22 December 2016).

33. The difficulties in returning from the quest is a common trope in many mythological traditions, explored by folklorists like Joseph Campbell. Joseph Campbell, 'Return', in *The Hero with a Thousand Faces*, Bollingen Series XVII Third Edition (Novato: New World Library, 2008), pp. 167–210.

34. Andrea Kann (ed.), *The Art, Science, and Technology of Medieval Travel* (Aldershot: Ashgate, 2008), pp. 115–26.

35. Ibid., pp. 1–15.

36. Lloyd Alexander, *The Book of Three* (London: Holt, Rinehart and Winston, 1964). This hero type seems to arise whenever a landscape is noted for being particularly harsh or difficult to traverse. See as examples in other literature, TV and film: Lawrence of Arabia or Paul Atreides from *Dune* become masters of desert landscape. Pirates occupy this space in the Early Modern seas – though the degree to which they are half-civilised and/or heroic depends on the story. Native Americans (or their white allies) tend to fill this role in early American or Western narratives, like John Dunbar in *Dances with Wolves* (1990) or Nathaniel Hawkeye in *Last of the Mohicans* (1992). Frank Herbert, *Dune* (London: New English Library, 1965).

37. Christopher Tyerman, *God's War: A New History of the Crusades* (Cambridge, MA: The Belknap Press, 2006), pp. 400–1.

38. David Watkin Waters, *The Iberian Bases of the English Art of Navigation in the Sixteenth Century* (Coimbra: University of Coimbra General Library, 1970), p. 5.

39. Alan Lee and David Day, *Castles*, David Larkin (ed.) (New York: McGraw-Hill, 1984), pp. 26–9; Gary Russell, *The Art of The Lord of the Rings* (New York: HarperCollins, 2004), p. 85.

40. A.J. Taylor, *The Welsh Castles of Edward I* (London: Hambledon, 1986); D.J. Cathcart King, *The Castle in England and Wales: An Interpretive History* (London: Routledge, 1991).

41. William Morris, *A Dream of John Ball* (Oxford: Kelmscott Press, 1892). Available at http://morrisedition.lib.uiowa.edu/dream.html (accessed 20

December 2016). For more on William Morris' socialist medievalism, see: Jennifer Harris, 'William Morris and the Middle Ages', in Joanna Banham and Jennifer Harris (eds), *William Morris and the Middle Ages* (Manchester: Manchester University Press, 1984), pp. 1–16.

42. The one exception is King Richard I of England, who makes a cameo appearance at the end of *Kingdom of Heaven*. However, he plays no role other than as a vehicle used to show that Balian is unwilling to repeat the mistake of crusade even at the behest of a king.

43. William C. Calin, 'Christianity', in Elizabeth Emery and Richard Utz (eds), *Medievalism: Key Critical Terms* (Woodbridge: D.S. Brewer, 2014), pp. 35–41, p. 35.

44. Ibid.

45. Eva Thury and Margaret Klopfle Devinney, *Introduction to Mythology: Contemporary Approaches to Classical and World Myths* (Oxford: Oxford University Press, 2005), p. 4.

46. The excised portion of this quote is a parenthetical that reads: '(and "No women", but that does not matter, and is not true anyway)'. While *The Lord of the Rings* does have some female characters, as explored above, they are relatively few, and only two (Galadriel and Eowyn) can be said to hold positions of power or agency. J.R.R. Tolkien, *The Letters of J.R.R. Tolkien*, Humphrey Carpenter (ed.) (New York: Houghton Mifflin, 2000), p. 220.

Chapter 7   Discussion, Conclusions, and Looking Forward

1. Anselm L. Strauss and Juliet M. Corbin, *Basics of Qualitative Research: Techniques and Procedures for Developing Grounded Theory*, Second Edition (Thousand Oaks: Sage Publications, 1998), pp. 266–8.

2. Richard Utz, *Medievalism: A Manifesto* (Kalamazoo and Bradford: Arc Humanities Press, 2017), p. 10.

3. Louise D'Arcens, 'Presentism', in Elizabeth Emery and Richard Utz (eds), *Medievalism: Key Critical Terms* (Woodbridge: D.S. Brewer, 2014): 181–8, p. 184.

4. L.P. Hartley, *The Go-Between* (New York: New York Review Books, 2002), p. 17.

5. Masahiro Mori, 'Bukimi no tani {the uncanny valley}', K. F. MacDorman and T. Minato (trans), *Energy* 7 (1970), pp. 33–5.

6. For example: Angela Tinwell, Mark Grimshaw, and Andrew Williams, 'Uncanny behaviour in survival horror games', *Journal of Gaming & Virtual Worlds* 2/1 (May 2010): pp. 3–25; Saint John Walker, 'A quick walk through Uncanny Valley', in Alison Oddey and Christine White (eds), *Modes of Spectating* (Bristol: Intellect Books, 2009), pp. 29–40.

7. Mori, 'Bukimi no tani, {the uncanny valley}', p. 34.

8. Ferguson, 'Humanist Views of the Renaissance' in Clare Simmons (ed.), *Medievalism and the Quest for the 'Real' Middle Ages*, 1–28, p. 28.

9. John Green (presenter), 'The Crusades – pilgrimage or holy war?: Crash course world history #15', 3 May 2012. Available at https://www.youtube.com/watch?v = X0zudTQelzI (accessed 6 January 2017); John Green (presenter), 'The Dark Ages ... how dark were they, really?: Crash course world history #14', 26 April 2012. Available at https://www.youtube.com/watch?v = QV7CanyzhZg (accessed 6 January 2017).

10. Three popular websites that feature medieval content are Medievalists.net, and the collaborative history blogs *In the Middle*, and *The Public Medievalist*. Peter Konieczny (ed.), Medievalists.net. Available at http://www.medievalists.net (accessed 30 May 2017); J.J. Cohen, et al., *In the Middle: Towards a Progressive Medieval Studies*. Available at http://www.inthemedievalmiddle.com/ (accessed 30 May 2017); Paul B. Sturtevant (ed.), *The Public Medievalist*. Available at http://www.publicmedievalist.com (accessed 30 May 2017).

11. For examples of historians relating their experiences as consultants, see: Robert A. Rosenstone, 'History in images/History in words: Reflections on the possibility of really putting history onto film', *The American Historical Review* 93/5 (December 1988): pp. 1173–85; Natalie Zemon Davis, '"Any resemblance to persons living or dead": Film and the challenge of authenticity', *Historical Journal of Film, Radio and Television* 8/3 (1988): pp. 269–83; Kathleen M. Coleman, 'The pedant goes to Hollywood: The role of the academic consultant', in Martin M. Winkler (ed.), *Gladiator: Film and History* (Oxford: Blackwell, 2005), pp. 45–52.

12. Utz, *Medievalism: A Manifesto*, p. 23.

13. Ibid.

14. 'Medieval: Total Realism Forums', Totalwar.org, n.d. Available at http://forums.totalwar.org/vb/forumdisplay.php?162-Medieval-Total-Realism (accessed 20 January 2017).

15. Helen Young, '"It's the Middle Ages, yo!": Race, neo/medievalisms, and the world of Dragon Age', *The Year's Work in Medievalism* 27 (2012), pp. 1–9. Available at https://sites.google.com/site/theyearsworkinmedievalism/all-issues/27-2012 (accessed 10 January 2017).

16. Mike Baker, 'History study needs facts first, analysis later', *Guardian* (18 January 2011). Available at https://www.theguardian.com/education/2011/jan/18/history-national-curriculum (accessed 20 January 2017).

17. William Woods, 'Authenticating realism in medieval film', in Martha Driver and Sid Ray (eds), *The Medieval Hero On Screen: Representations from Beowulf to Buffy* (Jefferson, NC: McFarland, 2004), 38–52, p. 47.

18. For example: Chris Berdik 'How to teach high-school students to spot fake news', *Slate* (21 December 2016). Available at http://www.slate.com/articles/technology/future_tense/2016/12/media_literacy_courses_help_high_school_students_spot_fake_news.html (accessed January 13 2017); Moriah Balingit, 'After Comet Ping Pong and pizzagate, teachers tackle fake news', *Washington Post*, Education Section, 11 December 2016. Available at https://www.washingtonpost.com/local/education/after-comet-ping-pong-

and-pizzagate-teachers-tackle-fake-news/2016/12/11/cc19d604-bd99-11e6-91ee-1adddfe36cbe_story.html?utm_term = .c76ea9a6166f (accessed 13 January 2017).

Appendix A   Using Social Science Methods to Study Historical Consciousness

1. This is a necessary oversimplification. The field of historiography and philosophy of history is broad and encompasses a variety of ways in which historians approach (and have approached) their topics of study.
2. For example, in order to achieve a margin of error of +/-5 per cent with 90 per cent confidence from an overall population of 100,000 people, a survey need only be completed by 383 people.
3. Thomas R. Black, *Doing Quantitative Research in the Social Sciences: An Integrated Approach to Research Design, Measurement and Statistics* (London: SAGE, 1999), pp. 136–7; Robert M. Groves et al., *Survey Methodology* (Hoboken, NJ: John Wiley & Sons, 2009), pp. 6–10.
4. Joseph Alex Maxwell, *Qualitative Research Design: An Interactive Approach*, Second Edition (Thousand Oaks, CA: Sage Publications, 2005), pp. 70–3.
5. For more on purposive sampling, see: Sharan B. Merriam, *Qualitative Research: A Guide to Design and Implementation* (San Francisco, CA: John Wiley & Sons, 2009), pp. 76–83.
6. For more on the topic of generalisibility and qualitative research, see: Maxwell, *Qualitative Research Design*, pp. 96–8.

Appendix B   Methodology of *The Middle Ages in the Popular Imagination* Study

1. A.J. Cañas and J.D. Novak, *The Theory Underlying Concept Maps and How to Construct and Use Them* (Ocala, FL: Florida Institute for Human and Machine Cognition, 2008).
2. While it might have been more expedient to show the participants only clips from the films, to have done so would raise important questions about validity. The selection of the clips could unduly influence the results of the groups. Presenting only clips, though faster, would be an artificial environment, which would over-structure the interview and potentially skew the responses. As a constructivist position was taken with regards to understanding of the Middle Ages, it would be inappropriate to choose which pieces of each film exemplify certain aspects of the period or the issue at hand and possibly produce undue moderator influence. Ideally, the viewing of the film should be as close to a 'natural' experience of watching the film as is possible considering the restraints of the research environment.

3. There are a variety of releases of each of these films. For the purpose of the focus groups, I showed the participants the theatrical release edition of each film, rather than any of the extended editions. Also, *Beowulf* was frequently seen in theatres in 3D. However due to technological limitations of home viewing, I could only show the participants Beowulf in 2D. This may have affected their understanding of the films, but it is difficult to comment on how without evidence.

4. Maxwell, *Qualitative Research Design*; Berg, *Qualitative Research Methods for the Social Sciences*.

5. David R. Thomas, 'A general inductive approach for qualitative data analysis', *American Journal of Evaluation* 27/2 (2006): 237–46. Available at http://journals.sagepub.com/doi/pdf/10.1177/1098214005283748 (accessed 1 June 2017).

6. The codes used to sort the data were either 'emic' (meaning, data-generated) or 'etic' (meaning researcher-generated). Emic codes, also called 'in vivo' codes, are codes that employ the actual verbiage of the subjects themselves, whereas etic codes are based upon the extrapolations and examinations of the researcher. Examples of emic codes included words or phrases used by the participants such as 'medieval-ly cone hats' and 'lack of hygiene' while etic codes included researcher-labelled codes such as 'medieval costume' and 'influence of Disney films'. Some overarching themes that emerged from the data were geography, education, childhood memory, and coincidence or conflict with previous knowledge. For a fuller explanation of emic and etic codes, see Thomas A. Schwandt, *Dictionary of Qualitative Inquiry*, Second Edition (Thousand Oaks, CA: Sage Publications, 2001), pp. 65–6.

7. For more information on the virtues of Qualitative and Quantitative research, see: Norman K. Denzin and Yvonna S. Lincoln (eds), *The SAGE Handbook of Qualitative Research*, Third Edition (Thousand Oaks, CA: Sage Publications, 2005), pp. 1–42; Richard A. Krueger and Mary Anne Casey, *Focus Groups: A Practical Guide for Applied Research*, Third Edition (Thousand Oaks, CA: Sage Publications, 2000), p. 11.

8. Andrea Fontana and James H. Frey, 'Interviewing: The art of sciences,' in *Handbook of Qualitative Research*, Norman K. Denzin and Yvonna S. Lincoln (eds) (London: Sage Publications, 1994), pp. 370–2.

9. David W. Stewart and Prem N. Shamdasani, *Focus Groups: Theory and Practice* (London: Sage Publications, 1990), p. 9.

10. Ibid., p. 10.

11. It is important to note that the responses in focus groups, unlike responses garnered from quantitative research methods or closed-ended qualitative methods, are given in the respondents' own words. This allows the researcher a far richer pool of data, where responses can be close-read to construct a more nuanced interpretation than would be possible by responses to a scripted survey or interview.

12. Rosaline S. Barbour and Jenny Kitzinger (eds), *Developing Focus Group Research: Politics, Theory and Practice* (London: Sage Publications, 1999), p. 5.
13. This post-film discussion and negotiation does not occur only immediately after the film, but also now via the internet through a myriad of discussion groups, chat rooms and fan web pages. Though this variety of post-film discussion and negotiation is interesting, the anonymity offered by the internet tends to warp discussion in ways that are particular to the internet; opinions are voiced more violently and contention can erupt more easily than they would in person. Additionally, transcripts of internet chat rooms and message boards cannot be asked follow-up questions or for clarifications in the same way that a participant in a focus group could. While reactions to films found on the internet are certainly an interesting avenue for exploration, a moderated focus group interview can offer far richer responses from participants who can be questioned face-to-face.
14. Stewart and Shamdasani, *Focus Groups*, p. 16.
15. Some of the participants reported taking English or history at GCSE and A-level, but none had studied medieval literature or history in those courses.
16. A comparative study of the 'Middle Ages' schemata of those people who are very familiar with visual culture and those who avoid visual culture could be very fruitful, but is beyond the purview of this study.
17. Those 22 films were either popular big-budget English-language medieval or fantasy films made during the lifetimes of the participants (and thus likely to have been seen by them), or enduringly popular earlier films, such as the Disney adaptations of *Sword in the Stone* and *Robin Hood*, or *Monty Python and the Quest for the Holy Grail*.

WORKS CITED

Aberth, John, *A Knight at the Movies: Medieval History on Film* (London: Routledge, 2003).

Age of Empires 2: Age of Kings (Microsoft, 2001).

Alexander, Lloyd, *The Book of Three* (London: Holt, Rinehart and Winston, 1964).

Alsultany, Evelyn, *Arabs and Muslims in the Media: Race and Representation after 9/11* (New York: New York University Press, 2012).

Altman, Rick, *Film/Genre* (London: BFI Publishing, 1999).

Ambroise, *The History of the Holy War: Ambroise's Estoire de la Guerre Sainte*, Marianne Ailes (trans) and Malcolm Barber (ed.) (Woodbridge: The Boydell Press, 2003).

Anderson, Richard C., 'Role of the reader's schema in comprehension, learning, and memory', in Robert B. Ruddell, Martha Rapp, and Harry Singer (eds), *Theoretical Models and Processes of Reading*, Fourth Edition (Newark, DE: International Reading Association, 1994), pp. 469–75.

Anderson, Richard C., Rand J. Spiro, and William Edward Montague (eds), *Schooling and the Acquisition of Knowledge* (London: Lawrence Erlbaum, 1977).

Anderson, W.S., *Pompeii* (TriStar Pictures, 2014).

Andrea Kann (ed.), *The Art, Science, and Technology of Medieval Travel* (Aldershot: Ashgate, 2008).

Angvik, Magne and Bodo von Borries (eds), *Youth and History: A Comparative European Survey on Historical Consciousness and Political Attitudes among Adolescents* (Hamburg: Körber-Stiftung, 1997).

Annaud, Jean-Jacques, *The Name of The Rose* (20th Century Fox, 1986).

Aronstein, Susan, *Hollywood Knights: Arthurian Cinema and the Politics of Nostalgia* (New York: Palgrave Macmillan, 2005).

Austin, Greta, 'Were the peasants really so clean? The Middle Ages in film', *Film History* 14/2 (2002), pp. 136–41.

Ashcroft, Lord Michael, 'How much do children know about the Second World War?', *Lord Ashcroft Polls* (25 June 2012). Available at http://lordashcroftpolls.com/2012/06/how-much-do-children-know-about-the-second-world-war/ (accessed 28 August 2016).

Ashton, Paul and Paula Hamilton, *History at the Crossroads: Australians and the Past* (Sydney: Halstead Press, 2010).

Axelrod, Robert, 'Schema theory: An information processing model of perception and cognition', *The American Political Science Review* 67/4 (December 1973), pp. 1248–66.

Baker, Graham, *Beowulf* (Miramax Films, 1999).

Baker, Mike, 'History study needs facts first, analysis later', *Guardian* (18 January 2011). Available at https://www.theguardian.com/education/2011/jan/18/history-national-curriculum (accessed 20 January 2017).

Balingit, Moriah, 'After Comet Ping Pong and Pizzagate, teachers tackle fake news', *Washington Post*, Education Section, 11 December 2016. Available at http://wapo.st/2gtyUT5?tid=ss_mail&utm_term=.1b11f4970419 (accessed 13 January 2017).

Barber, Richard W., *The Holy Grail: Imagination and Belief* (Cambridge, MA: Harvard University Press, 2004).

Barbour, Rosaline S., and Jenny Kitzinger (eds), *Developing Focus Group Research: Politics, Theory and Practice* (London: Sage Publications, 1999).

Barthes, Roland, 'The reality effect', in Richard Howard (trans), *The Rustle of Language* (Oxford: Blackwell, 1986), pp. 141–8.

———, 'The Romans in films', in Annette Lavers (trans), *Mythologies* (London: Vintage, 1993), pp. 26–8.

Bartlett, Frederic C., *Remembering: A Study in Experimental and Social Psychology* (Cambridge: Cambridge University Press, 1932).

Bartlett, Robert, *The Making of Europe: Conquest, Colonization and Cultural Change, 950–1350* (Harmondsworth: Penguin, 1994).

———, 'Medieval and modern concepts of race and ethnicity', *Journal of Medieval and Early Modern Studies* 31/1 (2001), pp. 39–56.

BBC, 'Press releases: Alexander the Great won the Battle of Hastings', *BBC Press Office*, 5 August 2004. Available at http://www.bbc.co.uk/pressoffice/pressreleases/stories/2004/08_august/05/battlefield.shtml (accessed 22 August 2016).

Beatty, Warren, *Reds* (Paramount Pictures, 1981).

Beaumont, Claudine, 'Call of Duty: Modern Warfare 2: Why video games can't be ignored', *Telegraph*, 13 November 2009, sec. Technology. Available at http://www.telegraph.co.uk/technology/video-games/6562828/Call-Of-Duty-Modern-Warfare-2-why-video-games-cant-be-ignored.html (accessed 12 October 2016).

Bechdel, Alison, 'The rule', *Dykes to Watch Out For*, 16 August 2005. Available at, http://dykestowatchoutfor.com/the-rule (accessed 22 December 2016).

Beers, Henry Augustin, *A History of English Romanticism in the Eighteenth Century* (London: Kegan Paul, Trench, Trübner, 1899).

Bell, J. Carleton and David F. McCollum, 'A study of the attainments of pupils in United States history', *Journal of Educational Psychology* 8 (1917), pp. 257–74.

Benshoff, Harry M., and Sean Griffin, *America on Film: Representing Race, Class, Gender, and Sexuality at the Movies*, Second Edition (Malden, MA: Wiley-Blackwell, 2009).

Berdik, Chris, 'How to teach high-school students to spot fake news', *Slate* (21 December 2016). Available at http://www.slate.com/articles/technology/future_tense/2016/12/media_literacy_courses_help_high_school_students_spot_fake_news.html (accessed 13 January 2017).

Berg, Bruce L. and Howard Lune, *Qualitative Research Methods for the Social Sciences*, Eighth Edition (Harlow: Pearson, 2014).

Berger, Peter L. and Thomas Luckmann, *The Social Construction of Reality: A Treatise in the Sociology of Knowledge* (Harmondsworth: Penguin, 1991).

Bergman, Ingmar, *The Seventh Seal* (AB Svensk Filmindustri, 1957).

Bernau, Anke and Bettina Bildhauer (eds), *Medieval Film* (Manchester: Manchester University Press, 2009).

Biddle, Martin (ed.), *King Arthur's Round Table* (Woodbridge: Boydell & Brewer, 2000).

Biskind, Peter, *Seeing is Believing* (New York: Pantheon, 1983).

Black, Thomas R., *Doing Quantitative Research in the Social Sciences: An Integrated Approach to Research Design, Measurement and Statistics* (London: Sage Publications, 1999).

Boggs, Francis, *Mephisto and the Maiden* (Selig Polyscope Company, 1909).

Bohlman, Philip Vilas, *The Music of European Nationalism: Cultural Identity and Modern History* (Santa Barbara, CA: ABC-CLIO, 2004).

Boorman, John, *Excalibur* (Warner Brothers, 1981).

Bradford, Claire, 'Where happily ever after happens every day', in Tison Pugh and Susan Aronstein (eds), *The Disney Middle Ages: A Fairy-Tale and Fantasy Past* (New York: Palgrave McMillan, 2012), pp. 171–88.

Branagh, Kenneth, *Henry V* (MGM, 1989).

Bresson, Robert, *Lancelot du Lac* (Artificial Eye, 1974).

Brewer, William F. and Glenn V. Nakamura, 'The nature and functions of schemas', in Thomas K. Srull and Robert S. Wyer (eds), *Handbook of Social Cognition* (Hillsdale, NJ: L. Erlbaum Associates, 1984), pp. 119–60.

Briggs, John, Christopher Harrison, Agnus McInnes, and David Vincent, 'The medieval origins of the English criminal justice system', in *Crime and Punishment in England: An Introductory History* (London: UCL Press, 1996), pp. 1–14.

Briley, Ron, 'Teaching film and history', *OAH Magazine of History* 16/4 (Summer, 2002), pp. 3–4.

'British Social Attitudes information system: Variable analysis, "Do you regard yourself as belonging to any particular religion?"'. Available at http://www.brits ocat.com/BodySecure.aspx?control=BritsocatMarginals&var=RELRFW& SurveyID=346 (accessed 26 May 2011).

Brooks, Mel, *Robin Hood: Men in Tights* (20th Century Fox, 1993).

Brown, Tony, 'Clearances and clearings: Deforestation in Mesolithic/Neolithic Britain', *Oxford Journal of Archaeology* 16/2 (July 1997), pp. 133–46.

Brown, William, 'Beowulf: The digital monster movie', *Animation* 4/2 (1 July 2009), pp. 153–68.

Brownlie, Siobhan, *Memory and Myths of the Norman Conquest* (Woodbridge: Boydell Press, 2013).

Bruni, Leonardo, *History of the Florentine People: Books 1–4 Volume 1*, James Hankins (ed.) (Cambridge, MA: Harvard University Press, 2001).

Buckley, Sandra (ed.), *Encyclopedia of Contemporary Japanese Culture* (London: Routledge, 2001).

Butler, Andrew C., Franklin M. Zaromb, Keith B. Lyle, and Henry L. Roediger III, 'Using popular films to enhance classroom learning: The good, the bad, and the interesting', *Psychological Science* 20/9 (September 2009), pp. 1161–8.

Butler, David, *King Richard and the Crusaders* (Warner Bros., 1954).

Calin, William C., 'Christianity', in Elizabeth Emery and Richard Utz (eds), *Medievalism: Key Critical Terms* (Woodbridge: D.S. Brewer, 2014), pp. 35–41.

Campbell, Joseph, *The Hero with a Thousand Faces* (Novato: New World Library, 2008).

Campbell, Martin, *Casino Royale* (Columbia Pictures, 2006).

Cañas, A.J. and J.D. Novak, *The Theory Underlying Concept Maps and How to Construct and Use Them* (Ocala: Florida Institute for Human and Machine Cognition, 2008).

Cantor, Leonard, 'Forests, chases, parks and warrens', in *The English Medieval Landscape* (London: Croom Helm, 1982), pp. 56–85.

Capra, Frank, *Mr. Smith Goes to Washington* (Columbia Pictures, 1939).

Carlin, Martha, 'Feast', in Elizabeth Emery and Richard Utz (eds), *Medievalism: Key Critical Terms* (Woodbridge: D.S. Brewer, 2014), pp. 63–9.

Carpenter, Richard, *Robin of Sherwood* (ITV, 1984–1986).

Carroll, James, *Crusade: Chronicles of an Unjust War* (New York: Metropolitan Books, 2004).

Carver, Martin, *Sutton Hoo: A Seventh-Century Princely Burial Ground and Its Context* (London: British Museum Press, 2005).

Chahine, Youssef, *El Naser Salah al-Din* (Assia, 1963).

Chance, Jane, *Woman as Hero in Old English Literature* (New York: Syracuse University Press, 1986).

Chang, Joseph T., 'Recent common ancestors of all present-day individuals', *Advances in Applied Probability* 31/4 (December 1999), pp. 1002–26.

Christiansen, Eric, *The Norsemen in the Viking Age* (Malden, Mass: Blackwell Publishers, 2001).

Clark, Anna, *Teaching the Nation: Politics and Pedagogy in Australian History* (Carlton, Vic.: Melbourne University Press, 2006).

Cohen, J.J., Karl Steel, Jonathan Hsy, Leila K. Norako, Cord Whitaker, and Mary Kate Hurley, *In the Middle: Towards a Progressive Medieval Studies*. Available at http://www.inthemedievalmiddle.com/ (accessed 30 May 2017).

Coleman, Kathleen M., 'The pedant goes to Hollywood: The role of the academic consultant', in Martin M. Winkler (ed.), *Gladiator: Film and History* (Oxford: Blackwell, 2005), pp. 45–52.

Collins, Robert G., 'Star Wars: The pastiche of myth and the yearning for a past future', *Journal of Popular Culture* XI/1 (1977), pp. 1–10.

Conrad, Margaret, Kadriye Ercikan, Gerald Friesen, Jocelyn Létourneau, Delphin Muise, David Northrup, Peter Seixas, *Canadians and Their Pasts* (Toronto: University of Toronto Press, 2013).

Constable, Giles, 'The historiography of the Crusades', in Angeliki E. Laiou and Roy Parviz Mottahedeh (eds), *The Crusades from the Perspective of Byzantium and the Muslim World* (Washington, DC: Dumbarton Oaks, 2001), pp. 1–22. Available at http://www.doaks.org/resources/publications/doaks-online-publications/crusades-from-the-perspective-of-byzantium-and-the-muslim-world/cr01.pdf (accessed 6 October 2016).

Couch, Julie Nelson, '"I couldn't help but wonder.": Sex and the City a medieval romance?' (presented at the International Congress on Medieval Studies, Kalamazoo, MI, 2010).

Couvares, Francis G., 'The paradox of protest: American film, 1980–1992', in Francis G. Couvares (ed.), *Movie Censorship and American Culture*, Second Edition (Boston, MA: University of Massachusetts Press, 2006), pp. 277–318.

Cox, Alex, *Walker* (Universal Pictures, 1987).

Curtiz, Michael and William Keighley, *The Adventures of Robin Hood* (Warner Brothers, 1938).

D'Arcens, Louise, 'Presentism', in Elizabeth Emery and Richard Utz (eds), *Medievalism: Key Critical Terms* (Woodbridge: D.S. Brewer, 2014), pp. 181–8.

Davis, Natalie Zemon, '"Any resemblance to persons living or dead": Film and the challenge of authenticity', *Historical Journal of Film, Radio and Television* 8/3 (1988), pp. 269–83.

Dean, Stephen, Della Hooke, and Alex Jones, 'The "Staffordshire hoard": The fieldwork', *The Antiquaries Journal* 90 (2010), pp. 139–52.

DeBruine, L.M., Benedict C. Jones, John R. Crawford, Lisa L.M. Welling, and Anthony C. Little, 'The health of a nation predicts their mate preferences: Cross-cultural variation in women's preferences for masculinized male faces', *Proceedings of the Royal Society B: Biological Sciences* 277/7 August (March 2010). Available at http://rspb.royalsocietypublishing.org/content/early/2010/03/13/rspb.2009.2184 (accessed 1 June 2017).

DeMille, Cecil B., *The Crusades* (Paramount Pictures, 1935).

Denzin, Norman K. and Yvonna S. Lincoln (eds), *The SAGE Handbook of Qualitative Research*, Third Edition (Thousand Oaks, CA: Sage Publications, 2005).

Department for Education, 'National curriculum in England: History programmes of study', *Gov.uk* (2013). Available at https://www.gov.uk/government/publications/national-curriculum-in-england-history-programmes-of-study (accessed 10 October 2016).

Department of Education and Science and the Welsh Office, *National Curriculum History Working Group: Final Report* (London: HMSO, 1990).

Driver, Martha W. and Sid Ray (eds), *The Medieval Hero on Screen: Representations from Beowulf to Buffy* (Jefferson, NC: McFarland, 2004).

du Maurier, Daphne, *Rebecca* (London: Arrow, 1992).

Dwan, Allan, *Robin Hood* (United Artists, 1922).

Ebert, Roger, 'Movie reviews: *The Hurricane*', *The Chicago Sun-Times* (7 January 2000). Available at http://rogerebert.suntimes.com/apps/pbcs.dll/article?AID=/20000107/REVIEWS/1070302/1023 (accessed 14 November 2016).

Eco, Umberto, 'Dreaming of the Middle Ages', in William Weaver (trans), *Travels in Hyperreality: Essays* (London: Picador, 1987), pp. 61–72.

———, *Remaking the Middle Ages: the Methods of Cinema and History in Portraying the Medieval World* (Jefferson: McFarland, 2011).

Eisenstein, Sergei and Grigori Aleksandrov, *October: Ten Days that Shook the World* (Sovkino (USSR)/Amkino Corporation (US), 1928).

Elliott, Andrew B.R., *Remaking the Middle Ages: The Methods of Cinema and History in Portraying the Medieval World* (Jefferson: McFarland, 2011).

——— (ed.), *The Return of the Epic Film: Genre, Aesthetics and History in the 21st Century* (Edinburgh: Edinburgh University Press, 2014).

Emery, Elizabeth, 'Medievalism and the Middle Ages', *Studies in Medievalism* XVII (2009), pp. 77–85.

Ferguson, Niall, *Civilization: The West and the Rest* (New York: The Penguin Press HC, 2011).

Ferguson, Wallace K., 'Humanist Views of the Renaissance', *The American Historical Review* 45/1 (October 1939), pp. 1–28.

Fink, Arlene, *How to Conduct Surveys: a Step-by-Step Guide*, Fifth Edition (London: Sage Publications, 2012).

Finke, Laurie A. and Martin B. Shichtman, *Cinematic Illuminations: The Middle Ages on Film* (Baltimore: The Johns Hopkins University Press, 2010).

Fisher, John H., *The Emergence of Standard English* (Lexington: The University Press of Kentucky, 1996).

Fiske, John, *Understanding Popular Culture*, Second Edition (London: Routledge, 2010).

———, *Television Culture* (Abingdon: Taylor & Francis, 2011).

Fletcher, Robert S.G., *British Imperialism & 'The Tribal Question': Desert Administration & Nomadic Societies in the Middle East, 1919–1936* (Oxford: Oxford University Press, 2015).

Flinth, Peter, *Arn: The Knight Templar* (Svensk Filmindustri, 2007).

Fontana, Andrea and James H. Frey, 'Interviewing: The Art of Science', in Norman K. Denzin and Yvonna S. Lincoln (eds), *Handbook of Qualitative Research* (London: Sage Publications, 1994), pp. 361–76.

Forster, Edward Morgan, *A Room With a View/Where Angels Fear To Tread* (New York: Alfred A. Knopf, 2011.

Fowler, Floyd J., *Survey Research Methods*, Fourth Edition, Applied Social Research Methods Series 1 (Thousand Oaks: Sage Publications, 2009).

Frank, Jane and Howard Frank, *Great Fantasy Art: Themes from the Frank Collection* (London: Paper Tiger, 2003).

Frank, Melvin and Norman Panama, *The Court Jester* (Paramount, 1956).

Frazetta, Frank, *Testament: A Celebration of the Life & Art of Frank Frazetta*, Arnie Fenner and Cathy Fenner (eds) (Nevada City, CA: Underwood Books, 2008).

Fugelso, Karl (ed.), 'Defining Medievalism(s)', *Studies in Medievalism* 17 (2009).

Fulk, R.D., Robert E. Bjork, and John D. Niles, 'Bēowulf's fight with the dragon' in R.D. Fulk, Robert E. Bjork, and John D. Niles (eds), *Klaeber's Beowulf and the Fight at Finnsburg*, Fourth Edition (Toronto, University of Toronto Press, 2008), pp. xlv–xlviii

Fuqua, Antoine, *King Arthur* (Buena Vista, 2004).

Gaiman, Neil, 'The monarch of the glen' in Neil Gaiman (ed.), *Fragile Things: Short Fictions and Wonders* (New York: Harper, 2006), pp. 284–340.

Gaiman, Neil and Roger Avary, *Beowulf: The Script Book* (New York: Harper Collins, 2009).

Geary, Patrick J., *The Myth of Nations: The Medieval Origins of Europe* (Princeton, NJ: Princeton University Press, 2002).

Gee, James Paul, *What Video Games Have to Teach Us about Learning and Literacy*, Second Edition (Basingstoke: Palgrave MacMillan, 2003).

Geronimi, Clyde, *Sleeping Beauty* (Walt Disney Studios, 1959).

Géza Gárdonyi, *Eclipse of the Crescent Moon*, George F. Cushing (trans), Sixth Edition (Budapest: Corvina, 2002).

Gibson, Mel, *Braveheart* (Paramount, 1995).

Gilliam, Terry and Terry Jones, *Monty Python and the Holy Grail* (EMI Films, 1974).

Gillingham, John, *Richard I*, English Monarchs (New Haven, London: Yale University Press, 1999).

Gillingham, John, and Ralph A. Griffiths, *Medieval Britain, A Very Short Introduction* (Oxford: Oxford University Press, 2000).

Glenville, Peter, *Becket* (Paramount, 1964).

'Global Middle Ages'. Available at http://globalmiddleages.org/research-and-teaching (accessed 29 May 2017).

Gove, Michael, 'I refuse to surrender to the Marxist teachers hell-bent on destroying our schools: Education Secretary berates "the new enemies of promise" for opposing his plans', *Daily Mail*, 23 March 2013. Available at http://www.dailymail.co.uk/debate/article-2298146/I-refuse-surrender-Marxist-teachers-hell-bent-destroying-schools-Education-Secretary-berates-new-enemies-promise-opposing-plans.html (accessed 22 August 2016).

Green, John (presenter), 'The Dark Ages . . . How Dark Were They, Really?: Crash Course World History #14', 26 April 2012. Available at https://www.youtube.com/watch?v=QV7CanyzhZg (accessed 6 January 2017).

———, 'The Crusades – Pilgrimage or Holy War?: Crash Course World History #15', 3 May 2012. Available at https://www.youtube.com/watch?v=X0zudTQelzI (accessed 6 January 2017).

Grossman, Dave, 'Video games as "murder simulators"', *Variety, Special Issue: Violence & Entertainment*. Available at http://variety.com/violence/ (accessed 12 October 2016).

Groves, Robert M., Floyd J. Fowler Jr, Mick P. Couper, James M. Lepkowski, and Eleanor Singer, *Survey Methodology* (Hoboken, NJ: John Wiley & Sons, 2009).

Halbwachs, Maurice, *On Collective Memory*, Lewis A. Coser (ed and trans) (Chicago: University of Chicago Press, 1992).

Hall, Stuart, 'Women in the Crusader States: The queens of Jerusalem (1100–1190)', in Derek Baker (ed.), *Medieval Women*, Studies in Church History 1 (Oxford: B. Blackwell, 1978), pp. 143–74.

———, 'Encoding/decoding', in Stuart Hall (ed.), *Culture, Media, Language: Working Papers in Cultural Studies, 1972–79* (London: Hutchinson in association with the Centre for Contemporary Cultural Studies, University of Birmingham, 1980), pp. 128–38.

Hamilton, Bernard, *The Leper King and His Heirs: Baldwin IV and the Crusader Kingdom of Jerusalem* (Cambridge: Cambridge University Press, 2000).

Hamilton, David L., *Cognitive Processes in Stereotyping and Intergroup Behavior* (Hillsdale, NJ: L. Erlbaum Associates, 1981).

Hanawalt, Barbara A., and David Wallace (eds), *Medieval Crime and Social Control* (Minneapolis: University of Minnesota Press, 1999).

Harris, Jennifer, 'William Morris and the Middle Ages', in Joanna Banham and Jennifer Harris (eds), *William Morris and the Middle Ages* (Manchester: Manchester University Press, 1984), pp. 1–16.

Hartley, L.P., *The Go-Between* (New York: New York Review Books, 2002).

Harty, Kevin J., *The Reel Middle Ages: American, Western and Eastern European, Middle Eastern, and Asian Films About Medieval Europe* (Jefferson, NC: McFarland, 1999).

Harty, Kevin J (ed.), *King Arthur on Film: New Essays on Arthurian Cinema* (Jefferson, NC: McFarland, 1999).

———— (ed.), *Cinema Arthuriana: Twenty Essays*, Second Edition (Jefferson, NC: McFarland, 2002).

———— (ed.), *The Vikings on Film: Essays on Depictions of the Nordic Middle Ages* (Jefferson, NC: McFarland, 2011).

———— (ed.), *The Holy Grail on Film: Essays on the Cinematic Quest* (Jefferson, NC: McFarland, 2015).

Harvey, Anthony, *The Lion In Winter* (AVCO Embassy Pictures, 1968).

Hathaway, Henry, *Prince Valiant* (20th Century Fox, 1954).

Haydock, Nickolas, *Movie Medievalism* (Jefferson, NC: McFarland, 2008).

Haydock, Nickolas and Edward L. Risden (eds), *Hollywood in the Holy Land: Essays on Film Depictions of the Crusades and Christian–Muslim Clashes* (Jefferson, NC: McFarland, 2009).

Helgeland, Brian, *A Knight's Tale* (Sony Pictures, 2001).

Henderson, Lucius, *Tannhäuser* (Thanhouser Film Corporation, 1913).

Heng, Geraldine, 'The global Middle Ages: An experiment in collaborative humanities, or imagining the world, 500–1500 C.E.' *English Language Notes* 47/1 (2009), pp. 205–16.

Herbert, Frank, *Dune* (London: New English Library, 1965).

Heritage Lottery Fund and VisitBritain, *Investing in Success: Heritage and the UK Tourism Economy* (London: Heritage Lottery Fund, 2010). Available at http://www.hlf.org.uk/aboutus/howwework/Documents/HLF_Tourism_Impact_single.pdf (accessed 22 August 2016).

Hern, Alex, 'Michael Gove revealed to be using PR-commissioned puff-polls as "evidence"', *The New Statesman*, 13 May 2013. Available at http://www.newstatesman.com/politics/2013/05/michael-gove-revealed-be-using-pr-commissioned-puff-polls-evidence (accessed 22 August 2016).

Higson, Andrew, *Waving the Flag: Constructing a National Cinema in Britain* (Oxford: Clarendon Press, 1995).

Hirst, Michael, *The Tudors* (Showtime/BBC, 2007–10).

Hodges, Richard and David Whitehouse, *Mohammed, Charlemagne, and the Origins of Europe* (Ithaca, NY: Cornell University Press, 1983).

Hume, David, 'Of national characters', in *Essays: Moral, Political and Literary* (New York: Cosimo, 2007).

Hume, Kathryn, 'Medieval romance and science fiction: The anatomy of a resemblance', *Journal of Popular Culture* XVI/1 (1982), pp. 15–26.

Huntington, Samuel P., *The Clash of Civilizations and the Remaking of World Order* (New York: Simon & Schuster, 1996).

Internet Movie Database, 'Internet Archive: IMDB Beowulf (2007)', 10 February 2007. Available at http://web.archive.org/web/20070905003741/www.imdb.com/title/tt0442933/ (accessed 1 May 2010).

Jackson, Peter, *The Lord of the Rings: The Fellowship of the Ring* (New Line Cinema, 2001).

————, *The Lord of the Rings: The Two Towers* (New Line Cinema, 2002).

————, *The Lord of the Rings: The Return of the King* (New Line Cinema, 2003).

Jameson, Fredric, *Signatures of the Visible* (New York: Routledge, 1992).

Jeffords, Susan, *Hard Bodies: Hollywood Masculinity in the Reagan Era* (New Brunswick: Rutgers University Press, 1994).

Jude, Dick, *Fantasy Art Masters: The Best Fantasy and Science Fiction Artists Show How They Work* (New York, NY: Watson-Guptill, 1999).

Junger, Gil, *Black Knight* (20th Century Fox, 2001).

Kamalipour, Yahya R (ed.), *The U.S. Media and the Middle East: Image and Perception*, Contributions to the Study of Mass Media and Communications 46 (Westport, CT: Greenwood Press, 1995).

Kant, Immanuel, *Critique of Pure Reason*, Norman Kemp Smith and Gary Banham (trans), Revised Second Edition (Basingstoke: Palgrave Macmillan, 2007).

Kapell, Matthew Wilhelm and Andrew B.R. Elliott (eds), *Playing with the Past: Digital Games and the Simulation of History* (New York: Bloomsbury, 2013).

Karras, Ruth Mazo, *Slavery and Society in Medieval Scandinavia*, Yale Historical Publications 135 (New Haven, CT: Yale University Press, 1988).

Kelly, Amanda, 'What did Hitler do in the war, miss?', *Times Education Supplement*, 19 January 2001. Available at https://www.tes.com/news/tes-archive/tes-publication/what-did-hitler-do-war-miss (accessed 1 June 2017).

Kelly, Kathleen Coyne and Tison Pugh (eds), *Queer Movie Medievalisms* (Farnham: Ashgate, 2009).

Kidwell, Mark et al., *The Fantastic Worlds of Frank Frazetta, Volume 1* (Portland, OR: Image Comics, 2008).

King, D.J. Cathcart, *The Castle in England and Wales: An Interpretive History* (London: Routledge, 1991).

Knight, Stephen, *Robin Hood: A Mythic Biography* (Ithaca, NY: Cornell University Press, 2003).

Konieczny, Peter (ed.), *Medievalists.net*. Available at http://www.medievalists.net (accessed 30 May 2017).

Krueger, Richard A. and Mary Anne Casey, *Focus Groups: A Practical Guide for Applied Research*, Third Edition (Thousand Oaks, CA: Sage Publications, 2000).

Landau, Les, 'Heroes and demons' *Star Trek: Voyager* (Paramount Network Television, 24 April 1995).

Landsberg, Alison, *Prosthetic Memory: The Transformation of American Remembrance in the Age of Mass Culture* (New York: Columbia University Press, 2004).

Lee, Alan and David Day, *Castles*, David Larkin (ed.) (New York: McGraw-Hill, 1984).

Lewis, Carenza, Patrick Mitchell-Fox, and Christopher Dyer, *Village, Hamlet and Field: Changing Medieval Settlements in Central England* (Manchester: Manchester University Press, 1997).

Liman, Doug, *The Bourne Identity* (Universal Studios, 2002).

Linenthal, Edward T., and Tom Engelhardt, *History Wars: The Enola Gay and Other Battles for the American Past* (New York: Henry Holt and Company, 1996).

Logan, Joshua, *Camelot* (Warner Brothers, 1967).

London Datastore, 'Census 2001 key statistics 02: age structure', 2003. Available at http://data.london.gov.uk/dataset/census-2001-key-statistics-02-age-structure (accessed 22 August 2016).

Long, Edward, *The History of Jamaica*, vol. 2 (London: T. Lowndes, 1774).

Lyman, Rick, 'Movie marketing wizardry; "Lord of the Rings" trilogy taps the internet to build excitement', *New York Times* (New York, 11 January 2001), sec. Movies. Available at http://www.nytimes.com/2001/01/11/movies/movie-marketing-wizardry-lord-rings-trilogy-taps-internet-build-excitement.html (accessed 15 November 2016).

Madden, Thomas F., *The Concise History of the Crusades* (Lanham, MD: Rowman & Littlefield, 2014).

Marcus, Alan S., '"It is as it was": Feature film in the history classroom', *The Social Studies* 96/2 (2005), pp. 61–7.

Marcus, Alan S., Richard J. Paxton, and Peter Meyerson, '"The reality of it all": History students read the movies', *Theory and Research in Social Education* 34/3 (Fall 2006), pp. 516–52.

Marcus, Alan S. and Jeremy D. Stoddard, 'Tinsel town as teacher: Hollywood film in the high school classroom', *The History Teacher* 40/3 (May 2007), pp. 303–30.

Marx, Karl, *Capital: A Critique of Political Economy*, Ben Fowkes and David Fernbach (trans) (Harmondsworth: Penguin, 1976).

Maslow, Abraham H., *The Psychology of Science: A Reconnaissance*, The John Dewey Society Lectureship Series no. 8 (New York: Harper & Row, 1966).

Matthews, David, 'Middle,' in Elizabeth Emery and Richard Utz (eds), *Medievalism: Key Critical Terms* (Cambridge: D.S. Brewer, 2014), pp. 144–5.

Matthews, Derek, *The Strange Death of History Teaching (Fully Explained in Seven Easy-to-Follow Lessons)* unpublished report, January 2009. Available at http://bit.ly/ 2bRZwKS (accessed 22 August 2016).

Maxwell, Joseph Alex, *Qualitative Research Design: An Interactive Approach*, Second Edition (Thousand Oaks, CA: Sage Publications, 2005).

Mayer, Richard E., *Computer Games for Learning: An Evidence-Based Approach* (Cambridge, MA: The MIT Press, 2014).

McGovern, Chris, 'The new history boys', in Robert Whelan (ed.), *The Corruption of the Curriculum* (London: Civitas, 2007).

McTiernan, John and Michael Crichton, *The 13th Warrior* (Touchstone Pictures, 1999).

'Medieval, adj. and n.', *OED Online* (Oxford: Oxford University Press, 1989). Available at http://www.oed.com/view/Entry/115638?redirectedFrom=medi eval (accessed 24 August 2016).

Medieval II: Total War (Creative Assembly, 2008).

'Medieval: Total Realism forums', *Totalwar.org*. Available at http://forums.totalwar. org/vb/forumdisplay.php?162-Medieval-Total-Realism (accessed 20 January 2017).

Méliès, Georges, *Faust and Marguerite* (Star Film Company, 1904).

Merriam, Sharan B, *Qualitative Research: A Guide to Design and Implementation* (San Francisco, CA: John Wiley & Sons, 2009).

Metzger, Scott Alan, 'Pedagogy and the historical feature film: Toward historical literacy', *Film & History: An Interdisciplinary Journal of Film and Television Studies* 37/2 (2007), pp. 67–75.

——, 'Maximizing the educational power of history movies in the classroom', *The Social Studies* 101 (2010), pp. 127–36.

'Middle age, n. and adj.,' *OED Online* (Oxford: Oxford University Press, 2016). Available at http://www.oed.com/view/Entry/118142 (accessed 13 October 2016).

Minghella, Dominic and Foz Allan, *Robin Hood* (BBC, 2006–9).

Mommsen, Theodor E., 'Petrarch's conception of the "dark ages"', *Speculum* 17/2 (April 1942), pp. 226–42.

Montangero, Jacques and Danielle Maurice-Naville, *Piaget, or, The Advance of Knowledge* (Mahwah: Lawrence Erlbaum Associates, 1997).

Mori, Masahiro, 'Bukimi no tani, [the uncanny valley]', K.F. MacDorman and T. Minato (trans), *Energy* 7 (1970), pp. 33–5.

Morgan, Gwendolyn, '*Beowulf* and the Middle Ages in Film', *The Year's Work in Medievalism* XXIII (2009), pp. 3–15.

Morris, Ronald Vaughan, *History and Imagination: Reenactments for Elementary Social Studies* (Plymouth: Rowman & Littlefield Education, 2012).

Morris, William, *A Dream of John Ball* (Oxford: Kelmscott Press, 1892). Available at http://morrisedition.lib.uiowa.edu/dream.html (accessed 20 December 2016).

Morrison, David E., *The Search for a Method: Focus Groups and the Development of Mass Communication Research* (Luton: University of Luton Press, 1998).

——, *Defining Violence: The Search for Understanding* (Luton: University of Luton Press, 1999).

Mosse, Kate, *Labyrinth* (London: Orion, 2005).

——, *Sepulchre* (London: Orion, 2007).

——, *Citadel* (London: Orion, 2012).

Musson, Anthony and Edward Powell (eds), *Crime, Law and Society in the Later Middle Ages: Selected Sources* (Manchester: Manchester University Press, 2009).

Nakou, Irene and Isabel Barca (eds), *Contemporary Public Debates over History Education* (Charlotte, NC: Information Age Publishing, 2010).

Nash, Gary B., Charlotte Crabtree, and Ross E. Dunn, *Culture Wars and the Teaching of the Past* (New York: Vintage Books, 2000).

National Curriculum Council, *National Curriculum Council Consultation Report: History* (York: National Curriculum Council, 1990.

——, *History in the National Curriculum (England)* (London: Department of Education and Science, 1991).

Nin, Anaïs, *Seduction of the Minotaur* (London: A. Swallow, 1961).

Nolan, Christopher, *Batman Begins* (Warner Brothers, 2005).

Ogden, Daniel, *Drakon: Dragon Myth and Serpent Cult in the Greek and Roman Worlds* (Oxford: Oxford University Press, 2013).

Olick, Jeffrey K., Vered Vinitzky-Seroussi, and Daniel Levy (eds), *The Collective Memory Reader* (Oxford: Oxford University Press, 2011).

Olson, Steve, 'The royal we', *The Atlantic*, May 2002. Available at http://www.theatlantic.com/magazine/archive/2002/05/the-royal-we/2497/ (accessed 22 August 2016).

Osprey Publishing, 'Essential history survey results (Internet archive)', 18 January 2001. Available at http://www.ospreypublishing.com/features/5">http://web.archive.org/web/200102031935/http://www.ospreypublishing.com/features/5 (accessed 22 August 2016).

Overing, Gillian R., 'The women of Beowulf: A context for interpretation' in Peter S. Baker (ed.), *The Beowulf Reader*, Basic Readings in Anglo-Saxon England 1 (London: Garland, 2000), pp. 219–60.

Pelteret, David A.E., *Slavery in Early Mediaeval England: From the Reign of Alfred until the Twelfth Century*, Studies in Anglo-Saxon History 7 (Woodbridge: Boydell, 1995).

Peters, Edward (ed.), *The First Crusade: The Chronicle of Fulcher of Chartres and Other Source Materials*, Second Edition (Philadelphia, PA: University of Pennsylvania Press, 1998).

Phillips, Helen (ed.), *Robin Hood: Medieval and Post-medieval* (Four Courts Press, 2005).

Piaget, Jean, *The Origin of Intelligence in the Child* (London: Routledge, 1998).

Pipolo, Tony, 'Joan of Arc: The cinema's immortal maid', *Cineaste: America's Leading Magazine on the Art and Politics of the Cinema* 25/4 (September 2000), pp. 16–21.

Pohlsander, Hans A., *National Monuments and Nationalism in 19th Century Germany* (Oxford: Peter Lang, 2008).

Pollard, A.J., *Imagining Robin Hood: The Late-medieval Stories in Historical Context* (London: Routledge, 2004).

Porter, Dorothy Carr, 'The Social Centrality of Women in Beowulf: A New Context', *The Heroic Age* 5 (Summer/Autumn 2001). Available at http://www.heroicage. org/issues/5/porter1.html (accessed 22 December 2016).

Porter, Edwin, *Parsifal* (Edison Manufacturing Company, 1904).

———, *Faust* (Edison Manufacturing Company, 1909).

Press Association, 'Gandalf finds a place in British history', *Guardian*, 5 August 2004. Available at https://www.theguardian.com/education/2004/aug/05/schools.highereducation (accessed 1 June 2017).

Pryor, Francis, *The Making of the British Landscape: How We Have Transformed the Land, from Prehistory to Today* (London: Allen Lane, 2010).

Pugh, Tison and Susan Aronstein (eds), *The Disney Middle Ages: A Fairy-Tale and Fantasy Past* (Basingstoke: Palgrave Macmillan, 2012).

Rackham, Oliver, *Trees and Woodland in the British Landscape*, Revised Edition (London: Phoenix Giant, 1996).

Raimi, Sam, *Army of Darkness: Evil Dead 3* (Universal Pictures, 1993).

Ramey, Lynn Tarte and Tison Pugh (eds), *Race, Class, and Gender in 'Medieval' Cinema* (New York: Palgrave Macmillan, 2007).

Rauer, Christine, *Beowulf and the Dragon: Parallels and Analogues* (Cambridge: D.S. Brewer, 2000).

Reitherman, Wolfgang, *The Sword In The Stone* (Walt Disney Studios, 1963).

———, *Robin Hood* (Walt Disney Studios, 1973).

Reynolds, Kevin, *Robin Hood: Prince of Thieves* (Warner Brothers, 1991).

Riley-Smith, Jonathan, 'Crusading as an act of love,' *History* 65/214 (1980), pp. 177–92. Available at http://dx.doi.org/10.1111/j.1468-229X.1980. tb01939.x (accessed 7 November 2016).

———, *The Crusades, Christianity and Islam* (New York: Columbia University Press, 2011).

Roberts, Brian K., and Stuart Wrathmell, *Region and Place: A Study of English Rural Settlement* (London: English Heritage, 2002).

Robertson, Bruce, *Techniques of Fantasy Art* (London: Macdonald Orbis, 1988).

Robinson, Fred C., 'Medieval, the Middle Ages', *Speculum* 59/4 (October 1984), pp. 745–56.

Robinson, Paul, *Opera & Ideas, from Mozart to Strauss* (Ithaca, NY: Cornell University Press, 1986).

Rosenstone, Robert A., 'History in images/History in words: Reflections on the possibility of really putting history onto film', *The American Historical Review* 93/5 (December 1988), pp. 1173–85.

———, *Visions of the Past: The Challenge of Film to Our Idea of History* (Cambridge, MA: Harvard University Press, 1995).

———, *History on Film/Film on History* (Harlow: Longman/Pearson, 2006).

Rosenstone, Robert A (ed.), *Revisioning History: Film and the Construction of a New Past* (Princeton: Princeton University Press, 1995).

Rosenzweig, Roy and David Thelen, *The Presence of the Past: Popular Uses of History in American Life* (New York: Columbia University Press, 1998).

———, 'The Presence of the Past survey website', 1998. Available at http://chnm.gm u.edu/survey/ (accessed 22 August 2016).

Rudolph, Conrad, *A Companion to Medieval Art: Romanesque and Gothic in Northern Europe* (Malden, MA: Wiley-Blackwell, 2006).

Rumelhart, David E., 'Schemata: The building blocks of cognition', in Rand J. Spiro, Bertram C. Bruce, and William F. Brewer (eds), *Theoretical Issues in Reading Comprehension: Perspectives from Cognitive Psychology, Linguistics, Artificial Intelligence and Education* (Hillsdale, NJ: Lawrence Erlbaum, 1980), pp. 33–58.

Russell, Gary, *The Art of The Lord of the Rings* (New York: HarperCollins, 2004).

Russell, J.C., 'Late Ancient and Medieval population', *Transactions of the American Philosophical Society* 48/3 (1 January 1958), pp. 1–152.

Sapochnik, Miguel (dir), 'Battle of the bastards', *Game of Thrones* (HBO, 19 June 2016).

Sawyer, Peter H., 'The Age of the Vikings, and Before', in Peter H. Sawyer (ed.), *The Oxford Illustrated History of the Vikings* (Oxford: Oxford University Press, 1997), pp. 1–18.

Scarlett, W. George and Dennie Wolf, 'When it's only make-believe: The construction of a boundary between fantasy and reality in storytelling', *New Directions for Child and Adolescent Development* 1979/6 (1979), pp. 29–40.

Schaffner, Franklin J., *The War Lord* (Universal Pictures, 1965).

Schonlau, Matthias, Ronald D. Fricker, and Marc N. Elliott, *Conducting Research Surveys via E-mail and the Web* (Santa Monica, CA: Rand, 2002).

Schwandt, Thomas A., *Dictionary of Qualitative Inquiry*, Second Edition (Thousand Oaks, CA: Sage Publications, 2001).

Scott, Ridley, *Kingdom Of Heaven – Definitive Edition DVD* (20th Century Fox, 2005).

———, *Kingdom of Heaven* (20th Century Fox, 2005).

———, *Robin Hood* (Universal Pictures, 2010).

Scott, Ridley, Diana Landau, and Nancy Friedman, *Kingdom of Heaven: The Ridley Scott Film and the History Behind the Story* (London: Newmarket Press, 2005).

Seixas, Peter, C. 'Confronting the moral frames of popular film: Young people respond to historical revisionism', *American Journal of Education* 102/3 (May 1994), pp. 261–85.

———, 'Introduction', in Peter C. Seixas (ed.), *Theorizing Historical Consciousness* (Toronto: University of Toronto Press, 2004), pp. 3–20.

Shaheen, Jack, *Reel Bad Arabs: How Hollywood Vilifies a People* (Northampton, MA: Olive Branch Press, 2009).

Shippey, Tom and Richard Utz, 'Medievalism in the Modern World: Introductory Perspectives', in Tom Shippey and Richard Utz (eds), *Medievalism in the Modern World: Essays in Honour of Leslie J. Workman* (Turnhout: Brepols, 1998), pp. 1–14.

Sid Meier's Civilization IV (2K Games, 2005).

Simmons, Clare A., *Reversing the Conquest: History and Myth in Nineteenth-Century British Literature* (New Brunswick: Rutgers University Press, 1990).

———, 'Romantic medievalism', in Louise D'Arcens (ed.), *The Cambridge Companion to Medievalism* (Cambridge: Cambridge University Press, 2016), pp. 103–18.

Simmons, Claire A (ed.), *Medievalism and the Quest for the "Real" Middle Ages* (London: Frank Cass, 2001).

Snyder, Zack, *300* (Warner Brothers, 2007).

Sobchack, Vivian, '"Surge and Splendor": A phenomenology of the Hollywood historical epic', *Representations* 0/29 (Winter, 1990), pp. 24–49.

Somerville, Angus A., and R. Andrew McDonald, *The Viking Age: A Reader* (Toronto: University of Toronto Press, 2010).

Sorlin, Pierre, *The Film in History: Restaging the Past* (Oxford: Blackwell, 1980).

Spielberg, Steven, *Saving Private Ryan* (DreamWorks, 1998).

Stallybrass, Peter, '"Drunk with the cup of liberty": Robin Hood, the carnivalesque, and the rhetoric of violence in Early Modern England', *Semiotica* 54/1–2 (January 1985), pp. 113–46.

Stearns, Peter N., 'Why study history,' *American Historical Association*, 1998. Available at https://www.historians.org/about-aha-and-membership/aha-history-and-archives/archives/why-study-history-(1998) (accessed 21 August 2016).

Stearns, Peter N., Peter Seixas, and Sam Wineburg (eds), *Knowing, Teaching and Learning History: National and International Perspectives* (New York: NYU Press, 2000).

Stevenson, Katie and Barbara Gribling, 'Introduction: Chivalry and the medieval past', in Katie Stevenson and Barbara Gribling (eds), *Chivalry and the Medieval Past* (Woodbridge: The Boydell Press, 2016), pp. 1–14.

Stewart, David W. and Prem N. Shamdasani, *Focus Groups: Theory and Practice* (London: Sage Publications, 1990).

Stock, Lorraine K., 'Now starring in the Third Crusade: Depictions of Richard I and Saladin in films and television series', in Nickolas Haydock and Edward L. Risden (eds), *Hollywood in the Holy Land: Essays on Film Depictions of the Crusades and Christian–Muslim Clashes* (Jefferson, NC: McFarland, 2009), pp. 93–122.

Stokes, Melvyn, *D.W. Griffith's* The Birth of a Nation*: A History of 'The Most Controversial Motion Picture of All Time'* (Oxford: Oxford University Press, 2007).

Stone, Oliver, *JFK* (Warner Bros., 1991).

Straubhaar, Sandra Ballif, 'Myth, Late Roman history, and multiculturalism in Tolkien's Middle-Earth', in Jane Chance (ed.), *Tolkien and the Invention of Myth* (Lexington-Fayette, KY: University Press of Kentucky, 2004).

Strauss, Anselm L., and Juliet M. Corbin, *Basics of Qualitative Research: Techniques and Procedures for Developing Grounded Theory*, Second Edition (Thousand Oaks: Sage Publications, 1998).

Sturtevant, Paul B., '"You don't learn it deliberately, but you just know it from what you've seen": British understandings of the medieval past gleaned from Disney's fairy tales', in Tison Pugh and Susan Aronstein (eds), *The Disney Middle Ages: A Fairy-Tale and Fantasy Past* (New York: Palgrave McMillan, 2012), pp. 77–96.

———, 'Medievalisms of the mind: Undergraduate perceptions of the "medieval" and the "Middle Ages"', *Studies in Medievalism* 26 (2017) pp. 213–37.

——— (ed.), *The Public Medievalist*. Available at http://www.publicmedievalist.com (accessed 30 May 2017).

Sullivan, Joseph M., 'Silly Vikings: Eichinger, Hickox, and Lorenz's Anglo-German-Irish Production of Hal Foster's *Prince Valiant* (1997)', in Kevin J. Harty (ed.),

The Vikings on Film: Essays on Depictions of the Nordic Middle Ages (Jefferson, NC: McFarland, 2011), pp. 56–71.

Tarantino, Quentin, *Pulp Fiction* (Miramax Entertainment, 1994).

Taylor, A.J., *The Welsh Castles of Edward I* (London: Hambledon, 1986).

Taylor, Christopher, *Village and Farmstead: A History of Rural Settlement in England* (London: George Philip, 1984).

Thomas, David R., 'A general inductive approach for qualitative data analysis,' *American Journal of Evaluation* 27/2 (2006), pp. 237–46. Available at http://journals.sagepub.com/doi/pdf/10.1177/1098214005283748 (accessed 1 June 2017).

Thomas, Hugh M., *The Norman Conquest: England After William the Conqueror* (Lanham: Rowman & Littlefield Publishers, Inc., 2008).

Thury, Eva and Margaret Klopfle Devinney, *Introduction to Mythology: Contemporary Approaches to Classical and World Myths* (Oxford: Oxford University Press, 2005).

Tinwell, Angela, Mark Grimshaw, and Andrew Williams, 'Uncanny behaviour in survival horror games', *Journal of Gaming & Virtual Worlds* 2/1 (May 2010), pp. 3–25.

Tolkien, J.R.R., *The Letters of J.R.R. Tolkien*, Humphrey Carpenter (ed.) (New York: Houghton Mifflin Company, 2000).

———, *The Lord of the Rings*, Fiftieth Anniversary One-Volume Edition (Boston: HarperCollins, 2004).

Toplin, Robert Brent, *History by Hollywood: The Use and Abuse of the American Past* (Urbana: University of Illinois Press, 1996).

———, *Reel History: In Defense of Hollywood* (Lawrence: University Press of Kansas, 2002).

Toswell, M.J., 'Lingua', in Elizabeth Emery and Richard Utz (eds), *Medievalism: Key Critical Terms* (Woodbridge: D.S. Brewer, 2014), pp. 117–24.

Trousdale, Gary and Kirk Wise, *The Hunchback of Notre Dame* (Walt Disney Studios, 1996).

Tyerman, Christopher, *England and the Crusades* (Chicago: University of Chicago Press, 1988).

———, *God's War: A New History of the Crusades* (Cambridge, MA: The Belknap Press, 2006).

———, *The Debate on the Crusades* (Manchester: Manchester University Press, 2011).

United States Census, 'Resident population data—2010 Census'. Available at http://www.census.gov/2010census/data/apportionment-dens-text.php (accessed 22 December 2016).

Utz, Richard, *Medievalism: A Manifesto* (Kalamazoo and Bradford: Arc Humanities Press, 2017).

Utz, Richard and Elizabeth Emery (eds), *Medievalism: Key Critical Terms* (Cambridge: D.S. Brewer, 2014).

Valente, Claire, *The Theory and Practice of Revolt in Medieval England* (Aldershot: Ashgate, 2003).

Vallejo, Boris and Julie Bell, *Boris Vallejo and Julie Bell: The Ultimate Collection* (London: Paper Tiger, 2005).

van der Veer, Peter and Shoma Munshi (eds), *Media, War, and Terrorism: Responses from the Middle East and Asia* (London: Routledge, 2004).

Vasagar, Jeevan, 'Michael Gove accuses exam system of neglecting British history', *Guardian*, 24 November 2011, sec. Education. Available at http://www.

guardian.co.uk/education/2011/nov/24/michael-gove-british-history-neglected (accessed 22 August 2016).

Vigarello, Georges, *The Metamorphoses of Fat: A History of Obesity* (New York: Columbia University Press, 2013).

Walker, Saint John, 'A quick walk through Uncanny Valley', in Alison Oddey and Christine White (eds), *Modes of Spectating* (Bristol: Intellect Books, 2009), pp. 29–40.

Warn, Jesse, Michael Hurst, and Rick Jacobson, *Spartacus: Blood and Sand* (Starz, 2010).

Waters, David Watkin, *The Iberian Bases of the English Art of Navigation in the Sixteenth Century* (Coimbra: University of Coimbra General Library, 1970).

Weiskott, Eric, 'Feeling "British"', *The Public Medievalist*, 28 March 2017. Available at http://www.publicmedievalist.com/feeling-british/ (accessed 30 May 2017).

William of Tyre, *A History of Deeds Done Beyond the Sea*, Records of Civilization, Sources and Studies 35 (New York: Columbia University Press, 1943).

———, *La Continuation De Guillaume De Tyr, 1184–1197*, Documents Relatifs à l'Histoire Des Croisades 14 (Paris: Librairie Orientaliste P. Geuthner, 1982).

———, *The Conquest of Jerusalem and the Third Crusade: Sources in Translation*, P.W. Edbury (ed.) (Brookfield, VT: Scholar Press, 1996).

Williams, David, 'Medieval movies', *The Yearbook of English Studies* 20 (1990), pp. 1–32.

Wineburg, Sam, *Historical Thinking and Other Unnatural Acts: Charting the Future of Teaching the Past* (Philadelphia: Temple University Press, 2001).

Wineburg, Sam and Daisy Martin, 'Reading and rewriting history', *Educational Leadership* 62/1 (2004), pp. 42–5.

Woods, William, 'Authenticating realism in medieval film', in Martha Driver and Sid Ray (eds), *The Medieval Hero On Screen: Representations from Beowulf to Buffy* (Jefferson, NC: McFarland, 2004), pp. 38–52.

Workman, Leslie, 'Preface', *Studies in Medievalism* 8 (1996), pp. 1–2.

Young, Helen, 'Approaches to medievalism: A consideration of Taxonomy and methodology through fantasy fiction', *Parergon* 27/1 (2010), pp. 163–79.

———, *Constructing 'England' in the Fourteenth Century: A Postcolonial Interpretation of Middle English Romance* (Lewiston, Mellen Press, 2010).

———, '"It's the Middle Ages, yo!": Race, neo/medievalisms, and the world of Dragon Age', *The Year's Work in Medievalism* 27 (2012), pp. 1–9. Available at https://sites.google.com/site/theyearsworkinmedievalism/all-issues/27-2012 (accessed 10 January 2017).

——— (ed.), *The Middle Ages in Popular Culture: Medievalism and Genre* (Amherst: Cambria Press, 2015).

Zemeckis, Robert, *Beowulf* (Paramount Pictures, 2007).

———, *A Hero's Journey: The Making of Beowulf* (Paramount Pictures, 2008).

Zucker, Jerry, *First Knight* (Sony Pictures, 1997).

INDEX

Printed in the USA
CPSIA information can be obtained
at www.ICGtesting.com
LVHW021516240823
756138LV00001B/56